GW00691219

NASSER
The Final Years

ABDEL MAGID FARID

ITHACA PRESS
Reading, 1994

Copyright © 1994 Abdel Magid Farid

All rights reserved. No part of this book may be reproduced in any form or by any electronic or mechanical means, including information storage and retrieval systems, without permission in writing from the publisher, except by a reviewer who may quote brief passages in a review.

First Edition

ISBN 0 86372 174 5

British Library Cataloguing-in-Publication Data.
A catalogue record for this book is available from the British Library.

Designed and typeset by John Saunders
Jacket Design by Mark Slader
Production by Anna Watson

Printed in Lebanon

Ithaca Press is an imprint of Garnet Publishing
Published by Garnet Publishing Ltd,
8 Southern Court, South Street,
Reading RG1 4QS, UK.

CONTENTS

FOREWORD

For those concerned with the tumultuous history of the modern Middle East, the period between the June 1967 war and President Nasser's death in September 1970 is bound to be of special interest. It was a time of deep apprehension but it was never dull. Nasser, the wounded giant, although humiliated and reduced by devastating defeat, continued to dominate the scene. Despite the disease, aggravated by diabetes, which was to kill him three years later, he had not lost his political will. He was capable of pondering his mistakes and attempting to rectify them. But above all he was determined to avoid provoking further disaster while he was laying the foundations of recovery.

The task was colossal. Egypt was in dire financial straits but it was on poor terms with the wealthier Arab states who could help. Nasser was convinced that the United States was determined to impose the utmost humiliation on the Arabs on Israel's behalf. The Soviet leaders, shocked and angered by the military collapse of their Arab friends, were reluctant to help Egypt rearm and were inclined at first to advise getting the best available deal from the Americans. At home Nasser was faced by the open rebellion of Abdel Hakim Amer, his former second-in-command, to whom he had unwillingly and so mistakenly delegated control over the Egyptian military some six years earlier.

Not all was black. Above all the majority of Egyptians remained loyal, if more questioning than before. Indeed few Arabs outside Egypt hoped for his immediate downfall if only because this would have marked the final triumph for Israel. The wealthy Arab states agreed to shore up Egypt and Jordan with substantial aid after Nasser and King Faisal of Saudi Arabia had settled their differences over the civil war in Yemen. The Soviet leaders soon decided that a US–Soviet agreement to settle the Middle East was not going to work and turned to helping Egypt to rearm.

In the ensuing war of attrition on the Suez Canal Egypt suffered severe damage, but it inflicted enough losses on the Israelis to alarm them seriously and Egyptian morale began to recover. Then in 1969 sympathetic regimes came to power in Sudan and Yemen providing Egypt with potential new strategic depth. Disaster loomed in the shape of a Palestinian/Jordanian civil war but Nasser had done his best to prevent it, warning both sides as it approached, and then threw all his reserves into Cairo summit meetings to end the conflict. The effort succeeded but it killed him; his last hours were his finest.

How fortunate it is that Abdel Magid Farid, who was secretary-general of the Egyptian Presidency 1959–70, with the rank of minister, should have kept these records of Nasser's meetings during those crucial last years. He was always at his side in a unique position to observe and record the discussions with foreign and Arab leaders as well as Egyptian ministers and military commanders.

Some of the discussions – especially with the Soviet leaders – lasted many hours, so these are not full texts. But the selections are clearly unbiased. Nasser does not always appear in his best light or as making the wisest proposals. Mr Farid's own introductions and linking passages are objective and unobtrusive but also vital. Above all the dramatis personae come vividly alive with the help of Farid's "stage directions". We have Nasser breaking into English with certain phrases (such as "forcing a settlement"), Brezhnev in angry exchanges with President Boumedienne of Algeria, interrupted by a more soothing Kosygin and King Faisal at the Khartoum summit, mentally withdrawing when the debate became noisy as he twirls the hem of his long black robe. At the final summit in Cairo King Husain and Yasser Arafat both arrived carrying guns. It was to Farid that King Faisal suggested that they should be given for safe keeping.

Many will find Chapter 4 on the Khartoum summit in September 1967 of special interest. Farid explains that Nasser had to be persuaded to go; he was reluctant to face the Sudanese man-in-the-street after his humiliating defeat. As it was, he received, as I observed myself, an amazing popular reception in the streets of Khartoum ("mais c'est un vaincu" said the astonished French journalist standing beside me as we watched the surging crowds applauding). But my colleagues and I were deeply frustrated by our ignorance of the Arab leaders' closed discussions. Now at last we know.

Another vital chapter (Chapter 3) shows Nasser criticizing the political "system" (the English word used again) he had created and advocating radical change such as the formation of two parties to fight election – the existing Arab Socialist Union and an opposition headed by Baghdadi and Kamal Husain, former Free Officer colleagues who had long since disagreed with the way the Revolution was going. Nasser's cabinet decided this was impractical, as it probably was, and the idea was abandoned. Liberalization of the economy was considered more important. So the seeds of *infitah* – Sadat's "open door" policy were sown.

This book reads rather like a script for a "faction" television documentary. But it is much more satisfactory to read it than to watch actors attempting the impossible. The expressions of the originals, their tones of voice and even their gestures can be imagined without difficulty. Abdel Magid Farid's achievement is invaluable; it has been worth waiting for it for nearly a quarter of a century.

PETER MANSFIELD

PREFACE

This book consists largely of records of meetings and conferences of Arab and other leaders held between 22 June 1967, following the Arab–Israeli war, and September 1970, the day before President Gamal Abdel Nasser of Egypt died. During this time I was secretary-general of the Presidency of the United Arab Republic (Egypt) and accompanied President Nasser to all these meetings, whose proceedings I recorded. The translation from Arab into English is not verbatim, but is close enough to retain the flavour of the Arabic idiom.

The records are prefaced and occasionally interspersed with my own observations, including some background information, in a manner that I intended to be as unobtrusive as possible, leaving the discourses of the individual statesmen and politicians to speak for themselves. It is hoped that these records will provide an insight into the attitudes and personalities of the main participants, as well as a vivid picture of how pressing issues of the time were handled.

The meetings and conferences are centred round the repercussions of the Arab–Israeli war of June 1967 and Nasser's drive to regain lost ground: to rebuild his shattered army and to regain the trust and support of the Soviet Union for that purpose; to overcome the stigma of defeat both at home and abroad, especially in the Arab world where he had been supremely popular; to heal internal divisions and to foster inter-Arab collaboration and reconciliation. As for the United States the problem was even greater, for not only was it Israel's champion and a superpower, but was actively pursuing an interventionist policy which Nasser could hardly ignore. For much of the time therefore he preferred to parley with it through the Soviet Union.

Nasser had another problem to contend with: heart disease which had afflicted him since Syria broke away from the union with Egypt in 1961 and which caused his death within sight of national recovery.

Chapter 1

POSTWAR OVERTURES
Nasser and Podgorny meet in Cairo

On 22 June 1967, two weeks after Egypt's defeat in the war with Israel, the Soviet President, N. V. Podgorny, arrived in Cairo with an official delegation for a meeting with President Gamal Abdel Nasser. When Nasser had announced his resignation on 9 June, only four days after the outbreak of the war, the Soviet political leadership had contacted him, urging him to change his mind and indicating that a high-level delegation would shortly visit Cairo to discuss Egypt's political and military situation in the wake of the defeat. It was understood from their cable that the Soviet Union did not intend to abandon Nasser, and I can say that this message played a substantial, though not the only role in persuading Nasser to withdraw his resignation.

This meeting between Egypt and the Soviet Union was different from any of the previous summits. The triumphs of Nasserism had been thrown into reverse, and the profound shock experienced throughout the country in the wake of the defeat had also affected Nasser. The six days of war had immediately added ten years to his life. Already suffering from diabetes, he was now having to cope with severe leg pains that left him unable to stand for long. He was disinclined to talk, and seemed deeply troubled. All of us who were close to him felt that because of his anger, grief and pain, the heart had gone out of him, and even though he said little, we knew what was causing him the deepest hurt. It was not so much the military defeat that affected him as the plotting of the army men who had formerly surrounded him, and the gloating of those he had regarded as his friends.

What particularly worried him and caused him sleepless nights was Egypt's vulnerability. The defeat had opened the country's skies to the enemy. Israeli aircraft could now fly over Cairo when and however they wished, and strike at any target inside Egypt and along the axis extending from the Suez Canal south to the Aswan High Dam. Indeed, knowing that there would be no serious resistance, Israel was now powerful enough to send its troops from the Canal all the way to Cairo. I don't know whether Israel was aware of all these details, but in the first few days after the war it certainly behaved as though it was.

Nasser's method of conducting affairs of state also changed at this time. He became more inclined to consult those around him, even summoning senior army officers and influential government officials who had long since retired. He listened a lot and said little, but the constant Israeli threat to Egypt's major economic installations – factories, railways, bridges – was always uppermost in his mind and explains why the first of the summit meetings with the Soviets was of particular significance. Before the outbreak of the war, which he had fought with Russian weapons, his only allies had been the Soviet Union, the socialist countries and the non-aligned states. Relations with the United States had been severed, relations with Britain were cool, those with de Gaulle's France were indifferent, and with some Arab regimes they were extremely bad. Podgorny's visit could be of great importance in resolving Egypt's predicament.

Podgorny arrived in Cairo at the head of the Soviet delegation whose most prominent member was Marshal M. Zakharov, chief of staff of the Red Army. The first session took place in the conference chamber of al-Qubbah Palace. Those present on the Egyptian side included Nasser, Zakariya Mohieddin, Ali Sabri, Lt Gen Muhammad Fawzi and Mahmoud Riyad. Nasser and Podgorny sat opposite each other with the Egyptian delegation on Nasser's left and the Soviet delegation on Podgorny's right. As on all such occasions, I took my usual place behind Nasser.

In spite of everything, Nasser was full of energy. Podgorny also seemed ebullient, several times expressing his thanks for the warm reception he and his delegation had received and for the outburst of popular sentiment he had personally encountered in Cairo's streets. In this cordial atmosphere the talks began.

The First Session, 22 June 1967

Nasser: I warmly welcome our friend President Podgorny and the members of the distinguished Soviet delegation. And since he is the esteemed guest of the people of the United Arab Republic, I propose that our friend President Podgorny begin the discussion.

Podgorny: I thank the fraternal Egyptian people and I thank you for this warm welcome. Let us get straight to the heart of the matter. We are certain that through mutual cooperation we will be able to overcome all the difficulties facing you at present. We were eager to meet you and to talk to you before Comrade Kosygin left for his meeting with Johnson in New York: they will probably be discussing three topics that include (1) the Vietnam issue and the solutions proposed for it; (2) the Middle East crisis and the issues connected with it; and (3) intercontinental missiles and defences against them.

Even though Johnson does not wish to consider the last of these, I expect that when the second topic is discussed the question of possible Arab concessions will be introduced. For our part, where this issue is concerned, we will not support Israel's demands to retain the occupied territories. We also know from you that the holding of bilateral talks between the Arabs and Israel is practically impossible. In general, we will not agree to any proposal as long as it is condemned by the Arabs. On the subject of Vietnam, I received a cable from New York a few minutes before I entered the hall and I gather there is much hope that some kind of solution to this problem will be reached, even if only in principle. This means putting an end to the air strikes in preparation for finally resolving the situation.

As for the initial exchange that I held with you personally after my arrival in Cairo yesterday, I have sent Moscow a cable that focuses on two points; namely, the issue of air defence and the issue of alignment and non-alignment. I've also informed Moscow of the request for some ships from the Soviet fleet to be dispatched to the Mediterranean, and I believe that there is preliminary approval on this issue. It will be very useful if the military men from our two sides can start discussions on important aspects such as how the ships will be supplied from ports, joint measures to be taken when ships are exposed to air attacks, and so forth.

At this point Podgorny asked the Soviet interpreter to explain clearly that the cable he had sent to Moscow covered the topics which Abdel Nasser had raised during their meeting on the previous day and which had been approved by the Egyptian leaders whom he had met after his arrival at the airport. Nasser smiled and I learned from him afterwards that he was aware of Podgorny's fears that his demands might not have had the unanimous approval of the Egyptian leadership. This is why he told Podgorny that these issues had indeed been discussed and approved by all the members of the Revolutionary Command Council [Supreme Committee], Egypt's ruling body, including those who were not present in the hall that day.

Podgorny: As for the subject of non-alignment, the Politburo in Moscow welcomes what your Excellency has said about standing with the Soviet Union in the future. However, they're considering in Moscow if it would be useful to announce this now or to postpone such a declaration, and our colleagues are also wondering about the reactions and the problems that might arise from this. Moscow has asked me what structure you are proposing our relationship with you should take. Is it the established form or is it to be a new agreement and treaty? How do you visualize future relations between us? Generally speaking, Moscow fully approves this issue in principle, but certain problems could arise because of this new relationship between you and us, particularly with respect to your relations with some Arab countries, including progressive states such as Syria and Algeria. Concerning the issue of air defence, this is currently being examined at the Ministry of Defence in Moscow, and discussion of the details will be initiated with the appropriate officials immediately after my return to Moscow. What is important here is that we believe it is vital to help Egypt in the matter of air defence.

Nasser: Concerning the issue of non-alignment, we are regarded as aligned to start with, which is why we were subjected to aggression in 1956 and again in 1967 and why we will be exposed to aggression for as long as we follow this line. The Americans are well aware of this. They wanted us to go along with them but we refused because we could see that their policy supported colonialism. We know that the Americans aren't going to leave us alone. But it's important for us to find out where our interests lie. As far as our relations with you are concerned, they have lacked one thing, which is military cooperation. During the fighting our people kept asking: 'Where are the Russians, our friends?' I know of course that you couldn't have had a military presence because no previous agreement had been made with you about such an arrangement.

I predict that the Americans will continue to be our enemies in the future. They are your enemies, too, and that is why we have to organize our cooperation: it is unreasonable that I should stand neutrally between the one who strikes me and the one who helps me. Arranging for our two countries to cooperate will require careful thought on our part because any action that Egypt takes will provoke an international response. The end result of an agreement between us will be a considerable shift in the world balance of power. Although we'll have made this decision objectively and even though it will have been arrived at as a result of intense study and discussion, I agree with you that such a declaration will also have considerable repercussions in the Arab world: it may prove divisive, and countries such as Saudi Arabia, Tunisia and Morocco may declare their alignment with the United States. In fact these countries are already aligned with America. By the same token, there are also certain African countries that are fully aligned with America even though they maintain formally that they belong among the non-aligned countries.

Podgorny: It's extremely hard to find a country anywhere in the world that is one hundred per cent nonaligned.

Nasser: We see this very clearly. But if we ask you to stand by us in time of war, then we have to stand with you too, in war as well as in peace. So now we have to discuss with you how our relations are to be organised. We are willing to conclude either a secret or an open treaty. What is important is that we now recognise that our main enemy is the United States and that the only possible way of continuing our struggle is for us to ally ourselves with the Soviet Union. There are difficult days ahead of us and it will be hard for us to overcome them by ourselves. So either we succumb, as Thailand has done, to the United States and they'll give us economic aid for as long as we submit to imperialism, or else we fight on. Here we are in agreement with the Soviet Union in our struggle against imperialism and in our support for national liberation. Before the fighting broke out, we were afraid that we would be accused by the Western media of being aligned, but nothing of that sort concerns us any longer. We are ready to offer facilities to the Soviet fleet from Port Said to Salloum and from al-Arish to Gaza.

Podgorny: Mr President, I agree with every word you have said. I believe that by working together we will find the best way of establishing cooperation between us. The logic is strong, understandable and entirely clear.

Nasser: On the question of air defence, I would prefer this to be a form of joint defence; in other words an Egyptian–Soviet defence arrangement. This means that our officers and troops will be able to share in the defence structure and the men will gain valuable experience through contact with your cadres. Another point is that because the Israelis are now in Sinai, we are building up our defences on the west bank of the Canal. If the Israelis refuse to leave peacefully, sooner or later we'll have to fight them to get them out. Of course the actual task of expelling them from Sinai will be our responsibility and not yours. What we are asking you to do is to take part in defending the territorial integrity of our republic.

There's another matter that needs to be looked at jointly and that's the possibility that Israel might cross the Suez Canal to attack us and then advance deep into the country. Dealing with this threat would come within the framework of our joint defence commitment. It's my belief that when the United States becomes aware of the nature of the alliance between us and when warships from the Soviet fleet have started to enter Egyptian ports, the Americans will lose their tempers and will push Israel into attacking us.

Naturally, there are people in Egypt who will oppose the agreement with you, and we will also be attacked by Western propaganda. This is only to be expected and it's a straightforward matter.

Zakariya Mohieddin: It is important that the joint arrangements for the air defence operation are put into effect as quickly as possible, because once the Americans get wind of what's going on they'll definitely try to obstruct them.

Ali Sabri: I also think that it's important to analyse the reactions that can be expected both domestically and abroad when it's announced that we have concluded an agreement with the Soviet Union. There is no doubt that the repercussions will be very considerable.

Podgorny: As soon as I get back to Moscow, I'll be bringing up all the points that everyone here has raised. Speaking generally we'd like to express our sincere thanks and appreciation to you on this matter.

Nasser: I put this subject to President al-Atasi of Syria, who told me that they would be discussing it and asked us not to take any decision on it independently. I sent him a message about it yesterday. I've also explained the situation to Bouteflika, the Algerian minister of foreign affairs, who was very surprised to begin with. However, I believe that sooner or later the Algerians will be forced to follow this line because of the attitude of the king of Morocco and of Bourguiba towards them.

Podgorny: I received a cable from Moscow this morning expressing the utmost satisfaction and approval of your statements as long as both sides take account of all the domestic and external reactions. On the whole I think that the issue of non-alignment is less urgent than the question of air defence. My colleagues in Moscow have agreed that the Soviet Union needs to cooperate in making the greatest possible efforts to strengthen your country's entire air defence system. Even though the standing of the United Arab Republic is well known throughout the whole world and even though nobody doubts that it will never accept subservience to any state whatsoever at any time, the presence of foreign military forces on the territories of a sovereign state is a sensitive issue especially in the domestic situation. Therefore, it is more appropriate for the air defence to be in Egyptian hands and for Soviet aid to be extended for that purpose.

Nasser: On the domestic front, of course, there'll be a lot said, because the country has experienced a major blow with this attack. But our people in Egypt are unshakable and their roots go deep. They have suffered such blows before and have ultimately surmounted them. At the same time, don't forget that we are in a state of transition from capitalism to socialism. Here at home this change has its enemies, some of whom were our companions in the revolution but who have shifted away from us because their line is now different from ours. I saw one of them three days ago [*Nasser did not mention the name*] and it was his opinion that we should agree with the Americans on all matters and that we should leave Yemen to King Faisal. Needless to say, there is a faction in the country that echoes this view, and that holds me personally responsible for everything that has happened because I undermined the relationship with America. At the same time, there is another trend that urges the necessity for firm agreement and full cooperation with the Soviet Union. There's also a third tendency that calls for a fully neutral position between the Americans and the Soviets. I consider that such demands are extraordinary. However, they will not go beyond simply being words because, as I have already remarked, the Egyptian people are solid and they have the capacity to endure and to fight. We are also distinguished in Egypt by having complete national unity. Because of this the domestic situation is, by and large, secured, especially as decisive measures were taken a few days ago to deal with the widespread slackness that has existed up till now in the armed forces.

Of course we will hear some people around the country saying that the British left through the door and the Soviets came in through the window. All this is mere rhetoric. However, once we are actually receiving your support, and when complete cooperation has been established between us, this will have a very good impact, both inside Egypt and in the Arab world.

Podgorny: I heard a radio report saying that China had declared that it was ready to send you weapons.

Nasser: China has in fact contacted us and confirmed that it is willing to assist us, but only with light weapons, and it has also condemned the ceasefire. Generally speaking, though, our Chinese friends do not know much about the type of terrain in Sinai or about certain other local conditions, which explains why they think that the fighting should not be stopped and that we should pull back to the Delta and fight with the Israeli aggressor in the villages. They also think that it is not particularly important to concentrate on defending Cairo and the other big cities. [*While Podgorny was in Cairo, the Chinese ambassador in Egypt asked to meet Nasser and was received by Ali Sabri. The ambassador said that China was prepared to send light weapons and grenades, but that it was unable to offer any kinds of aircraft or tanks.*]

Podgorny: China is engaged in propaganda attacks against us all over the place, and claims that the Soviet Union has betrayed the Arabs in the same way that it betrayed the Vietnamese. We are thoroughly familiar with their propaganda and well aware of their manoeuvres. They are now trying to make us lose Syria by pushing the Syrians into an unequal fight regardless of the entirely predictable outcome of such an encounter.

Nasser: I believe that China adopts radical positions, which is why it is serving America's strategies.

Podgorny: We are supposed to forget local differences when we are faced with major catastrophes, but they insist on sticking to their radical position towards us.

Nasser: In the past, they also used to attack Tito pretty fiercely.

Podgorny: Nowadays they describe him as 'the old opportunist'. Their latest term is the 'new opportunist', and I expect that when you announce our new relationship, they will call you 'the new opportunist'.

Nasser: It doesn't matter because we've become accustomed to all kinds of insults.

Podgorny: What is the situation with Arab oil?

Nasser: Certain Arab countries are still delivering their oil to the Americans in a roundabout sort of way and declaring the opposite.

Mahmoud Riyad: However, Kuwait has actually stopped the delivery of oil to the United States and Britain, and as a result is losing nearly 180 million pounds.

Nasser: Iraq has also stopped pumping oil, and in Libya work in the oil companies has stopped because of the strike by Libyan workers.

Here the discussion turned to weapons and Lt Gen Muhammad Fawzi handed over to Marshal Zakharov a list containing Egypt's requirements for Soviet weaponry. It was agreed that this issue would be discussed separately by the military men, Marshal Zakharov and Lt Gen Fawzi.

Podgorny: I would like to assure you that as soon as we return to Moscow, we will send all the equipment and weapons that are needed for immediate use. As for the weapons and equipment requested for stockpiling, they can be discussed by the special military committees.

At this point, Nasser brought up the subject of Egypt's request for economic aid from the Soviet Union.

Nasser: The closure of the Suez Canal has lost us nine million pounds in hard currency every month, in addition to the value of the oil that we have lost as a result of the occupation of the Sinai oil fields. To deal with these economic difficulties, we have slashed our budget heavily, but even so we will still have a shortfall in hard currency. This is why we are asking for economic assistance from you, and especially for wheat, edible oils and for certain other raw materials. The Americans, of course, stopped importing Egyptian textiles, which they used to pay for in hard currency, some considerable time ago.

Podgorny: It may be difficult to respond to these requests straight away, but we will make every possible attempt to lighten your economic burdens.

Nasser: Wheat is especially important, because we need to import two million tonnes annually to supplement our own production of 1.5 million tonnes, given that our annual consumption amounts to 3.5 million tonnes.

Podgorny: I hope that his excellency the president will rest assured that these requests will receive the closest attention. I, and the delegation accompanying me, give preliminary approval to all your requests but the final agreement will reach you shortly after we have returned to Moscow.

At this point everybody noticed Podgorny glancing surreptitiously at his watch.

Nasser: It seems that our meeting has gone on for rather a long time, so we will now adjourn our discussions until tomorrow. However, before we do so, I would like to make it clear to President Podgorny that we are all keen to strengthen relations and ties with you, and that the political leadership of the United Arab Republic is ready, with one condition, to align itself with you against the imperialist camp. But we have really taken too long, so let us postpone discussion of this until tomorrow.

The Second Session, 23 June 1967

The official talks between Gamal Abdel Nasser and Podgorny resumed at 10.00 on the following morning, Friday 23 June. Nasser, who arrived at the conference hall in al-Qubbah Palace 15 minutes ahead of time, appeared relaxed for the first time since the disaster of the Six Day War, and his cheerful mood was apparent in the short joking conversations he had with us. His good humour was undoubtedly due to his feeling, after the previous day's meeting, that he was no longer alone in the struggle and that the sheer presence of the Soviet leadership in Cairo would give the populations in Egypt and in the Arab world a considerable charge of optimism.

Podgorny arrived at the conference hall shortly before 10.00 accompanied by his comrades in the Soviet delegation, and we noticed that he too appeared relaxed and cheerful. While we were taking our places at the table, he cracked a couple of jokes which made Nasser laugh heartily, and everyone joined in the general merriment. In this genial and optimistic atmosphere the second session began.

Podgorny: At yesterday's session, his excellency the president invited me to start the discussion, and I was happy to comply. In this session, I invite him to start the discussion.

Nasser: I want to start with an important subject. The enemy's latest assault has badly affected the morale of the armed forces. A speedy replacement of the weapons we have lost will therefore have a very positive effect on the morale of the officers and men. With regard to the air force, we received 25 MiG-21 aircraft and 93 MiG-17 aircraft from you immediately after the battle, although some of these aircraft have only a limited amount of flying time – ranging from 50 to 100 hours – left in them. I have learned today from our military delegation that you have agreed supply us with 40 new MiG-21 aircraft. I would like to mention a technical point here, especially in the presence of Marshal Zakharov. The MiG aircraft has a short range when compared to Israel's Mirage, Mystère and Vautour aircraft, which can fly from their bases all the way to Mersa Matruh [*this was before America supplied Israel with sophisticated Phantom aircraft*]. This means that the

Israeli aircraft can reach to the heart of Egypt whereas our planes are unable to reach the interior of Israel. Because of this, we need a new kind of long-range fighter-bomber, otherwise Israel will remain unrivalled in its ability to strike at us while we remain unable to retaliate.

Another issue concerning the air force is that you should send us as quickly as possible – by air, not by sea – a number of the MiG-21 aircraft so that they can immediately take part in the air defence of the republic. I'm not revealing any secrets when I tell you that we now have a number of pilots without aircraft.

There is also a shortage of weapons in the infantry divisions and it is essential that weapons and equipment for these divisions arrive as speedily as possible. I would like to remind you of your and Prime Minister Kosygin's cables which were sent on 10 June after my resignation had been announced and in which you confirmed that the Soviet Union would hasten to rearm our forces. Now, I will not conceal from you that I expect Israel to launch an attack against us after the UN General Assembly meetings have ended. The question that I want to ask now is this: what assistance can you offer us in such an event so that the country will not fall into Israeli hands?

I gather from Lt Gen Fawzi that in his talks with you this morning the question of your participation in the air defence operation was discussed, and you are leaving for Moscow tomorrow, are you not?

Podgorny: I don't at present have detailed information on the agreement reached by Lt Gen Fawzi and Marshal Zakharov [*a meeting between the Soviet and the Egyptian military delegations had been held independently of the leaders' meetings*]. But I would like to stress an important point, which is that we still stand by our promise to you concerning the rearming of Egypt's armed forces. In spite of the great distance between our countries, we will dispatch the military support you need by air, by sea or by any other method, and as quickly as possible. As for the kind of aircraft, I believe that the military officials will decide on the most appropriate type so that your armed forces will be able to fight off any new attack against them and even launch a counter-attack.

But there is one point in your statements that I would like to have explained: are you asking for more aircraft with the intention ultimately of annihilating Israel?

Nasser: Let us ask ourselves: what is defence and what is offence? What are defensive weapons and what are offensive weapons? When war starts, there is no distinction between offensive and defensive weapons. In asking for aircraft with certain specifications we are keeping in mind that we want to be able to strike all of Israel's airports when military operations begin. As I have already told you, Israel is capable of hitting our airports as far away as Mersa Matruh.

Podgorny: I agree with you absolutely. When war begins, there is no difference between offence and defence. This is why we have collectively to exert the greatest effort to make the Arab armed forces capable of fulfilling their military obligations. As for having a larger number of pilots than of aircraft, this is always preferable. In the Soviet Union, we have two or three pilots for every plane. By and large, we are willing to meet your additional requests.

Nasser: Our situation is different from yours in the Soviet Union, because we have neither the resources nor the reserves that are available to you. We can live on only five per cent of our lands. As for the shortage of pilots, it is a crucial matter. During the 1956 campaigns our pilots would land one aircraft and immediately proceed to fly another. We know that training and grooming combat pilots is difficult and time-consuming, which is why we are now asking you for aircraft and also for pilots.

As for America's policy toward us, I never feel reassured by American statements. America is always working to deceive and mislead us. So far we haven't declared our political position, but the Americans know perfectly well what we will say, where we will proceed, and what we will do. Yesterday, one of the American UN delegates met our representative and told him: "You are correcting your mistake with another mistake." So they know our intentions. We also know theirs, and we don't believe their promises that Israel will withdraw from the occupied territories. On the contrary, in my view Israel will probably resume its offensive against us after the 27th of this month [*June*] for the simple reason that the Americans and the Israelis have not yet achieved their objective.

No peace has been made with the Arabs and the stability required for Israel has not been achieved yet. At the same time, they know that the UN emergency force cannot prevent the Arabs from moving against Israel again, once they have recovered from the shock of the defeat. I believe that the war has produced contradictory results in that it has pushed Egypt and Syria towards an even closer alignment with the Soviet Union. America therefore now has two options: either to attack us directly on any pretext, or to support Israel and push it into launching a new attack against us. This is why you should speed up the process of reinforcing our defences day by day and why you should meet our requests for MiG-21 aircraft. We should also have a new kind of long-range aircraft which we currently lack.

A final question: how will you help us if a new Israeli attack is launched against us at this time? It has to be borne in mind that we will not withdraw from our present positions and that we will defend them until death. You withdrew to the Volga River. For us, there is no Volga. There are only 100 kilometres behind these positions before the centre of Cairo is reached.

Podgorny: I support you fully, and I do not recommend any further withdrawal. However, I do not anticipate any immediate Israeli attack against you.

I would like to ask about the Israeli intelligence situation in Sinai. Israel has full information on Egypt. Does Egyptian intelligence have information on Israel?

Nasser: Israel has detailed information on Egypt through the Americans, French and Italians who are in our country. We are a tourist country and we consider tourism an important economic resource since it provides us with nearly 100 million dollars in hard currency annually. On the other hand, Israel is a closed country from the security and information point of view. Furthermore the Jews hold their tongues while the Arabs always let their tongues run away with them. This is why they have a great deal more information about us than we have about them.

Podgorny: But it is possible to take certain measures that will help in maintaining confidentiality. For example, we have heavily restricted access to our borders, whereas we find that your canal area, which is both a border and an operations area, is still open to all and sundry.

Nasser: The reason for this is because our country is small. But we have in fact closed the canal zone since yesterday and entry into the area is now prohibited except with permits. We have also completely forbidden the area to foreigners. Israel has been carrying out daily air reconnaissance operations over the country but since yesterday we have put a protective air umbrella into place over our territory.

Podgorny: Naturally it is difficult to conceal everything but it is possible to work in secret without the enemy realising that you are preparing for a quick retaliatory strike. Try to work quietly until you have completed all your preparations. Also you always have to be very wary of journalists who often breach confidentiality because they are competing to report the news.

Zakharov: On the subject of military preparation, you will receive 40 MiG-21 aircraft in two or three days' time, accompanied by their assembly and installation crews, in addition to six MiG-21 aircraft equipped for training purposes. There will also be 38 Sukhoi aircraft. In fact you will soon have a larger number of fighter aircraft than you had before the invasion. As for armoured vehicles, you will shortly receive 100 tanks, and we are prepared to send more armoured vehicles when you have more trained crews available. But we will not send tanks just to be kept in warehouses. I have an important comment to make, which is that hard training is going to be needed because so far I don't think your forces have been particularly well instructed.

Nasser: We need expertise in organisation and training because before the war our forces had not trained under combat conditions or in real manoeuvres. Unfortunately, given the true situation, the confidence in our military command was misplaced. We need quite a number of military experts whose leader will be in direct contact with me so that any difficulties that might arise can be sorted out and dealt with immediately. But I also hope that we won't have to pay their salaries!

Podgorny: I agree with your view because it is useless to rearm without meticulous organisation and competent training. We will send you high-level technicians and they will work very hard and conscientiously. This matter has been discussed at some length in Moscow and we have decided to send between 1,000 and 1,200 experts from the general command level downwards. Generally speaking, their number will be determined according to your needs. Even though the issue of experts always creates sensitive situations on the ground, this can be overcome with wisdom, understanding and good intentions on both sides.

There is another thing: I beg you to prevent the Chinese from engaging in hostile anti-Soviet propaganda in the United Arab Republic because they are undertaking this everywhere and claiming that we are in collusion with the imperialist forces, with America and with Israel.

Nasser: Egypt is different from the other Arab countries. Here we have a single nation and a single people, unlike Syria and Sudan where there are numerous sects and tribes. On the whole the Egyptian people are not in the least influenced by Chinese propaganda. On the contrary, China is always protesting about the publication of some report or other in our newspapers about the Red Guard. It is not Chinese propaganda that is influential here in Egypt but Western propaganda, especially among the bourgeoisie.

Podgorny: With regard to your requests for weapons, we will speed up delivery as far as we possibly can. Be assured that we in Moscow are affected just as much as you are by this crisis. Your concern is the same as our concern. What's more, we will not raise the subject of accommodation and financial costs with you.

Your armed forces are not capable at present of engaging the Israelis in any action; therefore, we ought to have a period of calm during which we can work quietly. You asked me what we would do if the Israelis launched a new attack. First, I think that your armed forces are so far not well enough prepared to face any such attack. Secondly, I believe that it is both undesirable and inconceivable that the Soviet Union should take part in the conflict at present. Therefore it's important to shore up your military facilities as fast as possible so that you will be prepared to face any surprises. The enemy is close by; he is no more than 100 kilometres away and you are worried and you can't sleep. We are exactly like you, in spite of the long distance between us.

Nasser: On the matter of the political agreement between us, there are several proposals and each has its merits and its drawbacks. What is without question is that deep in our hearts we want to advance by the side of the Soviet Union. There is a full alliance between us. We have been compensated for the weapons and equipment lost in the war free of any cost. We agree to any form of alliance that you wish to choose on the one condition that it will not affect our reputation and our leadership status in the Third World.

Podgorny: Naturally, this is a fundamental condition. I hope that you will be fully confident of our eagerness to maintain the position of the United Arab Republic in this part of the world.

Abdel Nasser then asked Zakariya Muhieddin to review the country's economic situation and its main requirements.

Zakariya Mohieddin: It is obvious that the economic battle must proceed side by side with the military battle. When considering the economic resources of our republic in relation to the size of our population, and our defence and foreign commitments, it becomes clear that these resources are extremely limited, which is why any crisis always affects our economy adversely. Our economy relies on two principal sources of income: agriculture and revenues from the canal. Industry and tourism follow. Our economic situation can be simply explained with a few figures. Exports from the agricultural sector used to bring us 170 million pounds in hard currency. We used to earn nearly 100 million pounds from the Suez Canal, and about 100 million pounds from industry and oil, bearing in mind that industry is always affected by the availability of the raw and partly-processed materials that we import from abroad. We also used to earn 40 million pounds in hard currency from tourism and other sectors. This means that our total revenues amounted to 410 million pounds. Taking into account the new conditions arising since the war and following the closure of the Suez Canal, these revenues will fall to 290 million pounds, leaving us with a deficit of 120 million pounds. I will give the official in the Soviet delegation in charge of economic matters a list of the essential commodities that are needed, such as wheat, flour, corn, sugar, oils and fats, as well as some industrial items.

Podgorny: We know from our own experience that economic needs increase after war. We have taken note of all your requests, which we will discuss in detail in Moscow and then send you what we can. Moreover, representatives of the socialist states are due to meet in the near future to coordinate their programmes. At this meeting we can discuss with them how to supply and organise the aid that you and Syria need.

Nasser: In concluding our meeting with you, I would like to record the gratitude both of the Egyptian people and of their leadership, for the support of the Soviet Union. The people of the United Arab Republic have long memories and they will never forget the friends who stood by them in the difficult times.

Podgorny: In the name of the Soviet leadership, I express my thanks and appreciation to you and your people for the warm welcome, both official and popular. We believe that the visit has been extremely successful and useful. We also feel great satisfaction about the reinforcing and strengthening of the relationship between our two countries. We are confident that it will be possible to stamp out the signs of the assault and that the Israelis will not remain on your land. But we should not set a date for the next battle yet, and whether it is to be in one month or in six months. What is important is to let reason rule when making this decision so that we do not provoke the enemy before we are ready to face him.

Mr President, we will continue our consultations for as long as our destinies are linked and, as a result, we will together be able to solve all the problems, regardless of how big they are.

I have a final question: does the president not think that it would be better if we visited Tito on our way back to Moscow to explain the details of the political and military situation to him, even though we're afraid that he will be angry when we mention the subject of alignment and nonalignment? I will also review the general situation and the important issues that have been brought up here at the forthcoming meeting of the leaders of the socialist countries.

Nasser: I believe that it would be a good thing if you were to pass by President Tito and acquaint him with the substance of what has taken place in these meetings. Now, what do you think we should announce about our meetings? Should we issue a brief statement or a long joint communiqué?

Podgorny: I propose that we don't issue a long joint communiqué and that we content ourselves with a short press statement, bearing in mind that this short press statement will cause a lot of speculation and debate around the world.

Nasser: I agree to the issuing of a short press statement, provided that it is announced simultaneously in Cairo and Moscow at six o'clock in the evening, Cairo time, tomorrow, Saturday 24 June 1967.

Chapter 2

SECRET SESSION
The Arab leaders meet and two
go to Moscow

The blow dealt to Egypt and to Nasser by Israel was bound to have a strong impact on Arab and foreign opinion of Egypt's leadership in the area. It seemed to us that more than one player had set the stage for so spectacular an outcome. The despondency of the Egyptians now contrasted sharply with the air of confidence which the Egyptian leaders had displayed a few days earlier. Circumstantial evidence hinted at some form of collusion: the United States had been stepping up arms deliveries to Israel; Israel had mounted fierce attacks on Jordan and later on Syria and, finally, in May 1967 had quite openly threatened Syria with all-out invasion.

Egypt had responded by amassing forces in Sinai and had had to move troops to the Gulf of Aqaba from which the UN forces had withdrawn. The stage had been adroitly set for an Israeli attack. Nasser tried to reassure America that Egypt would not fire the first shot, but in public he had to show confidence. Insinuations spread that the Arabs would be at the gates of Tel Aviv within hours, and the effectiveness of these rumours was enhanced by Nasser's comments at a press conference held shortly before hostilities began. He said that if war did actually break out, Israel alone would have to bear the consequences and that if the United States took part in the fighting, the Egyptian response would be much tougher than Washington might imagine. But when the first bullet was fired everything changed. The light that had dazzled the eyes went out and the real and bitter facts began to appear. After only a few days it was the Israelis who were the ones standing at the gates of Cairo.

The Arabs were shaken to the core. Everybody, even those who had disagreed with Nasser, felt that the defeat was not the defeat of Nasser alone, but of them all. As the Arab leaders headed towards Cairo all they could ask

*was: how did this happen? What is to be done and where are we to proceed?
Nasser put the facts before them. Egypt had lost most of its weapons and
equipment in the attack, the first strike having paralysed the Egyptian air
force and effectively removed it from the battle. This had happened on 5
June, the first day of the defeat.*

*This was the atmosphere in which four Arab leaders gathered in Cairo:
Presidents Abdel Rahman Aref of Iraq, Nur al-Din al-Atasi of Syria, Houari
Boumedienne of Algeria and Muhammad Mahjoub, foreign minister of
Sudan. (King Husain of Jordan had come and gone.) At the first brief session
of this meeting of the so-called steadfast countries, Nasser explained the
domestic, military and political situation, and described the talks he had had
with President Podgorny during the latter's visit to Cairo, and the Soviet
readiness to rebuild the armed forces. He suggested that the Arab countries
who maintained good relations with the Soviet Union should press Moscow
to speed up the delivery of the military equipment requested by Egypt.
Boumedienne and Aref then volunteered to go immediately to Moscow and
to speak with the Soviet leaders on behalf of the Arab presidents who were at
that moment meeting in Cairo, and everyone agreed to remain in Cairo
until the two presidents had returned to Egypt so that the appropriate
decisions could be taken in light of the talks with the Kremlin leaders.*

*The journey by the two presidents was shrouded in secrecy. They were
flown in a Soviet-made aircraft from Cairo to a military base near Moscow
where they were received by Brezhnev, Kosygin, Ponomarev (members of the
CPSU Central Committee) and Defence Minister Marshal Grechko, in
addition to the first deputy minister of foreign affairs and the head of the
Middle East Department of the Ministry of Foreign Affairs. They were then
taken directly to the meeting chamber at the Kremlin.*

*The meeting started at 20.00 on 17 July 1967 and lasted for five hours
without a break. The following day, Tuesday, it was resumed at 10.00 and
went on until 14.00, at which point everyone present had a light luncheon
and Boumedienne and Aref then boarded the same aircraft to be flown back
to Cairo.*

*I should note here that I was not one of the members of the delegation
which went to Moscow on this secret mission. However, I obtained the
original copy of the conference papers from one of the Arab ministers who
was a member of the delegation and who had attended the talks. The
exchanges between the two Arab presidents and the Soviet leaders were
heated and threatened at times to reach boiling-point.*

The Evening Session, 17 July 1967

*Having welcomed the two Arab presidents and their companions with a few
conventional phrases, Brezhnev went straight to the point.*

Brezhnev: We hope, gentlemen, that the talks will be useful to both sides.
We are ready to listen to you without delay, especially in these delicate
circumstances.

Aref: We bring you, comrades, the greetings of the Arab presidents who are
currently meeting in Cairo. We also convey the greetings of the free and
struggling Arab peoples to the Soviet people and to all socialist peoples.
The Arab peoples and the Arab presidents thank the Soviet Union for its
fraternal acts, and are truly appreciative of these worthy efforts, especially
under the critical circumstances that are being experienced at present by the
progressive Arab states. We also thank those who met in Budapest [*the
Eastern bloc countries*] for the outcomes that were produced there. This is
another proof of the firm friendship that strengthens the Arab peoples and
makes them aware that there are friendly peoples standing with them in the
struggle against imperialism. We are conscious that imperialism and the
countries that parade at the forefront of that venture are trying to
emphasise the fact that all the Soviet Union's plans and attempts to deal
with this issue will fail. We realise that they are attempting through this to
create coolness between the Soviet Union and the Arab countries.

   Gentlemen, the Arab presidents who are meeting in Cairo decided to
send a delegation consisting of brother Boumedienne and myself to bring
you the facts, so that you may know that the friendship between us will not
be broken. I also hope that you will recognise that the Arab countries are
now more closely bound than ever to each other. A proposal was made in
Cairo last evening to invite the Arab foreign ministers to meet and to
prepare for a big Arab summit conference. We hope too that maximum
efforts will continue to be made at the United Nations towards reaching a
solution suitable for the Arabs and with total disregard for what
imperialism and its agents might intend. Diplomatic solutions will
naturally give us time to prepare for the restoration of our rights. It is
hoped that our friends in the Soviet Union and in the socialist countries
will increase the supply of modern weapons and equipment to the Arab
countries, as well as the supply of economic goods that we need.

Brezhnev: I have a question for Comrades Aref and Boumedienne. What is
the real position of the Arab countries towards ending the current problem?
Let us look at things as they stand at the present moment. The enemy is at

a distance of 100 kilometres from Cairo, he is close to Damascus and is occupying the Golan Heights that overlook Damascus. The course of events has indicated that this aggressor has been preparing himself for this assault seriously and for a long time. For example, Israel's population amounts to 2.5 million and its army includes 350,000 troops. This means that 15 per cent of Israel's population carry arms. Let us now study the balance of powers. They were superior in military tactics, in their use of the air force, tanks and airborne infantry, and also in cooperation between the various sectors. This is in addition to the fact that they had also prepared their rearguard for the battle, whereas this did not happen on the Arab side. Let us take the United Arab Republic as an example: its population is 30 million, yet those under arms amounted to only one per cent. The situation was the same in Syria. Is it reasonable for countries to engage in war while they are in such a state? Some of our military commanders have been to your countries and studied everything on the spot. Grechko, our minister of defence, can give you all the details. We say this not to hurt you and not to hold anybody responsible, but so that it can be taken into consideration, bearing in mind that most of these details were previously stated by the military commanders in the United Arab Republic and in Syria.

It is very important to know why the offensive took place, who prepared for it and what its objectives might be. We in the socialist countries have met twice during this short period, which is not easy because we don't usually meet so speedily, even for our own problems. In these two meetings, we examined the Middle East situation both broadly and in great detail. We also discussed all the steps that Israel may take. The purpose of these two meetings was not for publicity purposes but for serious deliberation. We agree with you that American, German and British imperialism is the factor that pushed Israel to carry out this aggression. This needs no proof. The entire world has learned about it through the discussions at the UN General Assembly. But where are the roots of this issue? As a state, Israel has no weight where other countries are concerned because it lacks economic underpinning and lives on the aid that comes to it from outside. If the United States stops loans and aid to Israel, it will wither and vanish within a short period. So, why is America so interested in Israel? The answer lies in America's ambition in the Arab region, which contains 60 per cent of the world's oil reserves. Moreover, the United States makes millions of dollars in annual profits from this black gold. The aim of America and the West is to hold the Arab peoples in their grip, as they did in the past. But after the progressive Arab regimes emerged and after it became evident that the Arab peoples wanted to live freely, independently and follow the path of progress, imperialism found that this constituted a danger to its own interest and almost caused it to lose its authority. This is why imperialism has needed Israel. A direct imperialist attack against the Arab countries is almost impossible but an attack through Israel will always give it an appropriate solution. Imperialism has found the right opening this time and so has pushed the Israeli army from small skirmishes to larger operations, and then to a full-scale war.

We have hardly slept during this whole month. How do we stop the Israeli army's march to Cairo or to Damascus? We have received a cable to the effect that the Syrian Government will move to Aleppo and this is why they have asked for a cease-fire. For our part, we have exerted pressure on the United States, and the socialist countries have severed their relations with Israel. All these are serious steps and we have not taken any like them during the past ten years.

The current situation amounts to this. As far as the enemy is concerned, it is in his interest to remain in the territories that he has occupied and also that the United Nations adopts no resolution concerning the aggression. Therefore, it is not surprising that he will try to create dissent between the Arab countries or between the Soviet Union and the Arab countries on the draft resolutions that are submitted to the General Assembly.

We must examine the facts as they stand and we must study them in detail because they contain positive aspects, just as much as they contain negative ones. The war started on 5 June. On 8 June, the Soviet Union started to send its aircraft to carry weapons to the United Arab Republic and to Syria through the air space of pro-Western countries. We have been able to compensate for large amounts of the weapons that were lost in the war by way of 544 airlifts and 15 cargo ships. We've sent nearly 48,000 tons of military equipment, and we have also sent experts to provide training in the use of the weapons and equipment who are now carrying out this task very actively and sincerely on the instructions of the Party's Politburo and because they realize that this is what our people want.

Concerning the political solution, the socialist countries believe that if a resolution is passed calling for Israeli withdrawal from the occupied Arab territories, then a decision to end the state of war can also be taken, bearing in mind that we have consulted all the international law experts and they have said that ending the state of war does not mean recognising the Zionist State. The political solution will give the Arabs the opportunity to prepare and to strengthen their defence capability. Gaining time in this way will give all the Arab countries the opportunity to advance militarily and economically.

You want to rebuild the Arab armies. This will require time, and a large number of trained troops will be needed. When we fought Hitler and occupied Berlin, we had military forces that numbered 16 million fighters. In your war with Israel, you did not have any numerical superiority. So, how could you have won? We are very upset because we had put our reputation with yours and because we have found our latest aircraft and missiles in American research centres. Moreover, our latest tanks have been sent to West Germany. At the same time, we feel deeply hurt when we hear Israeli officers say that our tanks and aircraft that you abandoned are the best kinds of weapons.

On the other hand, the imperialist forces have achieved what they wanted, namely the failure to pass a resolution at the United Nations. In this way imperialism is preparing the same conditions that can lead to new acts of provocation and then to large-scale military operations against Syria and the United Arab Republic. The coming new operations will mean the downfall of the progressive regimes. If this happens and new regimes emerge, they will work to change everything and to recognise Israel, which will mean the loss of our reputation once again.

Currently and for a number of reasons we require some time. First is the need to strengthen the defence capability of the Arab countries. At their latest meeting in Budapest the socialist countries agreed to strengthen the Arab countries militarily, by which they mean supplying weapons, advancing loans, sending experts and reorganizing the armies according to the requirements of modern warfare, especially in air capability and tank formations. Regrettably, our military experts say that most of your tank drivers do not currently have any more than three to six hours' experience, which means that they do not have combat capability to use the tanks in battle.

Secondly, there is a need to prepare the population politically and to get them ready to struggle and to support their political regime and their government fully. This is considered fundamental for continuing the struggle in the future. Thirdly, it is necessary to build a sound economic infrastructure because modern warfare requires the presence of a strong economy. Without a sound economy, the battle cannot be continued for very long.

Seven socialist countries have recently expressed their readiness to advance the necessary aid to the friendly Arab countries and each of them is now deciding the details of what it can offer.

There is another issue. You are asking us to undertake the responsibility for air defence and to send 50 Soviet pilots for air security. Do you imagine that if this happens, all your problems will be ended? This is an incorrect view of the situation. There are many difficulties in actual implementation. The orders of our officers and your officers will be confused and will be difficult to understand and then operational chaos will result.

Boumedienne [*interrupting Brezhnev*]: This is a technical and not a political problem.

Brezhnev: I understand that. But there is another aspect to the problem. The pilots cannot be used on their own. Auxiliary units must take part with them or else it will be easy to shoot them down. This means that we would have to contribute more of our crews and regiments. What will reactions be in such a case? It is possible in these circumstances that the battles and the war will escalate at a time when we find the lines of communication between us are stretched. Moreover, this form of participation in operations means that foreign forces would be defending a country whose own national forces had not yet been trained. This is not the correct way, and that is why we presented the issue to our comrades in the socialist countries and discussed the whole current situation so carefully. We have found that the best way of achieving our main goal, which is to protect the safety of the progressive Arab regimes, is to follow the longer route, by strengthening these Arab states with whatever help they need, whether military, political or economic.

Kosygin: Our Party has been fighting imperialism for many years, which is why it is the easiest thing for us to help you and to stand by you. We want the Arab states to be independent and strong. You brought up a political issue when you said that the Arab countries did not agree to end the state of war and that you regard this as an impossibility. If we take your position and say what you say, what will be left? Nothing will be left except to continue the war, and the meaning of a continued war is that Israel will not withdraw and will be supported in this position by the United States, Germany and many other countries.

In this case, are you prepared for war? Have you discussed this matter in detail? On our part, we would like to adopt a position that would please our Arab friends and we would like to say to them: "Go ahead, advance." But after assessing your present military strength and capabilities and after familiarising ourselves with the reports of our military experts, we have concluded that this would be unrealistic. This is why I would like to tell you that you are following a policy that lacks flexibility. Such a policy cannot be used against imperialism. It can be used with us because we are friends. But it is also our duty to tell you things that may not please you or may not appeal to you. What is important is to be open with each other, because history will not forgive us in the future.

Boumedienne: We have come here to talk frankly and to reach an understanding as friends.

Kosygin: I think that at present revolutionary slogans might be against the interest of the Arabs themselves. Take China, for instance. China asks you to adopt a firm revolutionary stance and says to you: "Begin the war and we will support you." Afterwards, you'll have nothing but meetings and that will be all. Grandiose words, if not based on actual strength, amount to treason. We have to take some factors into consideration. First, you should seize the current opportunity and work for the unity of the Arab countries, provided that you avoid any action which might obstruct this undertaking and that you isolate all the persons who stand in the way of achieving this unity.

Secondly, and regardless of how hard the conditions are, all persons who stand against the revolution must be rigorously eliminated. Reactionism and progressiveness must be separated. Thirdly, the current opportunity must be exploited to build a strong army, keeping in mind that building and bolstering an army requires at least two years. Fourthly you should not adopt a rigid policy toward imperialism. It is necessary to maintain a flexible approach. It is not important to end the state of war. What is important is to gain the time necessary to strengthen the armed forces and to consolidate the regime. This will give you the ability and the faith to achieve your future plans.

Brezhnev: In this case, you will rely on your factions and your party and the people will understand your orders and your policy well.

Kosygin: I think that your big mistake is to believe that sending 50 of our pilots and 1,000 of our troops will bring you victory. This is an unsound assessment. You have said that this is a technical rather than a political issue. However, I want to explain this issue to you fully. If we send our forces to you, then inevitably the United States and Britain will send their forces to Israel. I don't mean by this that we are afraid, but I mean that we should think carefully of the consequences before we escalate the situation. In the latest war against Israel, no forces – that is non-Israeli forces – or aircraft took part with Israel. Why? The answer is because Israel was strong. We hear that some Arabs are saying that the Russians are afraid. But the truth is that we should think with cool heads. I want to assure you that the current political situation is encouraging, that many countries are on your side and that we stand by you. I have learned that a meeting will be held shortly by the Arab foreign ministers. I hope that you will form a subcommittee to discuss the oil issue. Try to split the imperialist ranks on the issue of oil by supporting one country at the expense of another. The same goes for the economic concessions given to the United States and to the West by the Arab countries. Politically, you can create problems for them and you can make use of these problems in a number of ways. Unfortunately, your present thinking is confined to one issue, and that is 'will the war continue or will it stop?' If the Israeli forces do not withdraw now, who would be the victor? In my view, you should move in other directions. You have to work against imperialism and against Israel from a position of strength and not from a position of weakness. The power is in your hands and you can direct it any way you like through political flexibility.

In my most recent conversation with Johnson, I felt that although he wanted to help Israel with all his might, at the same time he was afraid of losing the Arab world. Besides, ultimately, he doesn't want to sever his relations with the Arabs. This position must be exploited. Johnson knows that if he loses the Arab countries, he will also lose Africa. So by using political means, you can achieve big results. Talk to the Americans any way you like. Words are not important. We don't consider that the present Arab defeat is also a future defeat. Nor should you forget that political struggle doesn't mean final withdrawal and therefore defeat, because there may in fact be progress behind it.

Aref: On the question of ending the war, this would mean opening the Suez Canal for navigation and also negotiating with Israel, and this could be followed by peace.

Kosygin: Not at all. The negotiations can be carried out through the United Nations and if they don't withdraw, then the state of war will continue. In any event, I believe that you are closing the door that would enable you to get out of the crisis.

Boumedienne: So, what is new in our present discussion is the issue of the UN resolution. The Middle East conflict is not a simple war. As I have already said, it is just one battle in a long series launched by imperialism against other peoples. The wars raging in the world at present are well known, but the most important of them is the Middle East conflict for a whole variety of strategic and economic reasons, but especially where oil is involved. Regardless of how often it is said, in connection with this conflict, that the Arabs are fanatical, the truth is that they are victims of aggression and their lands are occupied. I don't want to talk about the defeat because no clear-cut encounters took place and because the causes of the defeat are well known. Nowadays we are in the position of the victim who has to pay the price. Let us review the UN issue. Will mere voting put an end to the serious problem of the Middle East? Let us assume that the Arabs will agree to ending the state of war. Will this mean an end to the problem and will it, very simply, mean Israel's withdrawal?

Kosygin: If they don't withdraw, the state of war will continue. We always stipulate the condition of Israeli withdrawal from the occupied territories.

Boumedienne: In my opinion the problem can't be judged so simply. Why? Because the Americans themselves have based all their calculations and all their analyses on the grounds that the winning card is in their hands and that they will not easily let go of it. They won't part with this card until the problem is solved in the way they want it to be solved. In our view, the Americans will not accept any resolution that does not reflect their viewpoint and needless to say they can obstruct the passage of any resolution they do not want. America's main goal is to destroy every progressive regime in the Middle East.

Brezhnev: The United States, Britain and Germany were against the UN meeting, but in spite of this the meeting did take place and we obtained many votes.

Boumedienne: The problem has two components. The first was caused by the 1948 war and its outcome, which is the so-called Palestinian issue, and the second by the 1967 war and its outcome, or the so-called aggression issue. America's policy is finally to resolve both parts of the problem in the interests of Israel and at the expense of the progressive regimes. The United States is now in a position of power and will not let the opportunity of toppling the progressive regimes in the UAR and Syria first and then in Iraq go by without exploiting it to the full.

Brezhnev: So what is the solution? We are thinking in the same way. Theoretically, this is true. But the enemy is close to you.

Boumedienne: We have two choices in front of us. Either we acknowledge the *fait accompli* and negotiate at the expense of the progressive regimes or we take firmer positions.

Brezhnev: What do you mean by the *fait accompli* at the expense of the progressive regimes?

Boumedienne: The problem is not simply one of voting on a resolution at the United Nations. The resolution may not produce any results. In the present circumstances, the United States is in a strong position. Some Arab countries may offer one concession after another, and then it will be impossible for the governments of these countries to survive. Let us examine the proposed draft resolutions. First there was the Soviet draft and then matters developed and concessions started being made and now we have reached the point of being pressed to end the state of war. I will not hide from you that this is a serious matter. We respect the opinion of the legal experts you referred to earlier but we believe that this means recognising Israel. The Palestinian issue is a sensitive matter and neither Abdel Nasser's government nor the Baghdad government can approve the proposed draft resolution. If this has to be done, then new governments will have to approve these steps.

Brezhnev: These comments imply that you don't really desire to continue the struggle.

Boumedienne: I have read the statement that was issued in the wake of the Budapest meeting. It was a powerful statement. It referred to the unity of the Arab countries. The question to be asked is, how can the contradictions between the Arab countries be reconciled within a single unity?

Kosygin: We understand what you are saying and we haven't forgotten that Morocco, for example, is causing you many problems on the borders.

Boumedienne: And then you accuse Algeria of being radical! [*The statement issued by the Eastern bloc countries meeting in Budapest had made precisely this claim.*] All these are difficult issues. We defended the revolution against reactionary forces and now we are being told to go along with those in a position of power and to resort to tactics and to flexibility. How?

Kosygin: You talk about the facts as they exist, but you offer no solution to the problem.

Brezhnev: I have followed the problem since its beginning. However, I understand that if you go on conceding the reality of the state of war, then this will lead to big problems. In my opinion, you need to separate two issues: the first is how to eliminate the traces of the aggression and the second is how we should explore the other problems afterwards. The important issue now is how the progressive Arab regimes should be protected and how the enemy is to be expelled.

Boumedienne: Comrade Brezhnev has mentioned the question of how to eliminate the traces of the aggression. In my opinion, this can be done either by reaching an understanding with our enemies according to the conditions they dictate, or by pursuing our struggle regardless of how long it takes. This means we choose either the first or the second solution. If we opt for the second solution, which is struggle, then we must reach an understanding with each other on how to carry on the struggle. To put it briefly, I believe that there will be a victor and a vanquished.

Brezhnev: Regaining land is not easy.

Boumedienne: If land is the only problem, then we can change our political position and regain the land by accepting the American proposals and conditions. But then the result would be the downfall of the progressive regimes, which is why I said at the outset that the choice was difficult.

Kosygin: How will you implement the second option?

Boumedienne: At this point I would like first to mention the view of the people who sent us because you may find my own opinion radical. We [*the Arab leaders meeting in Cairo*] have agreed to pursue all diplomatic channels, but at the same time, we will not neglect the struggle. The matter that both Syria and the United Arab Republic request you to consider urgently is that their defence capabilities be strengthened.

Brezhnev: The date of the final UN General Assembly meeting is 20 July 1967, which is in three days' time. You are free to express your opinions but the world is going to say that the Arabs are fanatical in their position.

Kosygin: Are you in fact against the idea of ending the state of war, even after the aggressors have returned to the former ceasefire lines? What is more important to you: recovering your land or going on with the struggle?

Boumedienne: This question cannot be answered with a 'yes' or 'no'. We do not believe that the problem will be settled with a UN vote.

Kosygin: Then how will you solve this issue militarily in the meantime?

Brezhnev: Generally speaking, if any resolution is adopted by the General Assembly, the Security Council will implement it. We have the power of veto there, so you should not feel uneasy about the resolutions. However, why do you exclude the possibility that the enemy will move again and attack the three regimes with all his force on the grounds that the state of war continues and that afterwards new governments might emerge according to the wish and the will of the Americans? We want you to be strong, and then you may talk any way you want. But now . . . [*and here Brezhnev spread his hands in an eloquent gesture whose meaning was entirely clear*].

Boumedienne: The choice today is a decisive choice, and the problem isn't just one of a UN resolution. There has to be a practical guarantee for ending the state of war. This is something that the Americans will accept at the expense of the progressive Arab regimes. What we want now is political backing and military support, bearing in mind that we have already received some weapons and that others are on their way.

Brezhnev [*interrupting angrily*]: But you don't have trained officers and troops at present. I suggest that our positions and opinions be put down in writing. History will judge who was right and who was wrong. We agree with you on the need to continue the fighting, but the conditions are ill-timed just now. We are now facing a *fait accompli.*

Kosygin: What do you think about de Gaulle's proposal for a meeting of the major powers? De Gaulle says it is the pragmatic answer to the problem, but we won't endorse the proposal because you, the Arabs, have not accepted it. However, if you approve it, we will change our position. But who will guarantee America's position?

Brezhnev: Let us assume that a resolution calling for an end to the state of war is passed. In this case, the Security Council will be asked to study how it is to be implemented, and there will be a proposal that UN observers and forces be sent to monitor the implementation. The Egyptians will also be asked to declare the freedom of passage through the canal. For our part we will continue to send you military experts and armaments and as a result you will have time to complete your preparations.

Boumedienne: Ending the state of war will give rise to serious consequences.

Brezhnev [*again angrily*]: If we analyse your opinions thoroughly, we'll either find them radical or leading towards a new defeat.

Kosygin [*trying to cool the heated atmosphere*]: If you want to strike Israel, then we are on your side, but the current conditions don't help this.

Boumedienne: Ending the state of war essentially means capitulation. Do we understand that the Soviet Union's position is entirely consistent with what was stated in the recent Budapest communiqué?

Brezhnev: Yes. We exchanged opinions at that conference with complete impunity and everyone's opinions were virtually identical. When we'd finished exchanging views, we conducted an analytical study whose findings were integrated in the communiqué. We did not go into the conference carrying any specific plan from Moscow. I want you to be satisfied that we do not impose our own opinions on the seven socialist countries. I also wish you to know that the general atmosphere in that conference invited optimism and not pessimism. Indeed, there was an obvious hope that victory would be yours in the future. Ending the state of war does not dictate the establishment of political relations between you and Israel.

Boumedienne: But don't you see that Zionism controls America, Western Europe and Britain? This is why their opinions always reflect those of Israel. We still see the world as incapable of condemning Israel. We, the Arabs, did not start the war. Slogans were not the cause. The war of aggression was started and Arab territory was captured and yet the General Assembly refuses to condemn Israel and has recognized the *fait accompli.* The world then says that we are fanatical. This might have been true before 5 June but it has became meaningless since then.

Brezhnev: Let us be realistic. Where were the 800 tanks and the 1,500 guns destroyed? They were destroyed at the borders. They were not destroyed in battle. The Israelis succeeded in portraying you to the world as having prepared an attack against them and in portraying themselves as having repelled the attack and then having pursued and defeated you. If we want to overcome the dilemma and to achieve victory, then we have to think calmly together. In any case, this session has gone on for too long. Let us leave the calm thinking for tomorrow's session.

The Second Session, 18 July 1967

The second session of talks was acerbic and heated. The Soviets, as I learned later, believed that President Boumedienne had come to Moscow having committed himself completely to the Chinese viewpoint, and proceeding from this assumption the Soviets showed what they thought about the Algerian president, by hints and by insinuations. It seemed at times during the talks that any convergence of views was virtually impossible. Whereas the Soviets concentrated on the need to end the state of war and felt that protecting the progressive Arab regimes should come before liberation of the land, the Arab delegation believed that liberation of the land came first and foremost. I was later told that by the end of the meeting, the atmosphere was very tense and that each side found the other's approach extremely exasperating.

It was 10.00, Moscow time, on Tuesday 18 July 1967, when the second meeting got under way at the Kremlin Palace, and the weather was unusually pleasant and warm. Kosygin started the session immediately. He looked at his watch first and then launched directly into discussion of the issue without any words of greeting and without the usual courtesies, which was contrary to Soviet custom.

Kosygin: We are all aware that the problem is difficult but we are looking for a solution. We are even more distressed than the Arabs about the current situation.

Brezhnev: Currently we are more preoccupied with Arab problems than with any other concerns. Iran's prime minister is visiting us tomorrow. What was their attitude towards you like?

Boumedienne: Their position has generally been favourable.

Kosygin: It may be appropriate for you to send cables of thanks to all the countries that have supported you.

Aref: This has already been done. We have sent personal cables to all of them.

Brezhnev: I'm not satisfied with yesterday's discussion. The views we heard suggest that there is no clear understanding of the situation. Moreover, we didn't hear anything about solutions. We know that your citizens are distressed by what has happened, but listening to people's feelings is not sufficient. Imperialism must be fought. Imperialism is sly and we must also be sly in confronting it. It's always important to know what is the most important thing. Struggle before independence is one thing and struggle after independence is another. For a month and a half, we've been talking and exchanging opinions with the leaders of friendly countries. We are all thinking of the interest of the Arabs. Those who voted for the draft resolution tabled by the non-aligned states [*one of the political resolutions submitted to the United Nations*] were on the side of the Arabs, but unfortunately the draft resolution did not win a majority. This doesn't mean the end of the struggle. But we must find the right path. For our part, we have severed our relations with Israel and we are ready to go and fight with you. Sacrifice with results is acceptable but sacrifice without results is not.

Gromyko cabled us from New York today to tell us that the UN General Assembly is going to end its session without having adopted any resolution. This is the worst possible state of affairs because it means that Israel will have a free hand to strike again. Regrettably, there is no Arab country that is prepared for resistance at this time. In my opinion, the situation will be difficult. Comrade Boumedienne, you are a long way from the battlefield so you may be able to see the broad situation more clearly.

Kosygin: I would like to add another thing, which is that after the General Assembly session has ended, nobody knows what will happen next. I beg you to think carefully. Your affairs are in your own hands and we have no right to exert pressure on you, but if you are persuaded by anything you have heard, you can contact Abdel Nasser and the Syrian president by telephone from here and explain the situation to them straight away. Time is short and we need a definite answer. In Gromyko's opinion, the Israeli forces should withdraw first and then we could link this to the issue of ending the state of war and free navigation through the Suez Canal. Actually, freedom of navigation is a purely theoretical issue as far as Israel is concerned because Israeli ships pass through the canal under different flags.

Boumedienne: On this particular point, the passage of the Israeli flag through the canal does in fact imply recognition of Israel.

Kosygin: This is a theoretical issue. The Germans were navigating through our waterways while we were in a state of war with them, but we accepted this because we benefited economically from such traffic.

Boumedienne: Let us go back to the main issue. Does Mr Kosygin see that the Palestinian problem must be solved, because this is the crux of the issue?

Kosygin: No. If you agree to what has been suggested, the Palestinian question would be presented separately. During my most recent meeting with Johnson, I asked him: "How do you view the solution to the Palestinian problem?" He replied: "All countries must take part in solving the issue. We will agree to receive a number of refugees in America and Canada agrees to take some. The United States is ready to shoulder all the expenses." My answer to Johnson was: "Such a proposal is like taking some

Americans to live in Siberia, for example. It is an impractical proposal." I also told him that the crux of the matter was that the Palestinians wanted to return to their homeland and that what he proposed was a deception and would not be accepted by any Arabs. Speaking generally, this problem of the Palestinians should be on the UN agenda, but if we begin discussing it today, we wouldn't have finished talking about it by tomorrow.

Boumedienne: After yesterday's and today's discussion, I personally feel an atmosphere of ambiguity about the Soviet position toward the problem.

Aref: If the progressive regimes are to survive it is imperative that we achieve some gains for them. Don't forget that there is a hostile propaganda campaign whose slogan is that it is these regimes that have led the Arabs into this situation of defeat. If ultimately we accept certain concessions, the people themselves will rebel against these regimes.

At this point, a Soviet official entered and handed a message to Ponomarev, who read it, wrote a few words on it and then handed it to Kosygin.

Kosygin: We've just received a cable from Gromyko in New York saying that all the draft resolutions that were submitted to the General Assembly were turned down an hour ago because the Arab delegations rejected them, and that another draft resolution has been submitted as a result of the contacts that he has made with certain delegations. If the Arab delegations approve this, it can be passed, even though it is being rejected by Israel. [*All draft resolutions that were put to the UN General Assembly at this time stipulated in one way or another the ending of the state of war between Israel and the Arabs.*]

Brezhnev: I want again to ask a question that I've already asked, and that is, if Israel deals a new blow to the United Arab Republic, Syria and Iraq, what will the outcome be? In such a case, we would find ourselves with new problems, the progressive Arab regimes would fall and the issue would then be put before the Security Council. Can you imagine this picture? We in the socialist camp cannot allow such a development because it would mean war against the West and would also mean the use of nuclear weapons with results that nobody can possibly predict.

Boumedienne: In my opinion, a major war with nuclear weapons would break out only over far bigger issues than the question of freedom of navigation in the Suez Canal or other matters of that sort. A major war would only break out over issues that threatened humanity.

Brezhnev: You don't want to agree to ending the state of war, even on paper, and Israel doesn't want to withdraw. There are also other problems, such as the freedom of navigation and so on. We are looking for a solution, while the enemy, for his part, is looking for a solution too. In the present circumstances, we may accept a paper with the words "ending the state of war" written on it in return for the survival of the progressive regimes and for continuing the struggle. For our part, we will help you militarily and the socialist countries will not stop their assistance to you. You, as military men, will understand very well that it is impossible to rebuild armed forces in two days, especially after the recent lesson you've had to learn.

We received cables from Prague and Bulgaria yesterday. They are sending you weapons and munitions. The value of the weapons and military equipment recently received by the Egyptians has so far amounted to $258 million, and no conditions have been attached to them. Moreover, we are ready to dispatch 2,000 of our best experts. But it's not in our interests to keep them there for a long time. In the end you must rely on your own institutions and training centres. Podgorny and Marshal Zakharov, our chief of staff, were with Abdel Nasser three weeks ago, and he told them that he does not have an army in the real sense of the word and that he is currently reorganizing it. We estimate that at least two years of constant work will be needed after which you can launch an attack, provided that morale is high and that there is a willingness to sacrifice and to die.

Grechko: The Egyptian army has nearly 220,000 troops, 900 tanks, 300 aircraft, and more than 1,000 guns and other weapons. All these weapons are in the hands of troops who cannot use them properly. Nearly 60 per cent of the troops are new because a large number of the officers and the trained soldiers have either been killed or captured, or have left the service. There is a 35 per cent shortfall in pilots and a 30 per cent shortfall in tank crews. Generally speaking, the army is currently able to defend only against small forces and not stand against a big offensive, and the air defence system for the major cities is still inadequate. This means that at present the Egyptian army is not ready to take offensive action and not even for defence.

Let me turn to Syria. Casualties were low, but the Syrian forces left 12,000 items of various sorts of weapon behind them. The Syrians are now capable of defensive action, but they are not yet ready to launch an offensive.

Frankly, the balance of forces between the United Arab Republic and Syria on the one hand and Israel on the other does not allow an offensive to be launched against Israel at present. However, it is possible to achieve this with time, and to prove what I'm saying, I'll give you some recent data on the military capability in the three countries.

The number of military personnel in the United Arab Republic and Syria together amounts to 350,000 officers and men, and in Israel the number is 300,000. There are 34 brigades in the UAR and Syria together, and 31 in Israel. The UAR and Syria have a total of 1,450 tanks and Israel has 1,250. The UAR and Syria have 2,200 guns and there are 2,700 guns in Israel. The number of aircraft in the United Arab Republic and Syria is 340, while there are 300 in Israel.

Brezhnev: In view of this report, we say that there must be time to transform these quantities into a quality that is capable of fighting. If this is done we can guarantee military, economic and political victory. If you agree to this, you'll thank us one of these days. Let us discuss the issue objectively. You Easterners are zealous. But there also has to be a foundation. What does it matter if the Israeli flag goes through the Canal or not? What is the significance of formalities when compared to a monumental undertaking such as the High Dam, a mammoth industrial project or a big agricultural project within the country?

Boumedienne [*sharply and sarcastically*]: So in this case, if we get tractors they will be more useful to us than tanks?

Brezhnev: Yes, you'll also get tractors and everything else, but logic and realistic thinking is needed. The Arab countries have made great progress and they have carried out important social reforms internally because the revolution paved the way for them to do this. Is it right to drop all this from our calculations? It would be a crime against the revolution. Under these circumstances what does it matter if a resolution to end the state of war is issued, provided that the withdrawal of the Israeli forces precedes it?

There's another point. I heard some new statements made by Boumedienne yesterday. You criticize the Americans, and so do we. However, you said that you will not talk to Israel but will talk to the Americans. This is something new to us. Israel is not enslaving you but America can.

Boumedienne: Your words are incomprehensible and ambiguous.

Kosygin: The words are quite clear. The interpreter is responsible for any ambiguity.

Boumedienne: What I want to make clear is that Israel is not the problem because Israel is in the hands of the Americans who are now in a position of power. We believe that ending the state of war will lead to our having to accept the terms dictated by Israel. Any policy that leads to recognizing Israel is unacceptable. We know that the United States does not allow attacks against Israel. We have been defeated and our lands are occupied, and yet we cannot get an international resolution condemning Israel. We do not recognize the introduction of changes on the world map, and especially the Middle East map, through force. Ending the state of war will inevitably lead to recognition of the Israeli presence. This is something that is very difficult for Cairo and for the others to accept.

Brezhnev: Let Israel withdraw and then interpret the resolution the way you want and not the way Israel wants. When you become strong, do whatever you want.

Boumedienne: So the issue can now be summed up to the effect that in your opinion a vote must be taken on a resolution, any resolution, regardless of whether it calls for ending the state of war or not, and that the General Assembly must come up with a resolution. On this basis, we will move ahead one step and the enemy will move ten steps. You also say that, for diplomatic reasons and in order to gain time, we must accept anything, no matter what it is. Frankly, I don't agree with you that a resolution terminating the state of war is merely a humble piece of paper. If the problem is put forward in this form, then we must examine the entire issue, meaning the entire Palestinian issue, so that it can be settled completely and so that peace can be achieved. In this case, withdrawal from the occupied territories becomes a part of this whole solution. This is how all our brothers see it. Is approval of the draft resolution a temporary diplomatic solution or is it the beginning of other ways of solving the problem?

Kosygin: It is a new beginning for the struggle.

Brezhnev: In fact, the issue is complicated and there are immediate goals and long-range goals. The forms of struggle change according to circumstances. We now believe that the major issue is the immediate one, which involves safeguarding the progressive Arab regimes. How can this be done? It can be done through terminating the state of war, through withdrawal of the Israeli forces and through gaining time to strengthen your defences. Afterwards, you will become a real danger to the enemy.

Comrades, we are being very frank with you. If no resolution is taken at the United Nations and if Israel launches an attack against Cairo in two weeks' time, what will the outcome be? This is not beyond the bounds of possibility. What we are telling you now does not represent our opinion only, because otherwise you could claim that we might be wrong. We have consulted with seven socialist countries and they have all arrived at the same view. We know that you are sensitive on certain issues but problems are not solved with emotions alone. Marshal Abdel Hakim Amer used to ask us for weapons and equipment and told us that he had the necessary schools and cadres, so we did not interfere. But we have now realised that we were wrong because we did not make sure how the weapons were to be used and what training was to be given in using them before the weapons were sent.

Boumedienne: The discussion has gone on long enough and we have understood your opinion. To conclude the session, I would like to assure you in the name of the brothers who are meeting in Cairo that we will make every effort to preserve the friendship between us. At the same time, I would like to draw your attention to the fact that relations with you are passing through delicate and critical circumstances and duty requires that we take this into consideration. Secondly, we have explained the viewpoint of our brothers in Cairo to you, and when we return we will give them a clear picture about the position in Moscow. Thirdly, we stress the need to focus on serious military training, along with strengthening defence capability in both the United Arab Republic and Syria. Fourth, Abdel Nasser stresses the urgency of strengthening him by giving him the means of defence – he talked to Podgorny about this matter – especially with regard to air defence in the form and manner that you consider appropriate and possible.

Aref: If we accept the proposal to end the state of war and then Israel insists on being recognised and on the freedom of navigation, what will your position be?

Brezhnev: What will your position be in this case?

Aref: Complete rejection.

Brezhnev: In that case, we will reject as well. As for military aid, there are currently a number of air defence experts in the United Arab Republic and as soon as they return home, we will pursue our decision regarding the aid that has been requested. I want to tell you an old story about our military experts that happened before the aggression. We had 400 military experts in the United Arab Republic and we had instructed them not to interfere in anything unless they were specifically asked. Our officers put in a request to the Egyptian military command to go and see Sinai to acquaint themselves with the deployment plan for the forces but their request was turned down.

There's one final matter before you return to Cairo. You told us that you had come here to convey the views of the Arab presidents who are now in Cairo. Have you adopted final decisions yet in Cairo or will you take what we have discussed here into consideration? In other words, have you come to bring us your decisions just for the sake of giving us information, and are the observations of the socialist camp of no value? We would like you to answer this question.

Boumedienne: We will pass on everything that has been said at yesterday's and today's meetings to our colleagues in Cairo.

Brezhnev [*getting up from his chair*]: Time is getting short. Come, let us have lunch quickly so that we can accompany you to the airport and see you off.

It was nearly 14.00 when the two delegations left the conference hall, having spent almost four hours in heated discussion. After a light lunch with the Soviet leaders in the banqueting hall of the Kremlin Palace, all the participants proceeded to Moscow's military airport where the Arab delegation boarded the special plane for the non-stop flight back to Egypt. Five hours later, the plane landed at Cairo and the delegation proceeded directly to the conference chamber at al-Qubbah palace where the other Arab presidents were assembled. At the beginning of his account of the meeting, President Boumedienne expressed his deep distress at the position taken by the Soviet leaders, saying: "Had I read the communiqué of the socialist camp before our departure for Moscow, I would not have gone. They are afraid of direct friction with the United States and cannot bear to hear the slogan of the armed struggle."

Muhammad Ahmad Mahjoub, Sudan's foreign minister, had also just arrived from New York, where he had been attending the meetings of the General Assembly. Mahjoub, who played a prominent role after the defeat in attempting to bring the views of Nasser and King Faisal closer together, conveyed to them the current political climate at the UN and so more or less shattered whatever nerves were left.

Chapter 3

DIFFICULT DECISIONS
Discussions towards a pan-Arab summit

Nasser was plainly uneasy during the two days that President Houari Boumedienne of Algeria and President Abdel Rahman Aref of Iraq were away in Moscow. He had many things on his mind, of course, but he was also turning over a scheme of some kind that he kept secret even from his most intimate associates, although those who knew him and who were close to him, of whom I am one, were aware that he was hatching a plan at that time. When he was told that the special plane carrying the two leaders had landed, his features visibly relaxed. I heard him say to those standing near him: "Now we'll know the real attitude of our friends in Moscow." On arrival Boumedienne and Aref were not taken to the guest-house to rest but went straight to the presidential palace although it was obvious from their faces when they entered the hall that both men were exhausted. I noticed Nasser gazing intently at Boumedienne in an attempt to read the latter's expression.

The problems and difficulties of the defeat had by now begun to take shape and to crystallize. Nasser, who had been urged by popular demonstrations in Cairo, Baghdad, Beirut and Damascus on 9 and 10 June 1967 to withdraw his resignation, was now quietly reviewing, examining and bringing people to account, and would allow no more mistakes even by those most loyal to him. The attempt by his close friend Abdel Hakim Amer to seize power so soon after the forces under his command had been so comprehensively crushed perhaps hurt Nasser more than the defeat itself. It was a time, one might say, when Nasser had to look in front of him and behind him and to sleep with one eye open. Before he could attempt to predict what might happen outside Egypt, he had to deal with the many problems inside the country, which was why the visit by Boumedienne and

Aref to Moscow was so important. The day before the two presidents returned to Cairo, I walked with Nasser, who seemed very preoccupied, in the garden of his residence. I said to him: "What is the matter, Mr President? These troubles will pass." He replied in a low voice: "What if the Soviets have changed their minds about what we agreed earlier? The American position is clear. They want to topple the regime and to destroy Abdel Nasser personally. But the Soviet position is less obvious. Are they ready to go with us to the end of the road or will international calculations and circumstances force them to stop at a certain point?"

In addition to Nasser, Boumedienne and Aref, the meeting was attended by Abdel Karim al-Jundi on behalf of the Syrian President Nur al-Din al-Atasi who had been obliged to return to Damascus, and the Sudanese minister of foreign affairs, Muhammad Ahmad Mahjoub, representing President Ismail al-Azhari who had also left Cairo for Khartoum. There was a profound silence in the hall as President Boumedienne started to speak.

The First Session, 18 July 1967

Boumedienne: As soon as we'd arrived at Moscow airport we headed for the conference hall at the Kremlin Palace where we began the meeting with the Soviet delegation; their delegation included Brezhnev, Kosygin and Grechko, and Ponomarev who is the Central Committee official in charge of the Arab region, as well as a number of their civilian and military aides. The Iraqi and Algerian ambassadors in Moscow also joined our delegation.

Aref: The discussions were lengthy and consisted of two sessions which went on altogether for nearly nine hours. They mostly revolved around two issues, one of which concerned Arab–Soviet relations and the possibility that these might be affected by the present delicate circumstances. We assured the Soviets that we were eager to continue, and even to develop and improve these relations. The second was related to the political plans submitted to the United Nations, and discussions on this issue took a long time, especially our exchanges on ending the state of war.

Boumedienne: Before we boarded the plane which was flying us to Moscow, the Soviet ambassador in Cairo handed us the communiqué that had been issued by the eastern bloc countries at the Budapest conference. What caught my eye in this communiqué was the statement that Algeria held radical opinions and that these opinions might cause problems for all the progressive Arab countries. I tell you frankly that if I'd read that communiqué before I got to the airport, I wouldn't have gone to Moscow myself.

The impression I get from our meeting in Moscow is that the Soviets want at any price to pass a UN resolution on the matter so that it will remain in the hands of the international lobbies, otherwise they'll have to shoulder the responsibility for the entire problem themselves. That's why they kept insisting throughout the discussions on the need for the resolution to be passed and stressing how serious the situation will be if the UN meetings end without a resolution being agreed. I also noticed during the conversations which we had with them that there are contradictions in their political analysis, especially since their analysis is always based on the political considerations that affect them specifically. For example, they insist on taking on and firmly challenging domestic reactionary forces in every Arab country. At the same time we find that they're emphasising the need for a complete Arab alliance regardless of the various trends that are to be found within the Arab community at present. They also went on at some length on how important it was to pass the UN resolution, irrespective of the provisions it contains concerning the passage of Israeli ships through the Suez Canal and the Gulf of Aqaba. I personally believe that the Soviets have adopted this attitude because, in addition to their original position towards Israel as a state, they are anxious to avoid the damage to Moscow's reputation that such a diplomatic defeat would inflict.

As for the armaments issue, they said that they'd already sent us large consignments of weapons and that they would continue to uphold this commitment. Personally, I feel that they will in fact carry on with this, although there will probably be some delay in delivering the weapons and equipment that are required.

In the supplementary meetings we had with Brezhnev alongside the two official meetings, we put forward the issue of arming Sudan, and Brezhnev agreed. As for our request relating to the dispatch of technicians and complete crews for various weapons and equipment, and particularly for Egypt's air defence, they told us that this poses numerous technical difficulties including, for example, the language problem between their personnel and the Egyptian officers and troops, and also the lengthy communication lines between Moscow and Cairo for the Soviet units that would be taking part in the arrangements. But at the end of the discussion on this subject, they told us that since there is currently a technical military committee in the UAR which is studying all the details with the officials concerned, a decision will be made shortly on the basis of its findings.

During discussions, the Soviets suggested the possibility of a nuclear war breaking out as a result of the Soviet military presence in the United Arab Republic. I told them that such a conflict was unlikely to erupt as a result of problems that only concerned Cairo or Damascus because there would have to be much more serious reasons than these to trigger off a nuclear war. The Soviets also advised us that it is practically impossible for us to carry out any military action against Israel in the next two or three years, and Grechko explained this to us with the help of detailed maps of the Arab–Israeli front and other documents. This is why they consider that it is necessary to resort to a political solution which will provide enough time for reconstruction and for preparing for military action.

In their talks with me, they said that the policy which Algeria is following is wrong and that it is dangerous to all the progressive countries. At this point, there were some sharp exchanges between me and Brezhnev and Kosygin, and I got the impression from this that the Soviets are afraid of a direct collision with the Americans in this domain. Moreover, they don't want to hear the expression 'armed struggle' at this time because from their point of view, the correct solution at present is the political solution. They are also against the destruction of the State of Israel.

At the same time, they assured us that the socialist camp was willing to offer all the aid that has been asked for, whether political, economic or military, and they are going to meet in Belgrade next month to coordinate the aid that is required.

Aref: I asked them what their attitude would be in the event of the enemy deciding not to withdraw even if we recognised the State of Israel and they replied that in such a case they would support us in rejecting this possibility. They repeatedly declared that adopting the political solution would give us the necessary time to make military preparations and that we would then be in a strong position to follow whatever course we thought appropriate. During our conversation, Brezhnev quoted the comment made by Lenin when he signed the well-known Brest treaty and gave up the Ukraine: 'A successful commander is the one who knows when to advance and when to retreat.'

Mahjoub: [*who had recently returned from New York after attending most of the UN General Assembly meetings there*]: We heard the same argument and the same opinion from Gromyko, the Soviet minister of foreign affairs, in New York. I believe that the Soviets want the Arabs to recognize the State of Israel. I must convey to the presidents and brothers who are meeting here what is currently being repeated by delegation members in New York, and that is that the Soviets are demanding a nuclear base in the United Arab Republic and the Arab countries as the price for offering effective aid to the Arabs. If we, as Arabs, hope to become a successful political force at the United Nations, we must all agree on a unified political line toward this issue because at present there are numerous differences in the positions of the Arab delegations to the UN.

Nasser: I'm aware that this session has gone on far too long and that the reactions to the talks have not yet been fully communicated. I can also see that the two presidents who have just come back from Moscow are tired. Therefore, I will end this meeting by thanking the two presidents and their delegations for the great efforts they have made and for the truly Arab dialogue which they have conducted with the Soviets in this decisive phase in the history of the Arab nation. I propose that the session be resumed tomorrow, Wednesday, at ten a.m., but before we leave the hall, I would like to tell you frankly about some of the problems that are worrying me at the moment:

First, it's obvious that the Soviets are really pressing to pass a resolution, any resolution, at the United Nations.

Secondly, the Soviets and the Americans have probably already come to an agreement on dealing with this issue, and there are three reasons why I suspect this: (a) in their discussions with our brother Boumedienne the Soviets said not to be worried about talking with the Americans; (b) they haven't told us what discussions took place in the meeting between Johnson and Kosygin during Kosygin's visit to the United States; and (c) Marshal Zakharov's agreement to support the air defence of the United Arab Republic was withdrawn two days later on the pretext that some technical difficulties existed.

However, we must have a few hours of rest, and then we'll meet at ten o'clock tomorrow.

The Second Session, 19 July 1967

At 10.00 the following morning the presidents and the delegation members met again to complete the review of the Moscow trip and to agree on the next steps to be taken. Nasser was careful not to dwell on details during the discussions. I do not know the reasons for this although I believe they were connected with his desire not to reveal all his cards, especially as this was not a summit meeting in the true sense of the word – that is, not all the presidents were in attendance and other people were deputising for them.

Boumedienne: As long as we are thinking seriously about a political solution, then I believe that we shouldn't tie this solution to the current UN General Assembly resolutions. We need to study the political solution as a whole and also look at all the details. If we find that it all leads to us having to liquidate the progressive regimes, then we will have to choose another path.

Aref: It's obvious that in this case the Soviets do not believe in fighting and in the inevitability of armed struggle. They want to gain time. They don't want to fail at the United Nations, and at the same time they don't want to lose their friends. I believe that from a practical point of view these are contradictory positions. We, as Arabs, have to decide on our position in view of this, and given that the enemy is now standing on the outskirts of two Arab capitals and likely to advance further. In spite of this fact none of the UN member states will stand with us, so we need to gain the time needed to manoeuvre and prepare. As for the question of recognizing Israel, it is a broad Arab issue that doesn't only concern the people meeting here.

Mahjoub: I believe that the situation has become clear to us. We can either act militarily, and this may be a suicidal solution at this time, or we can operate within the framework of a well thought-out political solution. This will require assembling the entire Arab nation to look for a reasonable political response.

Aref: I propose that brother Minister Mahjoub visit all the Arab countries to discuss the issue with them in preparation for accepting the appropriate political solution.

Nasser: Before I express the United Arab Republic's opinion on the fundamental issue, I would like to explain my understanding of one important point. I believe that what is behind the attitude of the Soviets to Algeria and towards President Boumedienne is their belief that Algeria's position is similar to China's. In fact today China has censured the commander of the Soviet fleet that is currently in Port Said for his negative attitude towards a military battle – which took place 20 kilometres away from where he is based – on the grounds that he'd made no move to take part with our troops in the operation.

As for the main issue, I believe that there is a difference between political action and a political solution. In my opinion the political solution according to the Russian or American approach is not a political solution but amounts to capitulation. Indeed it amounts to the elimination of the problem. When we speak of 'a political solution' we must realise that a price of some sort has to be paid. Thus, the path ahead of us is blocked and when the road is blocked, armed struggle becomes the only option.

I believe that the proposed Arab summit amounts simply to a political action and that we will not emerge from it with a political solution. We are now like a fish on a hook, which will have either to break the line or pull the fisherman into the water, otherwise the fisherman will pull the fish out of the sea to die.

We consider the Soviet decision at the United Nations unacceptable because we can and will not agree to end the state of war and thus make our defeat become two defeats. However, this position shouldn't preclude the continuation of political action which needn't come to an end when the UN General Assembly meetings are concluded. Convening an Arab summit conference will help to sustain political action in the region. But if there has to be a political solution, then I perceive it as being the solution to some limited marginal concerns and not as one that touches the critical issues.

During this initial phase let us try to mobilize every rifle and every voice to our side. For the time being let us put aside the issue of the progressive Arab countries and the reactionary Arab countries. Let us avoid unnecessary verbal battles, at least until the Israelis get out. Then whoever wants to say or do something can go ahead.

At the same time, we must work for armed struggle. When the Soviets discover that we insist on armed struggle, they will be obliged to go along with us in spite of their constant fear that armed struggle on our fronts may cause the entire region to ignite.

Finally, I have learned from our brother, President Boumedienne, that in Moscow the Soviets talked a great deal about our military defeat and that they were highly critical of the condition of the Arab armies that withdrew and left their weapons and equipment behind on the battlefield. As a leadership, we should not be particularly affected by what is said about us. We were indeed defeated and we are now having to drink that bitter draught. True leadership drinks not only from the sweet but also from the bitter cup if compelled to do so. The leadership of nations is not only leadership in victory. There is leadership in victory as well as in crises and setbacks. Just as it accepts the cheering of the masses in victory, it has also to accept the jibes of the masses in defeat. This is the law of life. As I have said, we do not refuse to drink the bitter potion. We say now that we will not capitulate. We will not surrender and there will come a day when the bitter cup will be empty and when we will once again drink from the sweet cup together.

With these words, Nasser ended the meeting. Several days later he began to hold regular meetings with the political leadership in Egypt. He had chosen to proceed simultaneously along two routes: rebuilding of the army and political action. The first involved substantial assistance from the Soviet Union in terms of military supplies of all types. Nasser also set up a strenuous training programme that in the short term would enable the armed forces to defend the country's own territory and in the longer term to prepare to launch the war of liberation. To gain time, Nasser used the Jarring mission as a cover for political action, while avoiding having to reach a political solution.

After the defeat, King Husain had been the first to request a comprehensive Arab summit, and had sent a number of West Bank and Jerusalem notables to Cairo to urge Nasser to convene such a conference as a matter of urgency. Nasser had initially rejected King Husain's request, but once the Soviet position had become clear he decided to hold a summit meeting and to confront his Arab opponents in defeat as he had once confronted them in victory.

At one of the meetings which he held with Egypt's political leadership to discuss the matter of the conference, Nasser commented: "With regard to the use of the oil weapon, I maintain that the business of withholding the supply of oil from countries that have cooperated with the enemy will generally be perfunctory. I told Podgorny this during a bilateral discussion I had with him before he left Cairo. As for our position in Yemen, the disagreement between us and Saudi Arabia has been going on for several years. The Yemeni revolution is now established and it is difficult for the monarchy to return to Sanaa. When the June war broke out we had eight military brigades in Yemen and we desperately needed those forces here to take part in the fighting. However, I refused to bring all of them back and I removed only two brigades and some artillery units, the reason being that I was afraid that if they were all withdrawn from Yemen this would mean that Britain would delay its withdrawal from Aden. Even if our troops withdraw from Yemen, we have prepared a special military force to go to Aden on 9 January 1968 [*the date set for the British forces withdrawal*] to protect and uphold Aden's independence.

"Concerning Saudi Arabia, the Kingdom of Morocco, and Tunisia, they are coordinating their positions against us. But the Tunisian people in particular are an Arab people, and they have moved politically in staging demonstrations in the major cities and setting fire to the US Embassy and thereby forcing Bourguiba to declare his readiness to help us.

"As for Syria and Algeria, they utterly refuse to cooperate with the reactionary Arab forces and are against any conference in which these forces participate.

"In Amman, King Husain is taking a patriotic line and insists on the convocation of an Arab summit. For my part, I will stand by King Husain in building up his deteriorating economy, even if it is at the expense of our own sustenance, because I will not forget his attitude toward us in the war.

"Where Riyadh is concerned, there is another opinion which King Faisal expressed during his meeting with the Arab ambassadors. It was Faisal's notion that the Arabs should put the Soviets among the ranks of the enemies, along with the United States and Israel. This is an erroneous opinion and it has to be discussed with him. This is the substance of the Arab situation. In any event, preparations now have to be started for a comprehensive Arab summit at which we will confront those who love us and those who hate us."

Chapter 4

CONSTRUCTIVE AGREEMENT
The Arab leadership in Khartoum, 1967

The Sudanese foreign minister, Muhammad Ahmad Mahjoub, was a poet who also occupied himself with politics. In spite of their political differences and notwithstanding Mahjoub's position on the issue of unity between Sudan and Egypt in particular and the issue of Arab unity generally, he and Nasser had a good relationship. Nasser enjoyed Mahjoub's company and used to relax in his presence, seeing him as a man who engaged in politics in the manner of a modern versifier. Mahjoub was aware of the position he held in Nasser's affections and this is how he came to play a prominent role in preparing for the Khartoum conference. To this end, Mahjoub moved from one Arab capital to another, eventually restricting his journeys mainly to trips between Cairo and Riyadh. In this respect he can be regarded as the first to have employed shuttle diplomacy long before it was adopted by Henry Kissinger. During his travels between Cairo and Riyadh, Mahjoub became aware of the vast disagreement between Nasser and King Faisal. From the outset, King Faisal had expressed reservations about attending the summit conference, and Nasser had countered these doubts by refusing to convene the conference altogether, believing that the time was not right for a meeting of this sort. However, Mahjoub, who considered the holding of an Arab summit conference in Khartoum as his main goal in life, did not appear to feel either tired or bored and continued to negotiate and negotiate until eventually the gap between the two Arab leaders had been narrowed, thus crowning his efforts with success.

While Mahjoub was openly engaged in organising the conference, King Husain was working more secretly towards the same goal. He was able to apply considerable pressure on Nasser who, because of Husain's stand in the June war, had quite a soft spot for the Jordanian king. Husain was touching a sensitive chord where the Egyptian president was concerned, aware that Nasser was very concerned about the future of the West Bank and Jerusalem. At an official meeting Nasser had said: "Israel may stay in the Sinai for ten years or more but ultimately we will expel it and push it back behind its borders. But the West Bank and Jerusalem are a different matter. There, the Arab population has fallen under Zionist control. More than a million Arab citizens are under the yoke of Israeli occupation and must be saved as quickly as possible, by any means and under any circumstances."

The truth is that Nasser was nervous about holding an Arab summit after the defeat. He despaired of the prospect of a unified Arab position being reached and he believed that to convene such a meeting in the aftermath of the débâcle would reduce the conference chamber simply to a platform for recriminations, for one-upmanship and for gloating.

At the private meeting with President Podgorny on 22 June 1967 Nasser had explained his view of the Arab situation after the defeat. Moscow attached great importance to a unified Arab position on stopping oil supplies to at least some of the Western countries, and Nasser told Podgorny that the embargo on Arab oil supplies to the countries that had supported Israel was expected to be perfunctory. He also noted that Cairo's position on Yemen was the cause of the disagreement between Saudi Arabia and Egypt, but that Egypt would nevertheless continue to support the Yemeni revolution. The refusal of Saudi Arabia in company with Tunisia to cooperate with Egypt was a problem, while Syria and Algeria declined to attend any Arab summit at all; however, King Husain's 'patriotic policy' was gratifying.

Nasser was even more convinced that it would be fruitless to hold an Arab summit when he heard that King Faisal had held a meeting with a number of Arab and Muslim ambassadors in Jeddah, at which he had unequivocally stated the Saudi position. During the course of this meeting Faisal had declared: "If we consider the United States and Britain partners in the aggression against us, then we must also consider the Soviet Union a partner in this aggression, especially since it deceived us when it pledged to help us. When the attack was carried out, the Soviet Union shirked its promises and showed its true character. Consequently, the Soviet Union must be considered treacherous, deceitful and also criminal . . . We will, of course, support our Arab brothers, but above all we must express our opinions frankly. For one thing, what is the use of shutting the oil wells and how can the Arabs build their economies and enable their armies to surmount these setbacks when some of them do not possess enough resources to buy a loaf of bread?"

However, because of the pressures that were being brought to bear on him, Nasser had eventually to agree to the convening of a conference although he decided that he would not attend in person. He told his colleagues, members of the Revolutionary Command Council: "I have decided to entrust to our brother Zakariya Mohieddin the task of attending the conference on my behalf. There are three reasons for my decision. The first is that I do not want to expose myself to a political defeat after the military defeat. The second is that at the conference I will be confronted by the gloating of those that I stood against throughout the Arab homeland. The third reason, and I will say this perfectly openly, is that in Khartoum I am afraid to face the ordinary man in the street."

Nasser did not elaborate but we understood what he meant. He was ready to endure anything and everything – military defeat, betrayal by his confidants and the gloating of friends – but he was unprepared to listen to popular dissent against him. From the beginning of his political career he had considered the multitude of common Arab folk to be his real army. What would he be left with if this army too was to abandon him?

When Mahjoub, and then King Husain, learned that Nasser did not wish to attend the conference in person they were horrified. The meeting would be doomed to failure even before it had begun since without him who could guarantee that King Faisal, King Hassan II of Morocco or any of the other kings and presidents would attend? His personal presence was the key that would unlock the door to Arab understanding. Recognising this, Nasser also realised that he could no longer delay facing up to what he feared on the Sudanese streets and that it would be better to know at once what sentence the man in the street would pass. When Muhammad Ahmad Mahjoub heard Nasser's decision he positively danced for joy, feeling that the dream of his life had been fulfilled.

Four days before the summit was due to convene, I went to Khartoum at the head of a political and administrative mission to supervise the preparations for the meeting. In truth I was concerned about the effects on Nasser of the experience he would have to face at the conference, since I was aware of the worries he was suffering and I was afraid that another shock would destroy him. But my concern gradually receded. The first thing I had been keen to do after arriving in the Sudanese capital was to tour the streets in order to find out the feelings prevailing among the Sudanese people. What I saw in the streets of Khartoum was actually very gratifying – the banners and signs welcoming Nasser covered windows, doors and walls, including the walls of the US Embassy, whereupon, reassured as to the outcome of Nasser's visit, I cabled my reactions to Cairo.

On the day Nasser's plane was due to arrive in Khartoum, I was waiting at the airport with a number of officials. Suddenly, the Sudanese minister in *charge of receiving the delegations (whose name escapes me) came up to me and said: "President Abdel Nasser's plane is now circling the airport. Can the landing of his plane be delayed so that King Faisal's plane may land first?" Surprised by this request, I asked him when King Faisal's plane was due to arrive and somewhat embarrassedly he told me: "In ten minutes." "Why?" I asked him. "What is the reason for taking this strange measure? You say that the President's plane is now flying over the airport and King Faisal's plane needs ten minutes to arrive. I don't understand this." To which the Sudanese minister replied: "I hope you will appreciate the situation. If we permit Abdel Nasser's plane to land now, the crowds are going to follow him and the streets will be completely empty. Therefore we'll find that there will be nobody to receive King Faisal. If this happens, the king may be upset and if he's not pleased this may affect the prospects for the success of the conference!"*

I was convinced by the Sudanese minister's logic and agreed that the landing of President Nasser's plane should be delayed, for which decision I took full responsibility. When I explained the matter to Nasser on our way to the guest palace, he said with a smile: "Now I know why my plane flew over Khartoum airport for ten minutes before it was permitted to land."

Nasser's disembarkation from his plane at Khartoum was an extraordinary and historic moment on a scale that I had never experienced before. All the arrangements which had taken the reception committee days to organise collapsed, and all the barriers put in place by the security agencies fell down. The masses stormed on to the tarmac and formed a human chain around Nasser, cheering and shouting for the long life of the hero and of Arabism, and demanding revenge against the United States and Israel. The President's motorcade proceeded slowly through the streets of the capital amidst a turbulent sea of human beings. The entire city had emerged to receive him, unaware that it was banishing the atmosphere of defeat in which he had been living, and without realising that it was giving him the strength to stand firm.

However, the mood of popular acclaim that Nasser experienced in he streets of Khartoum was somewhat different from the atmosphere he encountered inside the conference hall.

The Important Discussions of the Conference, 29 August–1 September 1967

The Khartoum summit, later known as the Three Noes conference, got under way on 29 August. The Arab delegations were represented by kings and presidents: Abdel Nasser (UAR), King Faisal (Saudi Arabia), King Husain (Jordan), Abdel Rahman Aref (Iraq), Prince Sabah al-Salim al-Sabah (Kuwait), Charles Hilu (Lebanon), Abdallah al-Sallal (Yemen), Crown Prince Hassan al-Rida (Libya), Ismail al-Azhari (Sudan) who was the conference chairman, Ahmad al-Shuqairi (PLO), Abdel Aziz Bouteflika (Algerian minister of foreign affairs on behalf of President Houari Boumedienne), Ahmed Benhima (Moroccan prime minister on behalf of King Hassan II), and al-Bahi al-Adgham (Tunisia, on behalf of President Bourguiba). Syria was absent, although Ibrahim Makhus, the deputy prime minister, was actually staying in Khartoum. Makhus was active when the conference was not in session but when the meetings were going on he would sit quietly on the terrace of the Grand Hotel.

The turning-point in the fortunes of the conference came during the morning session on 31 August when it was agreed that oil would continue to be pumped to the world provided that the oil countries would advance financial aid to the frontline states for military preparation and for economic stability. The conference agreed unanimously that the oil countries would advance a total sum of 135 million pounds (55 million from Kuwait, 50 million from Saudi Arabia and 30 million from Libya), of which 95 million pounds was allocated for Egypt and 40 million for Jordan. After this decision, it became evident to all that the Arabs had achieved a united standpoint and at the evening session, all eyes and ears were on Nasser to know what he would have to say following the adoption of the resolution on economic aid.

Nasser: We must take two main points into our calculations when we deal with the issue of political action, namely military preparation and economic stability. There is no doubt that the resolution on economic aid that was adopted at the previous session will help us a great deal to stand resolute. We must also take into consideration the fact that there is an agreement between the United States and the Soviet Union to solve the issue politically. This has been reflected in the Soviet–US draft resolution which depends on two main points – termination of the state of war and withdrawal from the occupied territories – in addition to other subsidiary issues such as the issue of Jerusalem and sea navigation. For our part, we have rejected the draft resolution at the United Nations, and the other

Arabs must now define their positions. I hope that it is understood by everyone that when we speak about political action, this means that we will not only take but that we will also give. Here, we must discuss what we will give. In other words, what can we give? The international situation is different now from what it was in 1956. In that year, both the United States and the Soviet Union agreed to confront the tripartite aggression. But in 1967, both the United States and the Soviet Union have agreed to Israel's right to exist and to live securely. They have also agreed on ending the state of war.

Political action is hard and it requires firm struggle. Our political situation in Egypt has changed radically since we adopted the resolution on economic aid for the frontline states at this conference. In Washington they thought that we would capitulate within six months but this aid will enable us to stand fast. The cutting off of our revenues from the Suez Canal after the aggression will not now affect us very much. This is why I am continually saying that our situation in Egypt is noticeably different from that of King Husain of Jordan. We can stand fast in Egypt for one year, for two years, or more, especially since we have solved the hard currency problem with the resolution that we adopted at this morning's session. As for the populated areas in the occupied territories, such as al-Arish, Rafah and Gaza, there is heroic popular resistance there against the Israeli occupation, and this resistance continues, in spite of the mass executions that were carried out a few days ago against the men of the resistance and in spite of the indiscriminate demolition of homes in the Gaza Strip.

We in Egypt are able, despite our situation, to resist, to struggle and to reject any suspect offer that does not meet our demands. We in Egypt can wait until we have completed our military preparations. We will then be able to carry out the only action that Israel understands well, and that is the liberation of land by force. This is why I am not concerned about Egypt's situation. But what does concern me is the situation in the West Bank. Here we must ask ourselves whether, as far as the West Bank is concerned, the element of time will be in our interest or not. I personally believe that it will not be in our interest at all.

I follow everything that is currently happening in Israel in detail. The three parties that represent the essence of radicalism in Israel have merged into one faction under the name of the Likud Bloc. This bloc insists on keeping the entire West Bank and vows not to relinquish a single inch of it. This is why we must move quickly and exert the utmost effort to regain the West Bank and Jerusalem with whatever means are available to us at present, because the West Bank and Jerusalem will not be recovered if there is any delay.

Here we must also ask ourselves another question. Can the occupied territories currently be retaken through a military solution? I believe that the answer to this question is clear, namely that this path is not open to us at present. Therefore, we only have one path before us at present – the path of political action for the restoration of the West Bank and Jerusalem.

When King Husain came to us in Cairo, I was aware of the real problem of the West Bank. I grieve for the West Bank and for its people. My feelings and my pain for them are many; my pain is also for Sinai, and because the West Bank with its crowded Arab population has now fallen into the grip of Israeli occupation at a time when we can do nothing for this population. Sinai is almost unpopulated. Even so, Egypt will not yield for a moment in its attempts to liberate Sinai even if we have to offer up tens of thousands of martyrs. But Israeli ambitions in the West Bank are long-standing and well known. The Israelis call the West Bank Judea and Samaria and consider it a part of the promised land. This is why I have told King Husain that he has the right to resort to any measures, except negotiating with Israel, to regain the West Bank. Because I consider that each day of the Israeli occupation of the West Bank is another step on the way to linking it to Israel, I've also told him that we have no objection to his efforts to continue to improve his relations with Britain and the United States for the same purpose. I said this to King Husain in Cairo in the presence of the Algerian delegation and I am repeating these words today in front of all of you in this hall, because any delay in regaining the West Bank and Jerusalem will serve to alter their features and will ultimately turn them into a part of Israel. For the same reason, I concurred with King Husain on the calling together of this conference and I agreed to attend it personally. In Egypt the pressure to which we are subjected by the Americans is greater than that to which King Husain of Jordan is exposed. Of course, as I have already said, we can struggle politically and reject the US–Soviet draft resolution. But we see no harm in accepting the Yugoslav draft resolution, given that we are at present unable to embark on any military action and that we have no option other than to take political action.

Gentlemen, we tried military force, but we were defeated. We tried to close the Gulf of Aqaba to Israeli navigation, but we failed. We spent ten years in military preparation for the liberation of the land that had been usurped, but ultimately we were unable to achieve that goal. We are not ashamed to mention all these facts because we have committed no treason. All that we did was to have tried and failed. But in spite of the defeat, we stand here before you and before history, and we pledge before you and before history, that we will not negotiate with Israel and that we will not abandon the rights of the Palestinian people.

President Tito informed me that he was ready to go to Moscow to negotiate an agreement with the Kremlin leaders so that the Yugoslav draft resolution could replace the United States draft resolution, but because it calls for restoring our occupied lands to us, the Americans will not approve the Yugoslav proposal. The Americans will not accept it because they want to humiliate us and because they are planning to facilitate Israel's domination of the Arab area. In my opinion Tito's proposals will produce an acceptable political solution, but the US proposals will lead to surrender and humiliation, which is why we cannot accept them. If we cannot reach agreement on a specific draft resolution here, then I suggest that King Husain should go and arrive at an understanding with the Americans and agree with them over the restoration of the West Bank. I am ready to affirm these observations publicly because the United States is the party that can order Israel to take its hands off the West Bank.

The Security Council will be meeting in September. The Russians contact us every day to ask what we are thinking. A decision must be taken now so that our position will be clear to our friends. I personally believe that Tito's plan is an acceptable proposition and we must express our opinion on it.

I will ask King Husain now: Can you liberate the West Bank using military means? If the answer is positive, then I will go along with you, regardless of the consequences. But if the answer is negative, then we have been trying fruitlessly for ten years to liberate occupied Palestine. This may be what God in His divine wisdom has willed, in which case we have to resort to the political solution until we become capable of resorting to the military solution.

I emphasize to you now that the liberation of Sinai is postponed forthwith until God brings what is inevitable to pass. As for the West Bank, there is no way of getting the Israelis out except through political action.

When Nasser had delivered his address, everyone's attention turned to King Faisal, since, after Nasser, it was he who held the key to the success or failure of the conference. Speaking for the first time and with everybody listening carefully to every word and concentrating on every gesture, King Faisal said in his quiet, deep voice: "Gentlemen, I propose that President Abdel Nasser's speech should be the conference's working paper and form the basis of the resolutions that will be issued by the conference in the future."

This short and decisive statement by King Faisal set the seal on the legitimacy of the Khartoum conference. The summit had succeeded, and here were Faisal and Nasser standing in the same line. This was the first surprise in King Faisal's speech, but it was not to be the last – indeed his speech abounded with surprises. The Saudi king announced that he had been in contact with the Americans all the time, both before and after the war, and confirmed that he had had a meeting with the US ambassador immediately before his departure for Khartoum. When Nasser asked him what he and the ambassador had discussed, King Faisal said: "By God, he did not tell me anything."

After the address delivered by Nasser at the preceding session and following King Faisal's brief comment on it, the overall temperature of the conference rose noticeably. King Husain's speech earlier had been the direct cause of tension. Ahmad al-Shuqairi, the chairman of the PLO, had interfered and threatened ultimate withdrawal from the conference, and it also became evident that the Algerian and Palestinian delegations were clinging to a certain plan whereas the other delegations were looking for a pragmatic solution amongst the international political currents and the entangled interests.

Nasser had attempted to check the passions that flared up in the conference hall but was unable to do so although he tried several times to ease the highly volatile situation. Eventually he allowed the discussion to take its course after making sure that these storms would not affect the positive results that had been achieved so far by the conference. However, this approach did not prevent him from stressing repeatedly that at that stage political action was permissible as long as military action remained impossible and that any political action had to be coupled with three principles: no negotiations with Israel, no recognition of Israel and no peace with Israel. It was the ultimate approval by the conference of these three declarations that gave the meeting its eventual title of the Three Noes conference.

The Closing Discussions

The conference hall did in fact become the battleground for a war of words. The Jordanian delegation, led by King Husain, and the Palestinian delegation, led by Ahmad al-Shuqairi, exchanged remarks that everybody else, especially Nasser, considered uncalled-for. For example, al-Shuqairi said furiously: "Nobody here, no king, no president and not even the PLO, is authorized to conclude an independent settlement with Israel for the West

Bank." King Husain retorted impatiently: "I have not come here to listen to anybody's advice." Nasser remained silent and when the argument reached its final stage, it was King Faisal who signalled to President Ismail al-Azhari to end the meeting.

The session started with an address by King Husain who, after praising Nasser and describing him as the representative of patriotism and loyalty in the Arab homeland, embarked straight away on the issue of the West Bank.

King Husain: The situation on the West Bank is extremely bad and very difficult. Even if we rebuild our military forces, we will not be able to liberate the land in the near future. At the same time, if we leave the West Bank in Jewish hands for a long time, it will be difficult for us to regain it. Nor is the issue one of the West Bank alone. There is also the future of Jerusalem, which not only concerns the Palestinians and the Arabs but also concerns the Muslims and the Christians. Since the cease-fire, the United Nations has issued several resolutions on Jerusalem but Israel has not observed any of them and has thus defied the entire world.

We stress that our people, whether in the West Bank or elsewhere, are one people and that certain elements must be provided in order for the West Bank to be restored, the most important of these being the cooperation of all of us and the degree of our ability to endure and to stand fast. If it is your opinion that Tito's plan is to be accepted, then I am with you because this plan is undoubtedly much better than others. But at the same time, we need to maintain some contacts with western and with eastern countries in order to make our position clear, and we must take into consideration that our unanimous agreement and united opinion concerning this issue will be of major importance and will gain us a large measure of international respect and support.

Before I conclude my remarks, I again express my thanks and appreciation to brother President Gamal Abdel Nasser for his openness and loyalty.

Nasser: During my meeting with some of the Arab presidents in Cairo last July, we sent a delegation consisting of President Boumedienne and President Aref to the Soviet Union to explain our positions to the Soviet leadership and to find out the Soviet position toward the issue. As for the United States, we have no contacts, and our relations with it are very bad. This is why I believe that the Arab states and the leaderships that have good relations with the Americans can contact them. I propose that His Majesty King Faisal should embark on promoting such contacts and act on our behalf to explain our point of view on the issue, especially since the whole matter is currently before the Security Council. We all know that the United Nations is ultimately the Soviet Union and the United States. I also propose that brother al-Bahi al-Adgham should take part with King Faisal in these contacts. For our part, we will continue our contacts with the Soviet Union and with France. However, we have no contacts with Britain at present.

King Faisal: I have listened to the words of my brothers with the utmost appreciation and attention. Allow me to express my opinion with complete candour. The goal, the wound and the catastrophe are the same [for all of us] and the only difference between us is in the means and the methods to be followed. This is why this meeting should not disperse without having reached a unified opinion. Moreover, it should issue resolutions and plans that are clear and understandable to all. As for what His Excellency President Gamal Abdel Nasser has said about the issue of contacts with the Americans, I would like to be wholly and absolutely frank and clear. We have been in almost daily contact with the Americans both before and since the catastrophe. I recently received a message from President Johnson which I answered immediately, telling him in my message that I, as a friend, advised the United States to condemn the Israeli aggression and to play a role, compatible with America's international weight, in securing Israeli withdrawal from the Arab territories. I also told him that such a measure would be the least that we would expect from a friendly and peace-loving superpower.

When I met General de Gaulle three days before the war, with Dr Rashad Faraon, we had a 90-minute conversation with him and we both explained to him the Arabs' rights, their just cause and the brutal Jewish aggression against the Arab territories. Unfortunately, we sensed confusion in de Gaulle's thinking where the Arabs' right to Palestine is concerned. He believes that the Jews have a right to Palestine, that they have returned to their homeland and that the Arabs have to acknowledge and coexist with the *fait accompli*.

We have also been in communication with the British and we held a meeting with the British prime minister at 10 Downing Street. We explained the Arab viewpoint to him and heard from him the British government's position towards the Palestinian question.

By and large, we have not stopped exerting pressure on the Americans, the British and the French. I believe that it is necessary for each of us to exert as much effort as he can. I also believe that none of us should adopt an independent decision or position toward the issue.

Nasser: I will return to the issue of the West Bank and say that if we have no military answer for its liberation at present, then King Husain should use his own experience to try to settle the issue, provided that this does not lead to recognizing Israel or to peace with it. As for my proposal that King Faisal contact the Americans, I hope that approval will be given to His Majesty to maintain these contacts in the name of the conference.

King Faisal: I am in constant contact with the Americans; I saw the American ambassador only a week ago.

Nasser: What was their opinion?

King Faisal: By God, the American ambassador told me nothing other than the five points contained in Johnson's plan.

Ahmad al-Shuqairi: The West Bank question is serious. The miseries to which our people are subjected shock all of us and make us apprehensive about the fate of the Palestinian issue. The PLO has defined its position in this regard in the six principles which it has distributed to the conference. We agree with you on the need for the enemy to withdraw from the Gaza Strip and the West Bank, and on the need to exert the utmost political effort to compel the enemy to withdraw. We also affirm that the Organization is setting no conditions or reservations. But the question we must ask ourselves is: what is the price that we have to pay? We all know Israel. Speaking entirely modestly, I have had long experience with Israel and I know its goals and ambitions as a result of prevailing practices. I hope that it is understood by you that our position in the Organization is not the product of obstinacy or extremism. The point that should preoccupy us is the price that we will have to pay to restore the West Bank. We believe that if this price is exorbitant then our acceptance of it will be a grave mistake. America's policy is ultimately to eliminate the Palestinian question. The five points contained in Johnson's plan are an exorbitant price for the restoration of the West Bank. Are we ready to pay this high price for the West Bank? I, as an Arab citizen and as a chairman, refuse to pay this price and hereby declare that I do not accept the plan. The Yugoslav plan seeks a final settlement and lasting peace in the area. I do not want to say any more. However, I wanted to explain our viewpoint to your distinguished assembly. We have distributed the six principles drawn up by the PLO for you. These sum up the Palestinian viewpoint relating to the future of the issue. Ultimately, we reject any formula that will lead to the final liquidation of the Palestinian problem.

Nasser: I disagree with al-Shuqairi on the phrase that he has mentioned concerning the final settlement of the issue. A final settlement means sitting with Israel around the negotiating table. This is what the United States actually wants. It would have been easier for me not to speak. However, in the past we had only one catastrophe whereas we now have two: the 1948 catastrophe and the 1967 catastrophe, which is why I have said that we are ready to pay a price for restoring the West Bank. All of us together are not able to regain the West Bank militarily. So, should we leave it in Israel's hands? What can be done at present? What is the alternative?

I could have remained silent and I could have spoken only about Sinai. But I will repeat what I have already said, namely that the West Bank is much more important to me than Sinai, even if the Israelis remain in Sinai for ten years. I have said that we must pay a price for the West Bank – and naturally I mean a reasonable price – as long as we cannot regain it militarily. We must not forget that one half of Palestine was lost in 1948 and the other half in 1967. If at present our goal is to regain the West Bank through political action, then the price has to be paid.

King Husain has had links with the Americans who were supplying him with weapons, and I believe that they are eager to maintain their connections with him. This is why I have spoken very clearly and frankly. Naturally, there will be a price but the price is not the liquidation of the issue. It may involve King Husain strengthening his relations with the Americans and moving closer to them. Even though the truth is always bitter, we have to accept it because we are currently facing a major catastrophe and we have to exert every effort to overcome it.

The issue is very simple and clear. There are two paths and not a third: political struggle and military action. When we are not capable of military action, we have to struggle politically. Though we have opted for political action because of our circumstances, I disagree with al-Shuqairi when he describes President Tito's plan as a liquidation of the Palestinian issue. There is a difference between political action and liquidation of the issue. If we do not hasten to act positively in order to restore the West Bank, the land occupied by the Israelis will gradually turn into Israeli land.

I say in conclusion that we have to struggle politically until the right time comes for restoring our rights by military action.

Mahjoub: I would like to deal here with three points which are that first it is possible to accept a political solution, provided that the Palestinian issue is not eliminated. Secondly, agreement to end the state of war means that Israeli ships will go through the Suez Canal. It also means our recognition of Israel. Thirdly, the economic resolutions approved by the conference will enable us to stand fast and will give us the opportunity to speak from a position of power.

Bouteflika [*Algerian minister of foreign affairs*]: Algeria's position towards the Palestinian issue is well known. As for the Yugoslav plan, I find that some of its provisions are appropriate and others are not. May I ask why President Tito hasn't submitted this plan to the Security Council or presented it during his tour of the Arab region?

This plan fulfils Israel's wishes. The East and the West have met together between its lines. Because Tito's plan is the plan of a friendly country that has always supported us, we should not remain silent about it, because silence means acceptance. We must respond now and tell our friends clearly that we do not agree to any plan that undermines the essence of the Palestinian issue. Israel now wants peaceful coexistence and this cannot be achieved except by eliminating the state of tension that prevails in the area. The ending of this situation can only be realized through the Arab states' recognition of Israel.

Another angle that I would like to point out is that certain states in the region have been subjected to savage aggression and are facing enormous external and internal pressures. These countries are suffering far more severely than those, such as Algeria, that are removed from the scene of the action. This is why it is being said that it is inappropriate for those who are thousands of kilometres away from the conflict to offer advice to those who are on the battlefield and who have to endure the hardships and pressures of occupation, however useful and valuable such advice may be. But as long as the issue is projected as fundamentally a pan-Arab issue, then we must listen to their views.

I believe that we are thinking with the mentality of the powerless. How I wish that the plan we are studying tonight were an Arab plan and not a Yugoslav, an American or a Russian plan. What is surprising is that the Americans do not recognize the People's Republic of China whose population amounts to 700 million, yet they put pressure on us to recognize Israel before any problems in the Arab region are solved.

I have heard tonight that Jordan and the other Arab countries are unable to embark on any military action which is why they are seeking a political solution. It is well known that any political solution calls for give and take. Consequently, if the political solution for the West Bank comprises giving and taking, then the danger lies in the fact that we may follow the same method where Sinai and the Syrian Golan Heights are concerned. We are now extremely perplexed because even though we agree on the goal, we disagree over the means. Moreover, we haven't yet found a way to recover the occupied territories without abandoning the issue of Palestine. If we now approve the principle of give and take in political action, it is still not clear to us how far the taking and the giving has to go.

Benhima [*Morocco*]: I thank President Abdel Nasser and congratulate him for his frankness. I also compliment the entire conference for its serious debate and discussions. It has become obvious to all of us that it is impossible to regain the Arab territories through war. Moreover, President Abdel Nasser has graciously put the West Bank ahead of Sinai. At the same time, King Husain has declared that no distinction should be made between the two domains. Indeed, all the discussions that have taken place at this conference have been positive.

It is true that we are far from the battlefield and that our land is not occupied. However, we believe that the Israeli occupation of the West Bank threatens all the Arabs and undermines their dignity, and this is something that we do not accept at all. In conclusion, I declare our full approval of everything that President Abdel Nasser has said and of what has been stated by King Husain. I also propose that King Faisal be given full powers by the conference to contact the Americans and to exert pressure on them to solve the issue politically within the framework of what has been approved by the conference until such time as we become capable of liberating Palestine by military means.

Ahmad al-Shuqairi: The PLO approves the exerting of the greatest energies towards solving the issue. But at the same time, it gives authority to no one.

King Husain: There is no doubt that our position will be strong if we can agree unanimously on one notion. We must not forget that the issue, as I have already stated, is the issue of all the Arabs and the issue of Arab existence. We cannot reach an acceptable solution simply through individual contacts by me or by others. The issue will always remain the issue of all of us. Within this framework, I am ready for any assignment and ready to shoulder any responsibility. But certain people [*here the king was referring to al-Shuqairi*] must understand that the issue is not one of upstaging others or of registering attitudes. We have heard al-Shuqairi speak about the six principles. Gentlemen, let us recall the resolutions of the first Arab conference. There was a specific assignment for al-Shuqairi.

I've another question: I should like to know who formulated these six principles and who made the decision on them?

I have heard a lot of words tonight and I hope that it will not be understood from what I am saying that I am angry on account of my personal dignity. The issue is much bigger than this. It touches on the dignity of all our Arab sons and citizens. The issue is not just of one party taking priority over another. The issue is that Jordan has now become the advance guard in the face of danger and I am speaking on this basis and from this starting-point.

Finally, I approve any opinion you consider appropriate or any duty you specify, but I am not disposed to listen to anybody's advice.

Abdel Rahman Aref: The issue is a pan-Arab one otherwise Algeria would not have come hundreds of kilometres to the battleground and Egypt and Iraq and others would not have offered thousands of their sons as martyrs.

Al-Shuqairi: The Palestine problem is a problem for us all. This is true. But nobody is delegated by us to accept a solution for it, not King Husain and not the Palestine Liberation Organization. If you want the Organization to be a mere listener, then there is no reason for our being here and we are ready to withdraw from the conference immediately. But before I leave this hall, I want to stress to you categorically, on behalf of the PLO, that no king or president is empowered to solve the Palestinian issue on his own. If such a person exists, then this is a serious shift on a national issue that concerns not only the present generation but also future generations.

> *At this point, a furious discussion erupted in which Ahmad Mahjoub, Abdel Rahman Aref and Ahmad al-Shuqairi took part. Nasser remained silent and occupied himself by exchanging whispered comments with various members of his delegation. King Faisal turned a deaf ear to the noisy debate and started twirling the hem of his flowing black robe.*
>
> *Finally, Aref and Mahjoub managed to quell the dispute and an atmosphere of calm was restored to the hall. At that moment, King Faisal started to look openly at his watch and then at Ismail al-Azhari. Al-Azhari, responding to the gesture, glanced quickly at the big clock on the wall of the chamber, and seeing its hands pointing to 2.00 o'clock in what was now the morning of 1 September, he promptly adjourned the session.*
>
> *One further brief session was held, which voted on the various resolutions, and the Khartoum summit then ended. To Nasser, this conference had represented the final testing of the ground following the defeat, and he emerged from the summit with his plans for the future complete. He had secured weapons from the Soviet Union as well as financial support from the Arabs. He had also installed a new command structure at the head of the*

armed forces whose objective, with the experience of the numerous and fatal mistakes of the past in mind, was to rebuild the military structure.

Nasser had at the outset to play all his cards, in order first to gain time, then to win over international public opinion and thirdly to rearm and retrain the army. While calling for a political solution, he was also promoting the slogan, 'What has been taken by force cannot be regained except by force', and at the same time that he was pressing the Soviet leadership to meet his requests for weapons, he was also keeping the door open to the American contacts who immediately after the defeat had begun actively to demand the re-establishment of relations with Cairo. Additionally, it was during this period that the Americans offered to dig Egypt a new canal on Egyptian territory, which would replace the Suez Canal and which they would run.

Chapter 5

DOMESTIC EXCHANGES
Nasser criticizes his own regime

It is to be hoped that by now the reader will have gained some idea of how Abdel Nasser dealt with international affairs during this period. In order to round out the political sketch of Nasser, it is necessary to introduce an account of some of his internal meetings and his discussions on domestic politics. One of the most impressive gatherings at this time was the meeting held on 3 and 4 August 1967 by the Supreme Executive Committee of the Arab Socialist Union (ASU) which was the regime's foremost command body. During the meeting Nasser openly admitted the disastrous events for the first time, expressing his candid opinion and criticism of the regime.

The ASU's Supreme Executive Committee was the pre-eminent authority in the government, and membership was by appointment; the committee consisted of the President and the Revolution Command Council members who remained with him in the regime, in addition to the prime minister. Thus the committee included Abdel Nasser, Abdel Hakim Amer, Zakariya Mohieddin, Anwar al-Sadat, Husain al-Shafei, Ali Sabri and the then prime minister, Sidqi Sulaiman.

In my capacity as Secretary of the ASU's Supreme Executive Committee, I personally attended all the meetings from the time of its formation until the death of Abdel Nasser in 1970. In reviewing the records of this committee's meetings in order to present the reader with a vivid picture of Nasser's political activities at the domestic level, I could find no meeting as lively and performance as polished as that held over a two-day period on Thursday and Friday, 3 and 4 August 1967. This meeting was held under extraordinary political circumstances and for a number of reasons had been specially convened.

To begin with, it was the first Supreme Executive Committee meeting to take place following the defeat of June 1967. Given that it was the highest political authority in the country both before and after the war, the committee had to shoulder more or less the entire responsibility for what had happened.

Secondly, the committee was meeting after 9 and 10 June; that is to say, after the Egyptian people, who had developed absolute confidence in Nasser during the 15 years of struggle, had insisted on affirming his leadership and on continuing the battle. This sweeping popular support, which surprised the entire world and for which some political commentators are still unable to find a clear explanation, was intended for Abdel Nasser personally and not for the regime or for its executive or political committees. The approval expressed by the masses on those two days in June was tantamount to a carte blanche signed by the Egyptian people to enable Nasser to restore their pride. Thirdly, the committee was meeting for the first time with only six members because the seventh was not present. The absence of Marshal Abdel Hakim Amer, who had shared the meetings and the responsibility with them throughout the preceding period, had an emotional impact on the other members especially when, on entering the meeting hall and preparing to take their seats, they contemplated Amer's vacant seat at Nasser's right.

The meeting was scheduled for Thursday evening, 3 August, in the meeting hall of the Supreme Executive Committee which was on the 11th floor of the Arab Socialist Union building on the Nile Corniche. As I waited with the members of the committee in the reception room next to Nasser's office I was aware that they were sitting in complete silence as though some bird of ill omen was hovering above their heads. There were no smiles, and even the informal remarks that they customarily exchanged before the appearance of the committee chairman were missing. When Nasser came in, he exchanged a few words with the members, which he had never been in the habit of doing before meetings previously, and then signalled to them to move to the meeting hall to begin the proceedings.

It was a stormy session. It went on until late that night, and I remember its words and I remember the reactions of the chairman and the committee members during those long hours. Because the discussions had not finished, the session was resumed the next day, Friday. Again, contrary to the usual procedure, no agenda had been drawn up for this particular session. However, it was obvious from the timing of the meeting so soon after the events which had befallen Egypt that it was to be a session for an extensive evaluation by the country's highest political leadership to discuss what had happened, how it had happened and where to proceed next.

I believe that had Nasser's observations on that occasion fallen on attentive ears, had they been made more widely available for analysis, and had any of them been acted upon, many things in Egypt might have been different from that time. But instead there were vociferous exchanges which drowned out the reasoned opinions voiced that night.

An important point mentioned in the discussions that follow and that needs some explanation is Nasser's relationship with the armed forces and his apparent aloofness from the command structure. His non-intervention in the general command's decisions has its roots in the period following the breakup of the union with Syria in 1961. The secessionists had used the misconduct of members of the military command based in the northern region (Syria) as an excuse to damage the alliance and to advocate secession among the Syrian forces, as well as exploiting other flagrant examples of bad decisions made by certain senior officers. At a meeting of the Presidential Council, which was at that time the highest authority in Egypt, Nasser asked for appointments to military positions to be ratified by decree from the Presidential Council rather than being left to the personal decision of Abdel Hakim Amer, the general commander. He also demanded the replacement of a number of the high-ranking personnel whose negligence recently had been proven and requested that the main criterion for the selection of military commanders should be military ability and not political attitudes or the degree of loyalty to the general command!

As soon as Abdel Hakim Amer read the resolution withdrawing his personal right to make military appointments and instead sanctioning the Council to do so on the recommendation of the general command, he challenged Nasser for the first time to his face, sharply criticising the resolution and attacking any interference with the authority of the commander of the armed forces. Although some of the Council members tried to calm things down, bitter and unproductive exchanges continued to the point where Nasser was finally compelled to leave the meeting, handing over proceedings to Abdel Latif Baghdadi.

Matters then proceeded to develop inside the armed forces. Marshal Amer had informed the high-ranking officers of Nasser's proposal, and senior military commanders began to speculate that there was a political plan to intervene in military affairs and to strip them all, including the general commander, of power. Nasser also learned later that an unofficial ballot had been conducted secretly among the military command structure to determine whether, in the event of the expected confrontation, loyalty would be to Abdel Nasser or to Abdel Hakim Amer, the general commander. Nasser who was of course aware of the degree of confusion prevailing among all the military commands, considered this to be an extremely serious matter that directly undermined the regime's security. Afraid that there would be a military coup or that a bloody clash might erupt between the army and civilian political forces, he was obliged to bow to the inevitable and agree to mediation and to reconciliation with Amer in order to save the regime.

Nasser was also compelled to abandon his proposal and to give in to Amer's demand that as general commander of the armed forces, he should continue to have sole authority to make appointments at all levels within the military command structure. Another concession that was not announced at the time was that Nasser would refrain from establishing contacts with the army through those of his aides who had originally been military officers; this meant that his only channel to the armed forces would be Abdel Hakim Amer himself.

From that moment, Nasser lost contact with the armed forces, and also lost day-to-day touch with what was happening within the army, except to the extent and in the manner allowed to him by Marshal Amer. From that time, too, the two men never regained the degree of understanding and coordination that they had previously enjoyed. Many disapproved of Nasser's negative attitude and criticised him harshly on the grounds that at the time, that is in the early 1960s, he was sufficiently pre-eminent and popular to have been able to present his conflict with Marshal Amer to the people in the full certainty that the entire population would back and support him. However, there are various factors and circumstances to be taken into account in arriving at a correct assessment of the stand taken by Nasser.

The session of the Supreme Executive Committee was opened by Nasser who, without any preamble, launched directly into an examination of the important issues.

The First Session, 3 August 1967

Nasser: Today we will be discussing the most important subject. This is why I have asked Abdel Magid Farid not to prepare any form of agenda. What we are going to consider, and which is much more important than all other matters, is an evaluation of the system of government that we are currently pursuing, because I believe that through following up and carefully analysing the events that have taken place recently, it will become evident to us that our system has not been sound. [*and here Nasser used the English word "system"*]. To clarify what I am saying, I will review the events that have recently taken place in our country in more detail.

You all remember that we attended a meeting of the armed forces general command in Madinat Nasr [*a district in Cairo*] shortly before the start of the military operations. I told the military commanders who were at the meeting that the political intelligence available to us confirmed that the enemy's major offensive would begin with the seizing of Sharm al-Shaikh and the isolating of the Gaza Strip. However, the basis on which the general command assessed its position was that it totally excluded the possibility of an all-out enemy attack on this front, and that even if such an attack were to take place, then it totally excluded the coastal route as a major axis of the attack. This is why the general command concentrated its forces in the south and left the northern sector near Rafah and Gaza exposed.

Zakariya Mohieddin: Indeed we do remember the discussion with general command operations staff that day after it had become apparent from general command's plan that the district of al-Arish and its surrounding area was weak, and we remember that after persistent urging the command agreed to reinforce the area of al-Arish with an armoured division and to strengthen the likely penetration zone near al-Shaikh Zuwaid with Saad al-Shazli's brigade.

Nasser: I regret to say that later on, on Friday 2 June, I learned from Abdel Hakim Amer that he had given orders for the armoured brigade to return to Nakhl and for Saad al-Shazli's force to go to the south, on the grounds that their estimates were that the major battle would take place in the south.

At that meeting I also told the armed forces general command, in front of the army and air force commanders, that I estimated that the war would break out on Monday 5 June, and that it was highly probable that the first blow would be struck against our air forces. Lt Gen Sidqi Mahmoud [*commander of the air forces at the time*] got annoyed and said that such a possibility would cause us great confusion!

As you know, the war did indeed begin on the Monday and the operations did start with the air strike against all our air forces. Moreover, the major attack took place in the northern sector and al-Arish collapsed. The enemy then moved along three axes, one of which was the coastal route, nor did the enemy divisions find their advance blocked by any of our military units because the general command had excluded the likelihood of any enemy movement along this route.

Let me go back to the first days of the war, which I followed from my office. From the Monday – 5 June – I did not visit the general command or intervene in any military instructions, until Thursday, 8 June! On that day Shams Badran, the minister of war, asked me to go immediately to the general command headquarters because Abdel Hakim Amer was in a state of total collapse and had asked his private secretary to bring him Sianor pills which are suicide pills. This is why I went to the general command headquarters and indeed found Abdel Hakim in a complete state of collapse. So I tried to calm him down, assuring him that I was personally responsible for what had happened and that I would step down as president. I then asked him who he thought would be a fit person to assume the presidency of the republic after me and he said that he thought the most suitable person for this position was Shams Badran.

I learned a few days later that after I had left the command headquarters, Abdel Hakim Amer held a long meeting with Shams Badran to reorganize the state and its civilian leadership. Both of them contacted certain political figures and ministers and asked them not to resign after I had stepped down so that they could cooperate with the new president of the republic.

On the following afternoon, 9 June, I telephoned Abdel Hakim before broadcasting my resignation statement and informed him that I had thought about the matter carefully and had concluded that Zakariya Mohieddin was the most appropriate individual to assume the position of president after me. This is where the problem of Shams Badran started. He considered himself president of the republic from 11 o'clock in the evening of Thursday 8 June until the time I announced my resignation on the afternoon of Friday 9 June. He also considered that by my nominating Zakariya Mohieddin for president, I had encroached on his legitimate position and dismissed him. While I was actually making my resignation statement from my office in al-Qubbah Palace, Shams Badran got in touch with Muhammad Ahmad [*Nasser's secretary*] and asked him to inform me that I should not continue to deliver the rest of the announcement. This, of course, was impossible.

Two days later, Shams Badran contacted me by telephone to tell me that there was a group of about 500 army officers surrounding Marshal Amer's residence in Hilmiyet al-Zaitoun and at the general command headquarters, and that they were insisting on the reinstatement of Abdel Hakim as general commander and asking me to make a decision on the issue immediately. I told him that I would make a decision the next day. On the following day when he telephoned me, I said to him: 'Shams, you know my opinion of the general command. If we sincerely want to rectify the situation, we must select a veteran military commander, and Abdel Hakim can stay on as the first vice-president of the republic. I have tried personally to bring the marshal to my office at home to explain matters to him, and I even asked Salah Nasr [*head of intelligence*] to help with fetching him because he wasn't at his own house but at Isam Khalil's flat [*Isam Khalil was one of the officers loyal to Amer*]. However, he has refused to come and see me. In the 2.30 news bulletin this afternoon I announced Fawzi's appointment [*Lt Gen Muhammad Fawzi*] to the post of general commander and then ordered him to arrest the officers who are mutinying and resisting.'

Then I met Abdel Hakim and tried unsuccessfully to persuade him that it was illogical for him to remain as general commander after the military defeat and that he should be content with being the first vice-president. He completely rejected my arguments and went off angrily to his home in al-Minya, from where he got in touch with Heikal [*Muhammad Hassanein Heikal, the minister of information*] and passed on his condemnation of all my actions. Shams Badran then came to my home and told me that the general situation was getting worse by the day, that the whole country was against me, and that the only solution was to reinstate Abdel Hakim Amer to his former position so that conditions would stabilize.

A couple of days later, I met Badran again, having in the meantime arrested the officers of the secret organisation that he had set up within the armed forces; most of them were officers who had graduated with Badran in 1948. I told him: 'Shams, I gave you my trust but I regret to say that you have worked for your own and for the marshal's interests behind my back. If you had been genuinely sincere and loyal when you established that group inside the army, you would have informed me at the time about its structure and told me the names of its members. But you have not been honest. As a matter of fact, I've had all the members of the organisation arrested.' He began to tremble and got very confused. The marshal came to my house last Monday, and our conversation was generally friendly. However, he suggested that he should go to the United States to arrive at an understanding with the Americans, and implied that the Russians are traitors. I did not comment on these unbalanced statements and just told him: 'We will think about it.'

Zakariya Mohieddin: This is naive, unwarranted and disgraceful reasoning.

Nasser: The reason why I have recounted this story in detail is that I want to underline an important question, which is that in view of the fact that all these activities have been carried out by the people closest to me and by the command structures closest to the regime, what sort of actions might not be perpetrated by others? What has happened requires discussion and deep thought. Abdel Hakim and I were the two people most closely bound to each other. Yet Abdel Hakim acted in this way, while Shams Badran's 1948 group and others were getting ready to take over the country. We can only conclude from this entire saga that the closed system will ultimately lead to a hereditary system. Therefore, we now have two tasks. First we have to seek a new system for ourselves, and secondly we have to determine the major faults that exist in the country at the present time and look for ways to correct them.

These days it is being said throughout the country that we are eating each other and that the system is eating itself. If this is so, the future will be very dangerous. So I think that we should immediately exert efforts to change the system because there are certainly faults in it. It is well known that in the single-party system, the struggle for power always occurs at the top. There are plenty of examples around the world, the clearest and the most recent being China and what happened there. I imagine that most of us are unlikely to last for more than ten years, especially me with my sickness and with the pressure and the strains that I am exposed to. This is why I believe that we have to adjust our present system to one that will prevent a politically unenlightened or ignorant person or clique from ruling the country which has placed its absolute and unbounded trust in us. Naturally, the sort of change that I am talking about would not affect our socialist commitment because we have in fact almost completed our socialist strategy in most sectors, apart from the contracts sector and the trade sector. Our work will focus on the development plans that we are drawing up and then we will concentrate on following up their implementation.

Ali Sabri: It is important for the future of our movement that we should safeguard the progress and the benefits that we have achieved so far.

Sidqi Sulaiman: While we are evaluating matters in this meeting, I hope that we can look at the position with regard to the public sector and the private sector, and clarify each one's sphere of activity and the relationship between them.

Zakariya Mohieddin: I want to explain my point of view in some detail, especially because I feel from what we've heard today in the president's statement that the overall picture is now clearer in his mind than ever before. I consider that 9 June was both a historic day and a day that saw a major transformation in the 23 July revolution. What the president has just said represents the discerning foresight and profound thinking that will lead us to the peaceful path that we wish this country to pursue. At the same time, it cannot be denied that the revolution has achieved numerous advances and triumphs during the past fifteen years.

As for the subject that the president has referred to concerning our system, it is well known that a closed system has a particular way of ruling and that the open system also has its own methods. I believe that the way our government has been run so far has been somewhere between the two systems. We have accomplished a great deal at the level of governmental structures but we have not managed to make a lot of progress at the popular level.

If we re-examine conditions in our country, we will find that geographically it is difficult for us to follow the closed system. Therefore an open system is better for us, especially because it allows an individual to develop his own personality and this is the basis of society. When we decide to follow the open system, we can determine the method of ensuring the individual's position in this society, regardless of whether we have one, two or even more political parties. We can also ensure the security of our society by defining its limits constitutionally.

Another point that relates to economic concerns is that we will not be able to provide full employment for all citizens in the public sector. This is why we should allow the private sector to operate more widely so that it can take some of the responsibility for providing employment in our society. This sector will also provide an alternative source of employment for individuals who are dismissed from the public sector.

On the issue of groupings, it is a factor from which all societies inevitably suffer, regardless of whether the system is open or closed.

Looking at the labour force, no group should feel that it is less equal than other groups as far as rights and obligations are concerned. I am thinking here of the people who would make investments because they are under constant attack from the Arab Socialist Union leadership – attacks that make them feel insecure and as a result make society insecure. One final point on production; the importance of expanding this sector is that we should provide all the guarantees needed to enable it to realise its full potential. We must stress that the yardstick for revolutionary labour is production and more production. The point of what I am saying is that I believe that our system should be an open system and that our elections should be open and not controlled.

Nasser: Of course you remember March 1964. The elections were completely open and security measures were guaranteed for all citizens. There wasn't a single detainee; we even released the convicted Muslim Brotherhood members. You know what happened in spite of all this.

Ali Sabri: I don't believe that the issue of democracy is simply confined to security measures, since national security procedures have not proved to be an obstacle to the realisation of democracy in any country.

Zakariya Mohieddin: I didn't mean the security measures that you are talking about, but rather the sort of measures that affect the way the citizen lives, such as faulty administrative procedures, the sequestration measures and the measures that were taken by the committee to eradicate feudalism.

Ali Sabri: Those measures were adopted entirely in line with the revolution's social criteria. The fault with the committee to eradicate feudalism is that in certain cases it failed to apply the principles and rules we had established for its work. I also believe that the National Assembly must take some responsibility because it could be of greater help.

Anwar al-Sadat: In fact, we can't say that the sequestration measures and the measures to eradicate feudalism were wrong. There were mistakes in some individual cases but not in all of them. Unfortunately, the mistakes made in this limited number of cases created a general feeling of alarm.

Husain al-Shafei: This is a really sensitive issue, and the mistakes that were made have been linked in people's minds to their confidence in the regime as a whole. I know of certain instances where the way the decisions of the committee to eradicate feudalism were applied infringed on people's rights. The security forces assigned to enforce the decisions also made such idiotic mistakes that they stirred up really hostile reaction to and bitter criticism of the authority.

Nasser: For the record and for future reference none of you, with the exception of our prime minister Sidqi Sulaiman, has ever made any remarks or offered any criticism to me before about either the committee to eradicate feudalism or the actions of Marshal Amer.

Zakariya Mohieddin: Personally, I was quite content to pass on my observations to Abdel Hakim directly. I didn't want to bother you. By and large, we are all responsible for the mistakes that were made in that period.

Nasser: So, we have all made a mistake. I wish, like the famous Soviet story, that we could speak the truth for three minutes. Just imagine – we are the members of the Supreme Executive Committee which is the highest political authority in the country, and there were only seven of us, and yet we did not speak out and tell the truth at the proper time, when Abdel Hakim Amer, the chairman of the committee to root out feudalism, was actually sitting here with us in his place. This means that the system deteriorated and gradually collapsed to the point where we were afraid to speak out and to tell the truth. For my part, I am prepared to criticise myself and admit that I made a mistake when I withdrew from supervising the army in 1962 and as a result lost contact with what was happening in it. My intention at the time was to reassure Abdel Hakim about myself. But I consider that it was an error on my part.

Zakariya Mohieddin: For the record, I too would like to say that my remarks to the marshal did not touch on fundamental principles. Moreover, none of us objected to the radical measures adopted by the revolution. The sequestration question was decided in 1962 and now we are in 1967. Any observations I made to the marshal were concerned only with its application. You ask me why I didn't speak about those mistakes two or three months ago. Of course this was wrong, but the reason, unfortunately, was that personal relations between us were very tense and particularly delicate.

What is important is the current situation. I propose that we give people the right to appeal against the decisions of the committee to eradicate feudalism before a special court. People will find this very reassuring. I also suggest that we introduce some modifications to our present system so that opinions can always be expressed freely and sincerely and without fear or hypocrisy.

Nasser: In my opinion the present system has reached its limits and there has to be a new system. I personally have certain proposals to make on this issue. First we, as the highest political authority, should free ourselves from fear and then we can rid the entire country of fear.

Secondly, if we truly want to provide security and peace, as you have said, then we should allow the presence of opposing views in the country. In forming such opposition groups, I don't imagine that we'll say that Zakariya should represent a certain tendency and Ali Sabri should represent another tendency in opposition to the first and that we will thus have government and opposition. If we were to do this, we would be creating theatrical opposition. Real opposition will be created by bringing in people who genuinely oppose us at present, such as Baghdadi and Kamal Husain who were both with us and who both approved the Charter, and allowing them to form an opposition party and publish a newspaper expressing that party's views. For our part, we should reorganize our ranks and create an Arab Socialist Union party, and then parliament should be dissolved and new elections be held in December this year on the basis of two platforms for the two parties. Whichever party wins the elections will take over government, while the other party will form the opposition, provided that the army and the police retain their position as professional agencies.

I believe that if we carry out this proposal we will cure the country of all the ailments that we are suffering from and each one of us, from the highest to the lowest, will be rid of the fear that has spread among us. I am against the one-party system because with a single party a particular group of individuals can often create a dictatorship.

My final words on this issue are that if we do not change our present system, we will be following an unknown path and we will not know who will take over the country after us. What has made us ashamed of telling the truth and not accepting criticism will lead us towards a dark future.

At this point, Nasser looked at his watch and found that it was past midnight. The other committee members also seemed anxious to postpone further discussion until they had had time to think more calmly about what had been said and to analyse the fundamental question of how the country should be ruled in the future. He therefore asked them to prepare their reactions to his proposal and indicated his willingness to listen to any other suggestions.

The session had lasted for six hours and the arguments and the statements made by the President had surprised the Committee. He had censured the nature of his own regime severely, its gains and achievements notwithstanding, less than two months after the military defeat that had shaken his reputation. This was enough to convince his colleagues that Nasser had not lost his nerve, that his revolutionary spirit remained steadfast, and that the severity of the defeat and subsequent events had made him a wiser politician who believed both in the fundamental reform and in outspoken criticism that began with himself and ended with the colleagues who had shared power with him. It remained to be seen, however, whether his proposal to change the system that Egypt had followed since the 1952 revolution, into a more open system permitting the presence of real opposition, would be approved by his fellow members of the Supreme Executive Committee.

The Second Session, 4 August 1967

The second session was held on the evening of Friday 4 August at ASU headquarters. Nasser again opened the discussion, repeating his proposal to transform the existing closed system of government into an open system that would permit genuine opposition, and noting that the example of Abdel Hakim Amer, among others, showed how the regime had been affected by relations between certain sections of the leadership.

Nasser: In my opinion the Arab Socialist Union should form a party, provided that another party representing the opposition is allowed to form as well. This political framework will not prevent conflicts occurring inside our ASU organization, but they will be of a different character because of the presence of another party competing with the Arab Socialist Union. As I said yesterday, we should let Baghdadi and Kamal Husain set up the opposition party, provided that we give them the same resources and facilities enjoyed by the ASU, including the right to issue a newspaper that speaks for their party. I believe that they are good men and will continue to act accordingly because they have been with us since the start of the Revolution.

As for the social concept of the regime, it will accord with the concept of whichever party will win in the forthcoming elections; these can be held in December after the current session of the National Assembly has been dissolved in November.

Zakariya Mohieddin [*He extracted a small notebook from his pocket, to which he made frequent reference in presenting his opinion. Among the members he played the largest part in debating Nasser's proposal, raising numerous points*]: I have put a great deal of thought into what the President said to us yesterday, and I will try, with the help of the hasty analysis I have made, to comment on the proposal that he outlined. I understood yesterday, and also from what the President has repeated today, that there will be two parties, one of them the Arab Socialist Union, which will abide by the charter. Certain issues which will be influenced by the presence of two competing parties, each of which will be lying in wait for the mistakes of the other, have already become apparent here. First there is the question of our economic system, certain aspects of which have evolved gradually and in a distinctive way during ten years of growth and development. Some problems have appeared during the application of economic policies and these now require a fundamental appraisal. It is necessary to re-examine a number of economic projects, especially with regard to production and to profits and also to overmanning. In my estimation these projects should be approached within the structure of economic guidelines, and every effort must be made to supply everything that is needed to ensure stability for the more effective administration of these projects.

Another economic aspect is the need to raise savings to 25 per cent, considering that deposits have so far not exceeded 13 per cent [*of total revenues*]. This is considered inadequate in relation to the annual population growth in our country. Another point is our failure to increase the volume of exports sufficiently to meet our substantial import demands.

A second issue concerns foreign policy after the aggression, and the question as to the best policies to follow so that our domestic goals can be achieved, as well as the issue of whether or not we should allow joint projects with the participation of foreign capital. Should we encourage the participation of Arab capital so as to raise the rate of annual growth from six to eight per cent, and should we limit wage increases so that they don't exceed two per cent?

All of these things, whether they are in the political or the economic sphere, require a quick decision and some will require a fundamental approach. I'm afraid that domestic political factors and the factional fighting that's bound to occur between the two parties may affect the way we choose the correct solutions. Here, a new notion starts to emerge with regard to our major economic projects and whether they can be made independent of the supervision and intervention of partisan ministers? But in this case, to whom would these projects and their organizations be accountable? Would it be to the National Assembly, to the government or to a special council formed from members of both parties?

Nasser: Zakariya, whoever takes charge of government will be responsible for the success of all the institutions. He will also be responsible for their failure. In other words, any failure in managing the organizations will lead to the government's downfall. To set up a special council from the two parties to supervise the establishments would be impracticable.

Don't forget that the goal of any party is always to gain power and that the other party will be lying in wait for the first party to make mistakes in its performance. So, how can you say that the opposition party can participate with the government party in a single council to supervise the economic projects? Whoever is in government will be responsible and will be the party that supervises and directs in all areas, including economic projects.

Zakariya Mohieddin [*with obvious feeling*]: I didn't intend to make a definite proposal. What I wanted to do was to highlight some of the problems that will result from the presence of two parties, such as the problems of one-upmanship and invective. As I've already said, each party will be lurking, waiting for the other party's mistakes and without considering their impact on the public interest, with the aim of stirring up the people and winning them to its side – mistakes on issues such as the dismissal of surplus labour and limiting wage increases, and so on.

I also expect the other party to dig up the past, and this may well be followed by the discrediting of the country's leadership and of the state presidency!

Nasser: This means that we are afraid and that we should therefore make no move. Why? In the past the leadership of the alternative party participated with us in all the steps that were taken by the regime. As for defamation of the leaders, this is happening at present but behind closed doors. It is much better for it to happen out in the open.

Zakariya Mohieddin: There are numerous other issues that will result from a change in the structure of the system, the first being the need to amend the constitution and the question of whether the state will become a presidential republic, or a parliamentary republic, or a presidential republic with some modifications. Will the top executives always be changed with the change of ruling party leaderships such as the governors, the directors of enterprises, under-secretaries and company chairmen? I ask myself, what is more important than this? What are the basic goals over which the two parties are expected to disagree? What is the social formation of each party's supporters? Can the ruling party amend the charter or does this require a certain degree of agreement by the two parties?

Nasser: It is assumed that all these questions will be answered when the new constitution is discussed and that the answers will be perfectly clear in its various articles and stipulations.

Zakariya Mohieddin: My final question is whether it is right to change the country's political structure while the Israelis are still occupying the east bank of the Suez Canal?

Nasser: If Zakariya has completed his review and finished all his questions, then can we hear another opinion?

Sidqi Sulaiman [*the prime minister*]: My opinion of the president's words is that it is impossible for an opposition party to emerge in our country at present because the sole objective of the opposing party will be to attain power. It is also a matter of fact that you will find all the devious and opportunist elements rallying around the other party. In this present situation, are we psychologically ready to swallow partisan invective? What will be the effect of such vilification on the main state agencies, and especially on the armed forces? Another important point relating to this issue is that the presence of the president of the republic at the top of the ruling party makes it almost impossible for the opposition party to win control. The presence of President Abdel Nasser in particular, with all the popular support he commands, in practice makes it impossible for the opposition party to attain power.

At this point, Husain al-Shafei joined the discussion and proposed that the president – in order to avoid the obstacle mentioned by Sidqi Sulaiman – should be above the two parties and not considered as belonging to either. But how, he wondered, could this be done in a presidential system?

Sidqi Sulaiman: I believe that what can be done now is to introduce some changes and some minor adjustments to the present system, such as accepting criticism, eliminating fear, making it possible to appeal before a judicial authority against any sentence, and clearly defining the relationship between the Arab Socialist Union and the government. And finally, any person who accepts the leadership of an opposition party under the present conditions is a madman!

Husain al-Shafei: In fact, since the President has crystallized his statements in the form of a definite proposal for changing the system, the issue with its various dimensions has become difficult; it is easy to talk about the negative aspects that appeared in practice but it is very difficult to proceed from the reality of these negative features to a new system. It may be essential to develop a system in which opposition is present. However, this issue raises numerous questions and reactions, the first being that if the Arab Socialist Union represents the alliance of the working people, what will the other party represent, keeping in mind that any party has to represent a certain concept or class?

If the two parties are in agreement over the charter, then what are the goals of each of them? But if the charter is amended, then the Arab Socialist Union will have less of a chance than the other party. We all remember that the National Congress members cheered a great deal when you made the remark about restoring Palestine, and mentioned the religious aspects, the abolition of some privileges given to certain leaderships, and so forth. This is why the other party will try to play around with slogans in order to engage in one-upmanship about the principles and foundations of the Arab Socialist Union.

I agree with Zakariya Mohieddin about the economic questions that will result from the presence of two parties, and I will end by saying that I do not envisage that our system should be changed before all evidence of the aggression has been obliterated.

Anwar al-Sadat: What I want to say goes back to 9 and 10 June when the Egyptian people, with their profound national instinct, rose up and insisted on clinging to the current situation. Every citizen came forward in his conviction that Abdel Nasser is a reflection of the picture of struggle and that Abdel Nasser is an expression of his desire for steadfastness. It is also my assessment that the entire regime fell on 9 and 10 June but that the masses reinstated it, demanding only the return of Abdel Nasser as president. This means that all the other agencies of the regime, including the National Assembly, have fallen. This is why I consider that the bickering and the discussions that have taken place in the National Assembly over the past fortnight are useless. However, they do give us an indication of what the bickering will be like for as long as the enemy remains entrenched in our territory and while his forces are still deployed at a distance of 100 metres from our forces. This is in addition to the murky impression left behind by Abdel Hakim Amer's extraordinary behaviour.

I will again ask whether it is reasonable to change our system and to form two parties while the enemy is still present on our land? What is more important now is to mobilize the entire country against the enemy, and this is why I do not agree with President Abdel Nasser's proposal to form two parties before evidence of the aggression has been wiped out. There would be no objection to our all stepping down from power and letting new administrations replace us. But in the present situation, dividing the country through the presence of the proposed opposition is unacceptable because our people are strong and loyal and they trust this man [*and he pointed in a very emotional manner towards the President*]. We are all confident that Abdel Nasser, our leader, is capable of leading us to safe shores.

Openness [*by which he meant the open system*] may be required. But for now there are things that can be done quickly. For now let us change our system a little bit. Let us look for all the existing mistakes and work to correct them. Let us hold new elections for the National Assembly in accordance with new concepts and rules. But to allow a system of opposition before removing all traces of the attack and to divide the country is unthinkable. I have full confidence in Gamal Abdel Nasser but I do not approve the process of opening up through a two-party system because it will open the door to the dogs that want to tear the regime to pieces! Let us form a new National Assembly and permit criticism within its framework. But I do not approve of creating an opposition until we have wiped away the marks of the invasion; at present we must concentrate our efforts on the battle because the battle is our destiny, whatever this destiny may be. Many peoples have fought and won hard battles, as happened in the valiant Leningrad.

To conclude my remarks, I repeat that there is absolute confidence in President Gamal Abdel Nasser. The question of two parties is improper because the new party will rely on one-upmanship. For example, the leader of the new party may raise the slogan that we should hand Yemen over to the enemies, regardless of the country's general interest. This is why I do not approve of having two parties.

Ali Sabri [*who was arrested by Sadat in the power contest of 15 May 1971 and sentenced to death. The sentence was later reduced to life imprisonment, and he was freed ten years later*]: As far as the past is concerned, it is my opinion that our system has not been as closed as a communist party system would have been. At the same time, it has not been as open as the systems that are found in Europe. As for the proposal to form two parties, it is well known that parties are established basically according to class affiliations. Therefore, if the Arab Socialist Union is established on the basis of the socialist concept, then the other party must be established on the basis of a different philosophy and of a new class. Even if we say that abiding by the charter is a basic condition, this is still not sufficient because it is always possible to deviate from the spirit of the charter in specific circumstances and the country may thus take a different direction.

I do not think we need to be afraid of this new experiment as long as Abdel Nasser is with us. The danger lies in what will happen after him. A prolonged class struggle will erupt, and we will also see the emergence of forces that support the socialist transformation as well as others that are opposed to it. This is why I am convinced that there should be openness and a greater measure of democracy, but not, I also believe, by way of the two-party system.

Abdel Muhsin Abu al-Nour [*who was also involved in the 15 May power contest. He received a 15-year prison sentence, spending five years in Tura prison before being released for health reasons*]: In our search for a new system we should not allow any individual or type of organisation to come and ruin or destroy the great edifice that has been built by Gamal Abdel Nasser. There can be no doubt that we must proceed towards forming an opposition but we want an opposition that builds and does not destroy, and an opposition that corrects any deviation, whatever it may be. I also believe that we should proceed along this path in stages, starting with a dissenting group inside the Arab Socialist Union, but provided that the leadership of the Union remains in the hands of Gamal Abdel Nasser. The system did actually collapse on 9 June but because the masses insisted on Gamal Abdel Nasser's leadership, he remains the safety valve for all of us. For this reason I propose the formation of two wings within the Arab Socialist Union – a supporting and an opposing wing. I do not approve the establishment of two parties because we will not obliterate the marks of the attack with a two-party system. Rather, we will have a heated battle between the two parties which will keep people preoccupied with its pronouncements and divert their attention from the fundamental struggle.

Nasser: I disagree with all of you – opposition cannot be fabricated, otherwise it becomes distorted opposition. The main reason why I have nominated Kamal Husain for the opposition is because he is genuinely opposed to us at present. As for opposition inside the party, you will always find this, but it is an internal opposition amongst the party's leadership and the people as a whole take no part in it. Take, for example, the Chinese party. It has recently become apparent that there was opposition between Mao Tse-tung's faction and Liu Shao-chi's faction, but this was opposition within the party. Even in our present meeting, there are various and conflicting tendencies. For example, Zakariya Mohieddin has a view that Ali Sabri, who holds a different view, is opposed to. There is no objection to this. What is important is that the leaders do not criticise and carp at each other because it is we, the high-ranking officials in the system, who have caused the system to crack. Each one of us is destroying what another one is doing whereas all of us, at every level, should be aware of our united destiny.

I now have to ask myself where we are going with this old system. When I met Anwar al-Sadat, the Speaker of the National Assembly, before the June war, I told him that there were numerous issues which would be difficult to solve within the framework of the present system, that we had to have an open system, and that we must have opposition. We also need to make it possible for the newspapers to write openly, because I believe that our revolutionary purity has suffered heavily after fifteen years. Even intellectual unity between us is non-existent. If there were another party and real opposition, there would be challenges for each and every one of us to face. Such challenges would oblige each person to refrain from discussing his colleagues and to avoid destroying their work. In such a case, Kamal al-Din Husain or someone from the other party would be lurking and ready to pounce on such an individual and on the other colleagues in his party. I feel that we have all failed in the responsibilities entrusted to us. Moreover, sensitivity among us has reached the point where we are afraid to criticize each other at meetings. I believe that the only solution is for us to create a real "challenge" in the true sense of the word, to hasten to correct the mistakes that have been committed, and to reorganize the agencies and departments of the Arab Socialist Union so that the Union will be able to deal with the new challenge facing it.

The issue in its simplest form can be summed up in precisely two ways. The first is to follow the single-party system, and I believe that it is now too late for us to form a sound single party and to proceed in a totally disciplined manner according to its principles and programmes. The second is to follow the system of political struggle and the survival of the fittest. When it was first formed there was a healthy political atmosphere within the Revolutionary Command Council: discussions among the members were at their most intense and final decisions were taken by the majority. But matters progressed and later the state broke down into several undeclared parties: Abdel Hakim's party, Zakariya's party, al-Sadat's party, Ali Sabri's party, and so on. Abdel Hakim wanted to build himself up by using the army. Zakariya wanted to build himself up using the police. Al-Sadat wanted to build himself using the National Assembly and Ali Sabri wanted to build himself up using the Arab Socialist Union. The system thus fell apart. Every group of us wanted to get rid of the other group.

This is why I have proposed the existence of real challenges so that it will become obvious to us all that any destructive action from within the system will cause the entire system to fall on all our heads. I may have been responsible for the lack of coordination and for the lack of collective participation in building up our political organization, the Arab Socialist Union. In any case, this is what has happened. Our enemies have been unable to dismantle a single brick in our internal structure in spite of all the efforts they have exerted whereas we, the ones who were responsible for building that structure, have gradually destroyed it. This is why it is impossible to continue as we were before 1967. If it becomes evident to us that our new rivals are better and firmer than we are, then let us declare with the utmost courage and honesty that we are leaving so that we can be replaced by others who are more eager than ourselves to serve the people and to serve the interests of the country. Our selection of an open system will also require a lot of change, otherwise it will be nothing more than words and the people will have no confidence in it. They will claim that we have propagated this slogan only for the flowers to bloom and so that it will be easy to distinguish them and pick them, as the Chinese proverb says.

I am sorry to have been so harshly outspoken in this session, but it is because I swore to myself on 9 June not to deal with the political issues through bargaining or through balances. I also swore to fight for my principles and to express my opinions frankly, even if it was at the expense of my own neck.

Sidqi Sulaiman: I believe, Mr President, that we are discussing this issue under the influence of the psychological pressures that have resulted from the military defeat, and that we are diagnosing our ailments and prescribing the cure for them during abnormal times. I believe that if we had triumphed in the military battle, our comments on our present system would have been that it is the best system. It is my view that all our present problems result from lack of coordination. Let us begin with a clear definition of the rights and duties of us all, and let us then bring everybody to account according to the degree to which he has abided by them.

Abdel Muhsin Abu al-Nour: Our duties and powers are defined, as, for example, with the powers of the governor, the ASU secretary and the director of security. Yet the conflicts between them persist and cause damage for the very simple reason that none of the three feels that they are under the same umbrella or believes that anything that hits one of them will also hurt the others.

Husain al-Shafei: I believe that it is difficult to create the 'challenge' and the required opposition before the traces of the assault have been wiped out. This is why I propose that the current phase be built on the basis of actual control and of reorganizing the process of constructive criticism at all levels.

Ali Sabri: I am still concerned that the formation of another party will mean a new philosophy and a new class. I wish we had implemented our originally-declared philosophy of 'democracy of all the people'.

Nasser: The democracy of all the people means that we are responsible for building up every citizen in a politically sound manner. It also means that we should not let one class dominate another class, whatever class or at whatever level it may be.

Zakariya Mohieddin: I think that it will be dangerous to implement the new proposal before we have eliminated all traces of the aggression. Moreover, it is worth carrying on with the experience gained by the Arab Socialist Union so far, provided that the Union and its agencies are reorganized. As for the formation of political wings inside the ASU, it is not right to do this until elections have been held throughout the organization.

There's another point, too. If it is decided that the two-party proposal will be adopted, why should we involve Gamal Abdel Nasser in local party contests given his status nationally and at the level of the entire Arab community? I still adhere to the opinion which I expressed at the beginning of this session.

The discussion between the president and the members of the Supreme Executive Committee went on for hours and hours that night too, but reached no final decision. However, it became obvious to Nasser from the debate among the members and from the critical opinions voiced concerning his proposal that they did not welcome his suggestions and that they believed that the proposed plan would cause numerous rifts throughout the entire political system. They were also unanimous in their belief that it would be dangerous to introduce any change in the system before the scars left by the June events had healed and before the territory on which the enemy was encamped had been liberated. At the same time, Nasser rejected any attempt on the part of the other members to divert his proposal from its stated goal and from the course he had set down for it, refusing as well to be satisfied with the creation of opposition inside the Arab Socialist Union. He rejected the setting up of a symbolic opposition, which he saw as distorted opposition, insisting that any such move would be to betray the confidence of his people who had unconditionally entrusted him with their destiny and the country's future.

Chapter 6

ARGUMENTS AND CONTRADICTIONS
Nasser and the Americans

After the Six Day War the tensions of the cold war began to heighten while the antagonism between Abdel Nasser and the Americans simultaneously died away. After Egypt's defeat, Israel had come to believe that Nasser would by one means or another take the initiative to contact Tel Aviv, and an Israeli leader was even quoted as saying: "We are waiting for a call from Cairo." America also felt that Nasser had thoroughly learned the lesson of the defeat and that because of this he would turn back towards the United States and divest himself of his past misjudgments by expelling the Russians from Egypt and by turning away from the socialist line. They anticipated that he would open the country's doors wide to Western capital generally and to American capital in particular, and that he would shed his Arab skin, isolate himself within his own borders and devote his efforts to development, tourism and to the provision of services.

Realising that their expectations were illusory and that their calculations were inaccurate, perhaps because of the cold logic according to which such political judgments are made, or perhaps simply because of their failure to understand his personality, and concluding that Nasser would neither communicate with Tel Aviv nor even contact Washington, the Americans decided instead to approach him. Initial contact was made between Cairo and Washington while Nasser was celebrating the final stages of the construction of the High Dam in Aswan. During the celebrations, in buoyant mood, he made his famous speech in which he said: "I thank God that I have lived to see the High Dam turn into a tangible reality for the prosperity of the Egyptian people."

It was at this time that the Americans requested the resumption of diplomatic relations, but Nasser stipulated that this would only happen if

"America formulates a clear position toward the Palestinian issue".

All subsequent events confirm that Washington, losing hope that any of Nasser's policies would change, then decided to resume its plots to overthrow the regime. Nasser was aware of this fact and was ready for all eventualities. At one of the cabinet sessions in 1969 he warned ministers of America's plotting, telling them that the US would spend huge sums of money during the year on promoting domestic opposition aimed at overthrowing the regime. And when Israel attacked Beirut airport on Christmas Eve in 1969, Nasser told a special session of the Egyptian Council of Ministers: "This operation proves that it is Israel which exerts pressure on America and not the other way round."

What was perhaps the final attempt to tame Abdel Nasser was made by Nikolai Ceaucescu, president of the Socialist Republic of Romania, when he offered to arrange a secret meeting in Romania or in a place of Nasser's choosing between the Egyptian leader and whatever Israeli leaders he might select. Nasser turned down this offer, informing his Council of Ministers that America and Israel were exerting the utmost effort to stamp out the Palestinian problem and that they were trying by every possible means to transform the question into an Egyptian–Israeli, Syrian–Israeli and Jordanian–Israeli issue.

The confrontation between America and Abdel Nasser is of considerable historic importance. Every Third World revolution against the Americans, whether in Africa, Asia or Latin America, was uncompromisingly supported by Nasser, and it was a great tragedy for these countries and for the Arabs when America finally defeated him.

The story of Nasser and the Americans is not a happy one, as the following extracts from his discussions with ministers and members of the Supreme Executive Committee will indicate.

Inside Egypt, 1968 was an eventful year. There was the so-called Marshal Amer case, there was the trial of military commanders accused of negligence during the war and there were widespread demonstrations. The workers went on strike in Helwan, Zakariya Mohieddin resigned as prime minister, and there were elections throughout the political establishment. Domestically, Nasser's main concern was to rebuild the country's political structure from within, and having achieved this he turned his attention towards military reconstruction, with the sole aim of liberating the occupied territories according to the precept that he had formulated earlier: What has been taken by force cannot be regained except by force.

Council of Ministers, 18 February 1968

On 18 February 1968, Nasser chaired a meeting of the Council of Ministers at which a report was presented by Mahmoud Riyad, the foreign minister. Riyad reviewed the latest political developments, explaining in some detail the mission of the UN mediator, Dr Gunnar Jarring. The importance of Riyad's statement lay in his conclusion that Jarring's mission would get nowhere. He also commented: "It is evident that America is extending its protection to Israel and to Israel's invasions as well. When the issue of Arab ownership in Jerusalem came up recently and when Jordan tried to present this matter to the United Nations, America exerted direct pressure on Jordan not to raise the question. The Jordanian Government complied."

Nasser: We have recently noticed an increasing American interest in the region generally and in Egypt in particular. The reason for this could be the growing stature of the Soviets here in the Middle East. I was told recently by an American that the US administration naively spends $30 billion in Vietnam to prevent the communist influence spreading in Southeast Asia while allowing the Soviets to gain a prominent position at the lowest possible cost in the Middle East. For our part, we can benefit from America's interest in us and in the region to gain more time for political action. All this will be for the sake of our military preparations. Mahmoud Riyad tells me that they [*the Americans*] have said they are willing to abandon the conditions they had stipulated so that they can resume relations with us, but I find that the time is not right for restoring links with the United States. The Americans want to return to the region at any price and they understand that they cannot return except through us. They have recently spent 10 million pounds in Sudan but to no avail, which is why they suddenly contacted us while I was in Aswan and insisted that the relations between us should be resumed. Their persistence reached the point where they had already prepared the communiqué that was to be issued as soon as the resumption of relations had been declared. However, I rejected their request, confirming that my sole condition for approving the restoration of relations was that the United States must adopt a clear position toward the Palestinian issue.

Speaking frankly, I can assure you, and I repeat my conviction, that Israel will not withdraw from our land as the result of the US applying pressure on it, nor will it withdraw as a result of the efforts of the United Nations. But it will withdraw when we become capable of carrying out military action to drive it out of the occupied land.

Council of Ministers, 7 April 1968

At the session of the Egyptian Council of Ministers held on 7 April 1968, this issue came up again in discussions. Nasser reviewed the situation in the region generally, focusing in particular on the position of the Americans.

Nasser: America's position makes it clear that they will insist on our meeting the Israelis, and regrettably the same message has been reaching us through the Soviets. From this, it is obvious to us that America and the Soviet Union have jointly agreed to submit a timetable for implementing the Security Council resolution. The Russians originally pressed us to accept a political solution because they believed that our armed forces would be unable to arm and to organise themselves for at least three years. However, all the Arab countries rejected the American–Soviet plan.

In the wake of that rejection, relations between us and the Soviet Union became strained. Then Mahmoud Riyad went to Moscow and explained our position to them, after which America refused to submit the joint plan to the United Nations. The Russians believed that the American–Soviet draft resolution would actually be implemented and that the Jews would withdraw from the occupied land. When Ali Sabri went to Moscow, Brezhnev told him: "It is important that you accept the present plan for a peaceful solution so that you can prepare militarily. We will continue to arm and to support you." What is extraordinary is that the Soviets contacted the Americans again in order to arrive at an understanding with them over the joint resolution. The Americans reversed their former approval on two points, the first being no withdrawal to the lines of 5 June, and the second being that the Arabs and the Israelis would have to meet in the presence of some mediator.

I have now received a message from the Central Committee of the Soviet Communist Party saying that they [*the Soviets*] have lost hope and that the Americans have misled and deceived them.

The fact is that our primary intention is to continue to pursue the political solution road in order to gain time for military preparation and to persuade the Soviets to supply us with all the weapons we need. I would like to repeat once again that as long as the Israelis cannot sign a peace treaty with us, Israel will not consider that it has won the war. The Zionist strategy is to force a settlement [*and here Nasser used the English phrase 'to force a settlement'*].

When I met him recently, I told the British ambassador, who I know is being pushed by the Americans, that we Egyptians utterly refuse to sit around a table and negotiate directly with Israel because such a table would be a capitulation table and not a negotiation table.

It is important for us to be militarily prepared and this is why we need time. In my opinion the length of time is not important as long as we come together with our people and explain all the aspects of the problem to them, and as long as our domestic front is stable. The Americans have tried to resume political relations with us yet again, and I have repeated to them that they have to adopt an even-handed political stance toward the issue, which they have refused to do. The reason why they persist is because they want, by resuming relations with Egypt, to secure an entry permit with which they can enter all the Arab countries. But we will make this impossible for them.

Dr Safiyeddin Abul-Izz [*minister of youth*]: Can we know the reason why Brezhnev will not visit Egypt, even though the visit has been announced?

Nasser: From the Soviet point of view, they have said that if Brezhnev comes to Egypt and nothing is achieved at the military or political level, then they – meaning the Soviets – will lose interest nationally. This is why they have been satisfied with sending the deputy chairman of the Council of Ministers at this stage. Broadly speaking, I find that we are the ones who need their aid and who make requests to them, and this is why I suggest that we go to them.

Dr Hafiz Ghanim [*minister of education*]: What is the likelihood of Jarring's mission succeeding?

Nasser: In my estimation, Jarring's mission will not lead to an honourable agreement as far as we are concerned. I also reckon that he will carry on for a year and a half, and that ultimately he will arrive at nothing. In fact, we need this time to prepare our armed forces. As for replying to the issues presented by Jarring, I made a number of points. I told him that concerning the right of survival, we in Egypt need this right just as much as Israel does. Where the borders are concerned, there are no problems between us and Israel in the first place, because the Egyptian borders are well known and have been fixed for hundreds of years. On the passage of ships in the Gulf of Aqaba, we reserve our right to submit this issue to an international court, and on the passage of ships through the Suez Canal, we agree to such passage, provided that Israel implements the UN resolutions on the Palestinians. Concerning demilitarized zones, we agree to such zones provided that they are on both sides of the border, and as for the presence of UN emergency forces, we agree to their presence, provided that they are also on both sides, here and there.

Jarring then went on to Israel and they refused to implement the Security Council resolution. They also rejected another plan submitted by the British that called for Israel's withdrawal to a distance of only 20 kilometres from the Suez Canal.

I am broadly of the opinion that we must benefit from Jarring's mission to gain time for military preparation. At this stage we must also carry out operations with the *fedayeen* in the occupied territories, and I have agreed with the military commander of the Fatah Organization on aid and coordination. I have information indicating that the Israelis are very disturbed by the *fedayeen* operations in the occupied territories, since around fifteen people are being killed every week, and this hurts the Israelis a great deal.

After having had all these political contacts, I want to make an observation about what is happening now. I find that the Americans want to make us follow a path that is different from that of the Security Council resolution. The resolution does not call for a joint meeting or for joint negotiations between us and the Israelis. I believe that the Americans, by going ahead with the steps in the way that they have planned, want to lead us to Israel's main demand. This means that we must review the American plans against us. These plans have gone through three stages. In the first stage, the military defeat was supposed to destroy the entire regime and to replace it by a pro-American regime. One of the reasons why I stepped down on 9 June was because I could not agree with the Americans. Later, of course, they remembered the events of 9 and 10 June and the determination of the masses [*referring to the sweeping popular demonstrations throughout Egypt and the Arab world urging him to withdraw his resignation*]. In the second of these stages they estimated that we would run out of money in December and be unable to provide the wheat for making bread for the people. But the resolutions of the Khartoum conference came as a shock to them and we acquired the economic aid which enabled us to get through this stage. The third and last stage is the one in which the Americans have turned to attempts to overthrow us internally through domestic instability. I estimate that next year they will spend between £E15 and £E20 million on certain domestic elements in order to achieve this goal. This is why I believe that we will have some internal troubles next year before we start military operations, and this is why it is going to be necessary to get a good grip on the country during this period.

Supreme Executive Committee, 28 October 1968

The president's declaration of 30 March 1968, approved by a referendum in May, called for the restoration of civil liberties, parliamentary control and the reform of the ASU. The declaration was in response to strong public reaction to the leniency with which a military tribunal had treated four air force commanders accused of negligence during the 1967 war: two had actually been acquitted. There had been widespread demonstrations in February in which many thousands of students and workers had taken part.

Following Nasser's declaration of 30 March and a subsequent decree, members of the ASU's Supreme Executive Committee were elected; they now comprised the President, Ali Sabri (who received 134 votes, the highest number of votes), Husain al-Shafei (130 votes), Dr Mahmoud Fawzi (129 votes), Anwar al-Sadat (119 votes), Ramzi Stinu (112 votes), Diya al-Din Dawud (104 votes), Abdel Muhsin Abu al-Nour (104 votes) and Labib Shuquair (80 votes). The outcome of these elections and the number of votes polled by each of the winning committee members produced a number of profound psychological effects which in turn caused consequences and complications from which Nasser was to suffer quite considerably.

Nasser: I have received a message from the Soviet Union, delivered to me by the Soviet ambassador in Cairo, which concerns new developments in the political negotiations between the Soviets and the Americans. Before I tell you about the contents of this message and about my proposed reply, I would like to summarize my current plan for dealing with the Americans and for talking to them. In my view we should make the Soviets enter into negotiations and arguments with the Americans. In this way, instead of having conflicts between Egypt and the Americans, the clashes will be between the Americans and the Soviets. Naturally, when the Americans and the Soviets, as superpowers, get together around the negotiation table, they use language that is different from that used between a major power and a small country, especially on the issue of a political settlement.

Now, concerning the message I have received from the Soviet Union, the Soviets are obviously afraid that we are about to push our armed forces into a new military operation before they have achieved capability at the manpower, training and morale levels, because if these forces are defeated again, the Soviets will have a serious problem on their hands in this region. I have reassured the Soviets on this issue and have told them that we will not become embroiled in a major war until we are completely certain that we have the military capacity to undertake one. This is why we repeatedly emphasise the need for them to arm us fully. Regrettably, we have not yet finished strengthening our mechanised military capacity to enable us to move eastwards after crossing the canal.

As for the topics and proposals contained in the Soviet message, I suggest that our reply includes the following points. First, where the holding of joint negotiations with Israel is concerned, it is impossible for us to embark on such a step. Secondly, concerning passage through the Suez Canal, this issue must be tied to the issue of the Palestinians. Then on the question of secure Israeli borders, I will repeat what I have already told them, namely that we cannot relinquish a single inch of land. Fourthly, the problem of Jerusalem can be discussed and debated, but Jerusalem cannot be relinquished. Concerning termination of the state of war, I will repeat to the Soviets that this question is firmly tied to full Israeli withdrawal, and that we will not end the state of war with the Israelis as long as they remain on a single inch of our land. Finally, concerning the subject of a referendum among the Palestinians living outside Palestine and the possibility that they will not wish to return, I believe the opposite to be the case. I predict that they will reject the no-return proposal.

For our part, we will continue to encourage the Soviets to press ahead with the political discussions and negotiations with the Americans, as long as we stress our view about taking advantage of this period to complete our military preparation along the lines already mentioned.

Dr Mahmoud Fawzi raised the issue of the prolonged discussions taking place between the Soviet and American foreign affairs ministers at the United Nations. Pointing out the danger of permitting a lengthy debate with Abba Eban, the Israeli foreign minister, he suggested that at this time it would be better not to specify a solution for the Palestinian problem, apart from Jerusalem, so that solutions could be reached on withdrawing Israeli forces from the occupied Arab territories. This should be done on the basis of the time factor and the question should always be asked whether the time factor favoured the Arabs or the Israelis.

Nasser: As regards the time factor, the main concern is the extent of our domestic capacity, the degree of our solidarity, the level of our economic development capability, and whether we are able to proceed as a state as far as industrialisation programmes, land reclamation, investments and our entire national plan are concerned. Is it a real plan or just a plan on paper? It is only on this basis that we can calculate whether the time element is to our advantage or our disadvantage.

They account for the time factor in a different way. It is in their favour on the basis that they anticipate that our domestic front will explode and then collapse.

Nasser believed categorically that Egypt was part of the Arab nation, and that Egypt's Arab stance was neither novel nor capricious. He held that Egypt's true interests were Arab interests and that Arab interests were the same as Egyptian interests, repeating to those around him that Egypt's Arabism was Egypt's destiny and that it was impossible to escape destiny. According to this principle, Egypt had therefore to play its role within the framework of this truth. He also used to say that the sole aim of the imperialist forces was to push Egypt off the Arab stage and far away from the problems of the Arabs and of Arabism so that the country would retreat into itself to deal with its own difficulties; that these imperialist forces wanted Egypt to devote itself to tourism, hotels and public services and to forget about the Arabs, but if Egypt were to do this it would be doomed to everlasting isolation.

Based on this perception and from this starting-point, Nasser was eager, even in defeat, to act without having to suffer the stabs of friends, let alone those of his enemies, and this is clear from the continuing discussions about the situation that took place during meetings of the Supreme Executive Committee and the Council of Ministers.

Supreme Executive Committee, 12 November 1968

Nasser: It seems to me that the activities of Jarring as the UN mediator are useless. I had previously estimated that his work in the area would last for eighteen months, in view of the fact that Israel's policy has proceeded and continues to proceed as planned, namely to force a settlement in their favour [*Nasser again said this phrase in English*]. For our part, we have offered the maximum concessions possible, under pressure from Jordan and for the sake of the West Bank. We cannot make any further concessions.

Here Dr Mahmoud Fawzi intervened to talk about the time that would be needed to solve the problem, about the possibility that Israel might be able to use nuclear warheads in 1970 and about expectations of the new US administration under Nixon who had to settle the problem of Vietnam as well as the Middle East. He then asked if it was possible to think seriously about resuming Egyptian–US relations, which would improve matters on both sides, mentioning a highly placed official of the Pan-American Petroleum Company who predicted the extraction of large quantities of oil from Egypt's Western Desert. Such an improvement would be reflected by gradual growth in the Egyptian economy, while even such simple indicators as the considerable rise in the value of the Egyptian pound on the Beirut market supported this assertion.

Nasser: We should never forget that Israel's goal has been and will continue to be to force us to consider the issue as an Egyptian–Israeli issue and not as an Arab–Israeli issue. We do not accept this view. As for restoring relations with America, there must be some basis on which this can be done. How can we restore relations when America has not approved the principle of withdrawal to the 5 June lines? The discussions on this matter have to be looked at with the other Arab countries, including Mauritania.

Dr Fawzi, there has to be a political price for restoring our relations with the United States. They have been demanding and insisting on this since February, but at the same time, they have not responded to our terms. In my opinion, therefore, we should proceed with caution and see what Nixon will do after he has formed his administration next January. We are of course continuing the political dialogue with the Americans through Ashraf Ghorbal [*who was head of the Egyptian Affairs Bureau in America*].

It is important for us to ask ourselves two questions. The first is, can we make more concessions than we have already made? and the second question is, can we accept the statements made by Israel?

When the Russians talked to us about the political solution, I told them that there were two issues that could not be cast aside. First, we would not abandon or cede a single inch of our territories. The second issue was the restoration of Palestinian rights.

Abdel Muhsin Abu al-Nour [*a member of the ASU's Supreme Executive Committee*]: I consider that the Israelis will not capitulate unless war is declared or until they believe that we are militarily strong. Therefore, both popular and military mobilisation have to continue because they are the only path.

Dr Labib Shuqair [*a member of the ASU's Supreme Executive Committee*]: Any further concessions will create domestic repercussions for the regime. The Israelis are fully aware of this, but the matter is not in Israel's hands alone. It is also in America's hands. It is in America's interest that the question takes a long time to resolve and that our regime fails through offering successive concessions. This means that a peaceful solution is impossible and that military confrontation is the only way.

Nasser: Military confrontation is not easy. I will tell you frankly that I have been hoping for a peaceful solution, even though our armed forces renounce such a solution in order to preserve their dignity and the dignity of Egypt. I told them [*the armed forces*] that war was not for the sake of war but that it was a means towards achieving the strategic political goal.

Another point is that the Israelis really do want to expand but they know very well what my opinion is on this matter, and they know that I will never allow this [*expansion*]. I have received a message from a member of the Tuqan family in the West Bank. It seems Moshe Dayan has said privately that they know the price of every Arab leader in the region and in the countries adjacent to them [*i.e. Israel*], except for Abdel Nasser whose price they have not found out yet. A further point is that the military in Israel have become remarkably affected by arrogance, in addition to Nixon's statement in which he said that the United States of America would always be keen to keep Israel superior to its Arab neighbours.

We should not forget that Britain and America both want and are exerting every effort to confine us within our borders in Egypt and that they are trying to turn the Suez Canal into an international naval corridor. They have been trying to do this since 1955 – after the evacuation agreement – by whatever means possible, and they have also tried to keep us inside the Egyptian borders.

Husain al-Shafei: As far as the time element is concerned, I believe that we can use this element in our favour as a way of planning moves rather than for giving further concessions. But we must launch a new political manoeuvre as a kind of smokescreen for the present waiting period which is being used for full military preparation.

Nasser: The issue of manoeuvres is not subject to discussion. Of course manoeuvres are needed and the Russians have repeatedly talked about them. But what is significant is that no contracts have been concluded for the weapon and equipment requests which I agreed with the Soviet Union last July. It seems to me that the issue of Czechoslovakia [*referring to the incursion into Czechoslovakia by the Warsaw Pact forces to overthrow the Dubçek regime*] has somewhat affected their relations with us, and I still believe this is the case even though Brezhnev and Grechko confirmed to Murad Ghalib, our ambassador in Moscow, that the Soviet Communist Party Politburo had approved all our requests. I've also been informed that the Russians told Murad Ghalib that they were now confident that Egypt will make thorough use of the Soviet weapons that are sent to us.

Our military situation at present is first-rate and I can disclose that we are now able to cross the canal, although we cannot move eastward after we have crossed. We should not forget that the Israelis are well trained in offensive combat and that it will take a long time, perhaps one or two years, for our forces to be skilled in this kind of fighting. Some of the Soviet leaders say that a peaceful solution is the only solution, whereas there are others in the Soviet Communist Party Politburo, as well as Marshal Grechko, who believe that the only solution to the problem is the military solution.

There is another matter which is related to Soviet loans. The instalments on all the weapons deals until 1971 amount to 106 million roubles, in addition to the High Dam repayment which amounts to 60 million roubles.

I will go back to the issue of military confrontation to say that it is a difficult question which requires long preparation. In this confrontation, too, we must not forget to protect our vital targets which at present are about one thousand in number.

Anwar al-Sadat: As far as making further concessions is concerned, I believe it has become clear that there is no place for any talk about making such concessions. The way I see it, America's problem with us started in 1965, specifically during Johnson's term when he started to harass us and to withhold aid from us. Generally speaking, the operation against us was politically planned and decided upon in America, and was enthusiastically carried out under Johnson and is now being carried out less enthusiastically under Nixon, which is why we cannot study ways of restoring relations with America in the prevailing atmosphere. This does not mean that we should embark on exchanging insults with Nixon. But it's important for us not to be deceived by their words. For their part they must show actions, and not just words.

The fundamental issue can be summed up as follows: Are the Egyptian people ruled from abroad nor not? The Americans are again insisting on ruling our people from abroad, as they did in earlier years. No, this battle is a fateful battle and we must stand fast to the end.

Concessions will mean the end and the disappearance of this regime. They will also mean that once again the people will be ruled from outside the country.

Let us examine what has happened to us in the fifteen months that have passed since last June [*June 1967*]. I personally was in a dazed state for three weeks or so. But then I found that we were gradually proceeding to the stage of steadfastness and then we moved to the *fedayeen* battle in the occupied territories [*i.e. the occupied Sinai territory*], to the gun battle, the air battle and the naval battle. This battle is our destiny. It is obvious to anybody with two eyes that after the last year and a half we are proceeding towards victory, God willing, and that we must endure, and that we must get together with our people and explain the situation to them and tell them how to stand fast.

Husain al-Shafei: There are some people who are concerned for the regime, for the revolution and for the armed forces and who believe that we should not move until we are fully prepared.

Nasser: Naturally, and this is clearly understood. But there is another factor that we should not forget, which is that it would be a big mistake on our part if the Israelis were left in their present positions undisturbed. It is my view that within one month from now we should be operating seriously in the occupied territories and also inside Israel. We should let patrols go there, stay for two or three days and then come back. In this way we will be initiating sustained campaigns of attrition against them.

Dr Labib Shuqair: If the situation cools down, it will be in the interest of the Israelis, and if it heats up, it will be in our interest. If the issue remains heated, the Arab peoples will remain incensed and as a result it will be difficult for any Arab government to withhold the agreed financial aid at this time. There is another aspect, which is that we are superior to the Israelis in numbers, a factor which we did not put to good military use in our previous confrontations with them.

Nasser: I have already spoken about the human element, when I said that this element required a firm base [*here Nasser used the term 'firm base' in English*] from which to operate. This is what we have gradually begun to prepare for. The second thing is that in order for us to translate the human element into work and production, we need money. There is one further point that concerns the human element. On the whole the terrain in Egypt does not provide our infantry fighters with the protection they need. The land is not like the Vietnamese or Algerian territory. In Sinai, for example, the soldier has to carry weapons, ammunition, water and all the food he needs because Sinai is largely a barren, unpopulated desert where infiltrators can easily be detected unless they are in small numbers.

Council of Ministers, 29 December 1968

On Sunday 29 December 1968 the Egyptian Council of Ministers met to discuss the raid which the Israelis had carried out against Beirut Airport on the previous day, 28 December.

Nasser: This Israeli operation provides us with a number of significant signals. Lebanon considered itself to be under American protection, and this may indeed be the case. Even so this American protection did not prevent Israel from carrying out a military operation against Beirut Airport – an operation which has inflicted enormous losses on Lebanon amounting to nearly 40 million pounds. What happened in Beirut might equally well be carried out in the form of a surprise operation against Egypt, for example in the Helwan district. Therefore, we must prepare ourselves, and our defence must cover all the vital targets in our country. It is obvious from the Beirut operation that Israel is the party that exerts pressure on America and not that America is the one exerting pressure on Israel.

Mahmoud Riyad [*minister of foreign affairs*]: Without any doubt the raid against Beirut Airport confirms that a peaceful solution is not to be anticipated, indeed is even impossible. A peaceful solution means that the Israelis have to withdraw from the occupied land, whereas at present Israel is trying to expand at the expense of Arab territory. It is also obvious that America always tries to help Israel to maintain its current military superiority over the Arabs, which is why it has armed Israel with more Phantom aircraft. As for ending the state of war with Israel, I have carried out a detailed study on the consequences of terminating hostilities and on the many benefits that Israel will derive from such an outcome – benefits that include the ending of the Arab boycott. This means that Israel will gradually turn into the Switzerland of the East, since it possesses the experience and the technology and can attract foreign capital. Moreover, America has an underlying interest in supporting Israel. You know very well what this interest is, and there is no place for discussing it now. All this means that there will be no political solution.

Nasser: We have information confirming that Israel has become desperate about reaching an understanding with us [*here Nasser used the word 'desperate' in English*], that the *fedayeen* activity is causing them [*the Israelis*] a lot of trouble and that their failure to reach an understanding with the Palestinians is also causing them a lot of concern. As I have already mentioned, Ben Gurion's strategy is to force a settlement [*here Nasser used* *the phrase 'to force a settlement' in English]*. Israel has not been able to achieve this, and this is why it is worried and desperate.

During Gromyko's recent visit, he briefed us on the latest Soviet contacts with the Americans. He also proposed that the Soviets should undertake new initiatives within the framework of the peaceful solution and of the Security Council resolution, in addition to setting out a timetable for implementing the resolution and for Israel's withdrawal from the territories it is occupying. In my opinion, this plan contains nothing new. It is also the view of the Soviets that Mahmoud Riyad should present this new plan to Jarring, the UN representative. However, I asked Gromyko if the Soviets would present the plan to the Americans because I am certain that Israel will refuse to withdraw. I am convinced that there is no leader in Israel capable of adopting this plan, especially since their elections will take place next year, that is in 1969. Added to this is the fact that I am sure that the Americans will reject such a plan. Should this happen, the Soviets will be angry and affronted, and then they will provide us with the weapons we require, will respond to us and will make every effort to meet all our requests.

Another matter that I would like to present to you is that Ceaucescu, president of the Republic of Romania, contacted us some time ago about Israel. He has been in touch with us again recently to suggest holding an unofficial meeting, even a secret one, between us and Israel in Romania. Naturally, this offer will be rejected because we are committed at the Arab level not to hold any independent contacts with the enemy, quite apart from the fact that even if such a contact took place secretly in Romania, it is likely that the Israelis would exploit the fact.

America and the Israelis persist with their repeated attempts to transform the problem into an Egyptian–Israeli, a Syrian–Israeli and a Jordanian–Israeli problem so that it will stop being an Israeli–Arab problem. American endeavours against us also continue in various forms. A leading American company recently offered to carry out a major project in Egypt that involved opening a new navigation canal that would extend from Port Tawfiq to the town of Rummanah on the Mediterranean. This firm employs an Egyptian who was once arrested and whose name is M. A. [*only the initials of the name mentioned by Nasser were given*]. Details of the project were sent to me through Abdel Latif al-Baghdadi [*a member of the Revolutionary Command Council*]. Naturally I have turned his project down because they are clearly using it to establish a state within the state.

Dr Sarwat Okasha [*minister of culture*]: Can we know the reason for the delay in delivering the Soviet weapons that have been requested and what the Soviet position is towards supplying us with weapons and military equipment?

Nasser: The reason for the delay in delivering the equipment and weapons requested from the Soviet Union is the Soviets' preoccupation with the Czech problem. They have been obliged to form new Soviet units so that their own key defences will not be affected and to avoid disrupting their military commitments to Eastern Europe. This, of course, is in addition to the financial burdens placed on them as a result of our numerous and successive requests. The army officers who recently visited Moscow told us when they came home that the Soviets had promised them that all the weapons and equipment asked for would be sent. I believe that there is some disagreement inside the Soviet leadership on the subject of the Middle East, and in addition the Americans have played games with them and have double-crossed them. This is why we find that sometimes the Soviet leaders are inflexible and at other times they are easygoing with the Americans. Sometimes too we find that they are optimistic and at others pessimistic.

As for Gromyko's most recent visit to us, I think that the main reason why he came here was because our army officers have been holding daily discussions and debates with the Soviet experts, and have indicated their resentment over the non-delivery of the weapons and equipment that the Soviets had promised me. I also think that Gromyko came to reassure himself about the domestic political situation in the wake of the student demonstrations in Mansura and Alexandria a little while ago. [*These student demonstrations were protestations about purely local issues to do with attendance schedules, syllabuses and so on.*]

Supreme Executive Committee, 30 December 1968

The first phase of the new plan for solving the crisis called for Israel to withdraw to a distance of 40 kilometres east of the Suez Canal. A month later, Israel would withdraw its forces to the 5 June line. Agreement would then be reached on the two issues of the Palestinians and of passage through the Suez Canal and in the Gulf of Aqaba, with the affirmation that the Gulf of Aqaba was an international waterway open to all.

Nasser: I am of the opinion, of course, and I have already stated this, that we should not submit the plan ourselves because this might be seen as a starting-point for further concessions. I have suggested to the Russians that they should put the plan forward. I consider that our domestic reconstruction and our military preparation is more important than these plans. The leader of the Soviet experts has told me that the new aircraft will be delivered to us at the beginning of next year. The Israelis are currently in a state of tension and anger and they are dying to take any sort of action. Their military operation against Beirut Airport certainly indicates a degree of recklessness. As for us, we will begin the *fedayeen* operations in Sinai as soon as we have finished organising protection for our critical targets. Then we'll begin our strikes immediately. Of course we will be hit at the same time. The Israelis say they want secure borders. When we ask them what these borders are, they say: "We want to negotiate with you directly." Unfortunately, Israel has been terrorising the Arab world as a result of the Beirut operation. In the face of this we must be patient and we must stand fast. War is war. We must strike and we must be ready to endure the blows that will be struck against us.

Chapter 7

FELLOW LEADERS
Three important meetings, 1968

Although Gamal Abdel Nasser was deeply preoccupied with domestic affairs, which involved the rebuilding of his armed forces, and the reorganising of the country's political system in a manner that would permit and indeed guarantee it greater responsiveness and flexibility, he did not stop for a moment his pursuit of foreign affairs. He took every possible opportunity to meet other world leaders and explain his position to them, and continued to exert his influence with Egypt's friends and to manoeuvre against his country's enemies while pursuing all possible moves to counter the American–Zionist plan for the Middle East.

Nasser used to enjoy meeting people with whom he felt comfortable, and profited from discussions and exchanges with them. He also used to make a point of meeting those with whom he felt less comfortable because he considered that dialogue was essential, even if it was at the expense of his personal convictions and emotions. He used to be annoyed by having to meet certain individuals but he was always the very model of the courteous host and of the speaker who also listens well, and people in whose presence Nasser felt impatient never once noticed his true feelings.

President Tito of Yugoslavia was the world leader closest to Nasser's heart. Tito's experiment in the Yugoslavian Republic was one of the few experiments from which Nasser benefited and which he used as an example. Tito was Marxist but he followed an independent policy which was a long way from Moscow's line. He was the only leader in the socialist camp who defied Stalin while the latter was at the peak of his vigour and power. Tito never wavered in his defiance of Moscow's line and remained steadfast in the face of all pressures. After Stalin had gone, his successors went to Belgrade and addressed Tito as "great comrade", thereby repudiating Stalin's denunciation of Tito as "a rebel against Marxist–Leninist principles".

For this and for other reasons, Tito's experiment in Yugoslavia attracted Nasser's interest and elicited his admiration. The Yugoslav leader had established his system on the twin foundations of a public and a private sector, and had succeeded in achieving a state of equilibrium between them so that neither predominated. More important was the fact that Nasser had great confidence in Tito's foresight, his sound judgment and his deep understanding of events that were occurring throughout the entire world. Indeed Tito was the mastermind behind the countries of the neutral and non-aligned camp, while Nehru was this group's philosopher. Gamal Abdel Nasser became the third member of the trio, in spite of the difference between him and the other two leaders in age and in experience, achieving eminence through his formulation of a policy for the Third World that could actually be put into practice.

Tito for his part also thought highly of Nasser, admiring the Egyptian leader's courage, his honesty and even his youth. On one occasion when he and Nasser were sitting together on the beach on the Yugoslav island of Brioni he said: "Believe me, I envy you. You are a younger man and you will live to see the fruit of your labours." Tito could not have foreseen the fate that awaited Nasser and the day that he himself would walk in the funeral procession of the young Arab leader.

A feature of the meetings between Nasser and Tito was the complete frankness of their discussions. The encounter which is recorded here took place under the extremely complex circumstances of Israeli intransigence, American plots at home and abroad, and an Arab situation that was characterised by ambiguity and instability. Tito had arrived in Cairo after a long tour of the Far East where he had encountered Kosygin who was also visiting the Indian capital. Nasser was keen to hear the Yugoslav leader's view of the situation, and especially to know what Indira Gandhi's position was on the Middle East.

The Meeting between Nasser and President Tito, 5 February 1968

At this meeting between the two leaders, which took place in Aswan in Upper Egypt on 5 February, Nasser steered the conversation towards the subject of the Middle East crisis, anxious to bring his friend up to date with developments.

Nasser: Since last August we have been making positive moves to deal with Israeli aggression. We attended the Arab summit conference in Khartoum and it became obvious during the sessions that it would be better for us not to cut off the oil flow, as long as the oil-producing countries would advance financial assistance to us and to Jordan as the confrontation states. We have therefore obtained financial support in the form of foreign currency amounting to 95 million pounds, even though as a result of the war we have the equivalent of 180 million pounds in hard currency. Certainly the amount of aid that has been allocated to us will be of tremendous help in enabling us to stand fast and to confront Israel. If the loans and commercial credits that have been advanced to us by the Soviet Union and by the socialist camp as well as the French and Italian loans are added to this allocation, then we can see that we will double our share of hard currency. However, we still need another sum of money to purchase raw and semi-processed materials that are necessary for our plants. By and large I think that the results of the Khartoum conference were to encourage us to continue to persevere and battle on. As far as the United Nations is concerned, as your excellency knows, our minister of foreign affairs has undertaken certain political actions of which you have already been informed. What I want to do here is to make certain observations to you.

First, the position of Goldberg, the American delegate, is one hundred per cent identical to Israel's position. Secondly, after we had approved the so-called US–Soviet plan [*the draft resolution*], the United States withdrew its approval of the plan. Thirdly, America's aim at the present stage is to freeze the situation and to leave it unresolved. Then fourthly, America and Israel are fully aware that at present we are not prepared militarily, and this is the reason for Israel's arrogance and indifference.

As for our armed forces, we have now arrived at a position that enables us to defend Egypt. But we are not ready for an air attack to liberate the land because of the shortage of pilots, and in the meantime the United States has strengthened the Israeli air force with more squadrons of modern aircraft. Israel persists with the requirement that we sit and negotiate with it directly and it believes that it will achieve this objective as long as we remain incapable of liberating our land by force.

With the Soviet Union and the question of weapons, our most significant problem is our need for a new kind of modern aircraft. At the present time we have MiG-17s, MiG-19s and MiG-21s, as well as Sukhoi-7s. These aircraft are considered to be short-range aircraft and they cannot reach all the Israeli targets. For example, the MiG-17 can only reach the Israeli borders and the MiG-21 can only reach the southern part of Israel.

The Sukhoi is a long-range aircraft but its combat capability is limited. On the other hand, we find that the French-made Israeli aircraft can reach most of our airports while the American Skyhawks can reach every inch of our country. This is why we have asked the Soviet leadership for a long-range fighter-bomber. We also asked for expertise and help in training, and they have actually sent us army, naval and air force experts. I'm delighted to be able to confirm that the cooperation between these military experts and our officers is excellent.

On the subject of political movement among the Arabs we suggested convening a new Arab summit conference with the aim of mobilizing the military and economic resources of the Arab nation against Israel, but the Syrians have vetoed the idea. What's more, the Saudis are also opposed to holding such a conference so that they can avoid becoming involved in new financial commitments. As for the Syrians, they refuse to cooperate with Saudi Arabia and Jordan. Our relations with the Saudis have been overshadowed by the Yemen war, and remain lukewarm even though we agreed at Khartoum that we would withdraw our troops from Yemen and did actually do so. The Saudis have now refused to recognize Qahtan al-Shaabi's government in Aden. Here it is important to make the point that we did not withdraw our forces from Yemen until we were certain that the British had left Aden and Southern Yemen.

At the same time, we have told Saudi Arabia that we support its position in the Arab Gulf and that we will send any aid that it might ask for to resist Iran's ambitions in the area, even though at one time the Saudis had entered into an agreement with Iran against us within the framework of the Islamic Alliance. However, that situation changed following Britain's decision to withdraw its forces from the area, and disagreements cropped up straight away between Saudi Arabia and Iran. As far as these disputes are concerned, we support Saudi Arabia, as a fraternal Arab country, against Iran.

On the question of freeing the ships that are trapped in the Suez Canal, we had already taken action to facilitate the process of releasing them, and we did this at the request of the countries whose flags these ships fly. I received four messages from Mr Brown, the British Foreign Secretary, on this subject. However, when we actually started to carry out the operation to free the ships, we were challenged by the Israeli troops stationed on the east bank who opened fire on the people carrying out the task, and as a result we decided not to proceed. [*Nasser had responded to pressure from the British foreign secretary to free the thirteen trapped ships, most of which flew the British flag, the real reason for his response being that George Brown had adopted a neutral position at the United Nations and had refused to succumb to the American pressure for absolute support for Israel. For this the foreign secretary was attacked by the British press.*]

Tito: I would like to know what the situation is like for Egypt's oil since the war in 1967.

Nasser: We have lost the oil in Sinai, which was valued at nearly six million pounds annually, but we now have a new source which will give us nearly the same quantity. As your excellency is aware, the Israelis attacked the oil refinery at Suez, and this is why we have begun to refine our oil in the refineries in Aden.

Tito [*having reviewed his Far East tour to India, Pakistan, Afghanistan and Cambodia*]: I have noticed that in general these countries sympathize with the Arab cause, despite the pressure applied on some of them by the Americans. And Mrs Indira Gandhi, for example, is subjected to severe pressure from the rightist wing in the Indian Parliament. I met Comrade Aleksei Kosygin who was also in India and we had a discussion on the Middle East crisis. Kosygin told me that they have decided in Moscow not to allow the Americans to replace the British in the Middle East region, in spite of the rumours that were circulating when Britain withdrew from Aden. Kosygin confirmed that the Soviets will remain in the area until a specific national power has emerged there, and assured me that what Western circles are repeating about a vacuum in the region that needs to be filled is simply imperialist jargon and that the Soviet Union will not permit anyone from outside the region to fill it. He also assured me that the Soviet Union and the other socialist countries will stand by these people and give them help and support, and added that the non-aligned countries must also support the region's populations.

Nasser: In his discussion with you did Kosygin deal with the political solution that has been proposed for the Middle East crisis?

Tito: I understood from my conversation with Kosygin that the Soviets are planning on the basis that no acceptable political solution can be reached unless the United Arab Republic is strong militarily. We must not forget that you are currently enjoying the sympathy of a large number of countries as a result of Israel's intransigent attitude. This is why I believe that when it becomes impossible to arrive at a political solution, the world will then understand why you have chosen the other solution.

The Meeting between Nasser and Abdel Rahman Aref, 10 February 1968

The Iraqi President Abdel Rahman Aref arrived in Cairo on 10 February 1968, following an official visit to France where he met President de Gaulle. Aref wished to bring Nasser up to date with the outcome of his talks with the French before returning to Baghdad.

Aref: As soon as we began our talks with de Gaulle we realised that he is under considerable pressure from the Zionist forces in France, but he is determined to proceed with his new policy to win over the Arabs. De Gaulle assured us that France is prepared to give the Arab countries whatever help they need without delay, and confirmed that France's new policy is not based on sentiment but has been formulated according to France's own interests.

In his statements de Gaulle touched on the need for Israel's withdrawal from the occupied territories, provided that later on the two sides would discuss their border problems and the issue of maritime navigation. But in the subsequent session, members of the French delegation intervened in the discussion and withdrew this clear-cut stipulation, and instead suggested proposals only for an agreement on peace in the region generally. When we brought up the subject of the Arabian Gulf, de Gaulle side-stepped this issue and it was obvious that there are strong ties linking him to Iran. He contented himself with stressing the importance of consulting Saudi Arabia, Kuwait and the adjacent countries on matters concerning the Gulf.

De Gaulle expressed France's readiness to provide all the aid and other requirements including weapons and military equipment that might be requested, and to demonstrate his goodwill he ordered an amendment to the delivery schedule for the Mirage aircraft for which a deal had been made with Iraq so that every month three aircraft would be handed over instead of two.

In a personal discussion with me, de Gaulle told me that on the basis of information he possessed on the quantity and quality of Israel's weapons, he was sure that Israel would defeat the Arab armies. De Gaulle also pointed out that we, as Arabs, should consolidate our political positions because Israel holds one single opinion on every issue whereas the Arabs have several. He said that if we developed a unified viewpoint, then this would help France, given its international authority, to play a major role in the Middle East dispute.

General de Gaulle complained about the control of the French news media by international Zionist forces. He thought that the reason for this might be because of the isolation of the Arab countries and their consequent failure to use the right methods for reaching out to European public opinion.

Ismail Khairallah [*Iraq's minister of foreign affairs*]: When we met the French minister of foreign affairs, he summed up the political aspects of the Middle East problem in a few clear words. He said: "Don't forget that solving this problem will always depend on the relationship between the Soviet Union and the United States of America. The solution will appear in the light of the relations between these two major powers."

Nasser: I thank you for passing through Cairo to exchange views with us on the current situation. I think that there have been some important military and political developments in the period between the June war and the present time. As far as the military situation is concerned, the situation of our armed forces is now considerably better than it was before the Israeli offensive. For example, we had two full divisions in Yemen and these have now been returned to the Egyptian front. We also had five other divisions and we have rearmed and retrained these, in addition to rebuilding all our armoured forces. We have also developed the military conscription system and this has enabled us to make use of a large number of soldiers who have graduated from universities and higher institutes to operate the modern equipment and vehicles, including radar systems, the air defence weapons and submarines. We have recently decided to increase the number of divisions and to arm these additional divisions, and we now have the Soviet experts who were sent in response to our request for operational training for our troops. What we fundamentally lack is the means to supply our armed forces with vehicles and with halftracks.

We are now capable of defending Egypt but we cannot launch an attack in Sinai as yet. The air force and the air defences have improved a great deal since 1967, but we are still suffering from a shortage of pilots. We have also asked the Soviets to supply us with new long-range aircraft.

Politically, we have not rejected the Security Council resolution, so that the world will be reassured that we are not obstructing the efforts that are being made to establish peace in the region. Through political moves and through Mr Jarring's visits, I have become fairly certain that the issue will not be settled for the present, the main reason being that Israel knows that we cannot launch an offensive to liberate the land. Consequently, we have no alternative other than political action. The Americans for their part are making every effort to maintain the situation in the area as it is at present. The belief in Washington is that the Arab masses will become increasingly impatient and anxious, that with time they will inevitably move against their governments, and that there will be flare-ups within the Arab regimes that are opposed to American policy in the region. This is why I propose that we should exert all kinds of pressures on the Americans to make them aware that their current position will have the gravest consequences for their interests in the region.

Soviet aid is still flowing to us. The Soviets had previously agreed with Ali Sabri to provide us with 100,000 tons of wheat, and we have recently asked them to send us another consignment amounting to 200,000 tons. We have also received other commodities valued at approximately 65 million pounds.

We have asked for an Arab summit to be held, but Syria has rejected the holding of such a conference, and there are various reasons why Saudi Arabia does not want this conference to be held either. Unfortunately, the military situation on the eastern front is very poor. Syria cannot stand alone, and Jordan lost all its aircraft in the war. Therefore, all the resources that are available in Iraq, Syria and Jordan must be mobilised to build up the eastern front so that when the next battle begins Israel will be forced to fight on two fronts and not just one. We have to be sure of the capability of our armed forces before we start the fight since unhappily we did not appreciate Israel's true strength in the previous war. Let everyone know that we will not endure another defeat by Israel.

I wish, as de Gaulle has said, that the Arabs were a united front and that they maintained just one single outlook. Tito visited me five days ago and advised us to focus attention on our domestic front, especially among the workers and the educated, to discourage the Americans from attempting to create any internal changes.

I believe that your visit to France and your talks with de Gaulle have been of considerable importance. We must make a great effort to link French and Arab interests. I know that France is going to need nearly 200 million barrels of oil in 1980 and that it is hoping to be able to rely on Iraq and Algeria to supply this quantity without the US trying to act as middleman and interfering in the arrangement.

The Meeting between Abdel Nasser and King Husain, 6 April 1968

King Husain of Jordan arrived in Cairo on 6 April at the head of a high-level political and military delegation. This was the Jordanian king's first official visit after the battle at al-Karamah village (see Chapter 8) which had occurred on 21 March 1968 and in which the Palestinian guerillas fought together with the Jordanian army.

Husain: I have come to consult with you as to what should be done at this point, especially in view of the important political developments that have taken place recently. Your message to us on 21 March – the day the attack on al-Karamah happened – was the first Arab message we received. This is why we are always proud of you, of your stand in the struggle, and of your place among the front-ranking leaders. There is now a trend in Israel that insists on keeping all the Arab territories which it occupied in the June war. There are also some who are calling for a total occupation of our territory so that there can be nothing but impregnable desert between them and Iraq and another impregnable desert between them and Saudi Arabia.

Bahjat al-Talhuni [*Jordanian prime minister*]: We have received a message from Hikmat al-Misri, who lives in the West Bank [*al-Misri, a Palestinian, was the Speaker of the Jordanian Chamber of Deputies in 1956 and was among President al-Sadat's entourage when he went to Jerusalem in November 1977*]. His message confirms our information on the possibility that Israel will launch a new military operation east of the Jordan River after which it intends to force King Husain to accept a local Palestinian government consisting of various Palestinians who live in the West Bank and cooperate with the occupation authorities.

Abdel Monem al-Rifai [*Jordanian foreign minister*]: It is noticeable that Israel's political activity has begun to veer away from the content and the provisions of the Security Council resolution. Israel has turned down the proposal we made to Jarring about adding a clause to the resolution stating that the parties concerned were willing to implement it. The Americans came to us in Amman yesterday and advised us not to stick to this clause otherwise matters might get complicated. It is of course clear from this that Israel has territorial ambitions in the Arab lands. We believe that Jarring will terminate his mission and take the issue back to the Security Council.

Nasser: The important issue is not Jarring's proposals but whether we should agree to meet the Israelis openly or in secret somewhere and what would be the effect of such an agreement after we have publicly rejected any such meeting. As far as my country is concerned, we cannot agree to any sort of meeting. Don't forget that I have agreed with you only about the formula of the resolution given to us by Jarring, in spite of opposition from Algeria, Iraq, Sudan and Saudi Arabia. I adopted this standpoint for the sake of continuing the political momentum.

I say again that we must now discuss whether we should agree to go to Rhodes or Geneva. For our part, we reject this proposal. As far as America is concerned, I anticipated that its attitude towards you would be different from its attitude towards us, on the basis that there is personal hostility between me and the Americans. The behaviour of the Americans towards you was supposed to be compatible with your position as their friends.

Our people here in Egypt want war and they reject this kind of peace, even though I can understand how tired and resentful they have become of all these conflicts and the heavy burdens that they are having to shoulder. Our people have become very unsettled and the general situation has become very difficult.

Recently we have acted on the domestic front: the declaration of 30 March was issued, a referendum was conducted and elections were held. We will continue to act politically until we are ready for military action. The Khartoum conference gave us aid of 95 million pounds to support our resoluteness. At this point we should ask ourselves: If we agree to what America is planning and Israel is proposing, wouldn't the Arab countries be justified in withdrawing this aid? We here in Egypt need this aid to sustain our determination, even though we have increased our tax revenues to approximately 250 million pounds. Moreover, our military budget has reached 300 million pounds. Israel insists on its demand for direct negotiation. Will your domestic situation be strong enough for it? As far as our circumstances are concerned, I will tell you straight out that we could not cope with this.

Mahmoud Riyad: I asked Jarring a straightforward question during his most recent visit: What is our delegate who would be going to Cyprus or to Geneva for the proposed negotiations actually going to sign? After a long discussion with him on the finer points of the answer to this question, Jarring became convinced that our delegate would in fact be signing a capitulation agreement. He admitted to me that the United States had sent him a special envoy a few days before to convey Washington's displeasure over the possibility that his mission might end in failure. The envoy also told him that the Israeli cabinet included thirteen moderately-inclined ministers and only five who refused to agree to returning a single inch of occupied Arab territory, and said that Eshkol [*the Israeli prime minister*], was unable to adopt a decisive stand on this issue in the Council of Ministers because such a move might topple his cabinet. I told Jarring that we had heard almost the same account from the Soviets through their ambassador in New York.

As for adding or deleting certain words and phrases in Jarring's proposals, we have covered a lot of ground in this respect in order to gain time and to please international public opinion. The question to be considered now is: Is it useful to carry on with the game of words and phrases? Will it guarantee a postponement of the anticipated attack against Jordan? Is it in our interest that Jarring should take the subject back to the Security Council on the basis that this would prevent Israel from embarking on military action?

Husain: Concerning this issue, the Americans contacted me yesterday with the excuse that they were saving Jarring's mission from failure, and advised me to conclude a separate peace treaty with Israel. My reply to them was that this subject cannot be discussed because it has not been mentioned in the Security Council resolution.

As for the occupation of Jerusalem, having examined the position internationally, we feel that we have no support on this matter from most of the Muslim countries. Moreover, the Russians have informed me that they are ready to support us politically. They have also promised to supply us with Russian weapons in case all our attempts to acquire weapons from Western sources fail. We are now trying to obtain Western weapons and armaments from certain fraternal Arab countries to make up for the shortages we are suffering. Regrettably, no military coordination has so far been made on the eastern front and the Syrians refuse to cooperate with us. In fact, there are varying degrees of feeling for the matter in the Arab world, and if we in the Arab world continue to be as we are at present, then the initiative will always remain in the enemy's hands. We need coordination between us on many issues and we need a unified position towards the issue of Jerusalem and towards the issue of UN observers on the borders.

Nasser: I said what you have just said in a public speech, and I also said that there is no common Arab plan and no Arab coordination. I believe that many Arab countries want to avoid becoming involved in new commitments. The Syrians have asked for a joint command with us but I told them that any such joint command must be between themselves, Jordan and Iraq and that the greatest possible use had to be made of Iraqi army capability. Naturally, there are suspicions between the Syrians and the Iraqis because of various factional differences. But we must exert the maximum effort to create the eastern command. We must also be patient in solving our domestic problems. But to agree to negotiate with the Israelis either directly or indirectly is not acceptable.

The Americans asked us last February to resume relations with them and we turned them down. We will not resume relations with them until they have clarified their position towards the Arab cause, even if it is only by way of a statement on the rights of the Arabs. But they have refused, and so have we refused.

Bahjat al-Talhuni: What will be the position of the United Arab Republic in the event of an Israeli attack against us?

Nasser: I asked Lieutenant-General Fawzi on the day of the attack on al-Karamah to assess the position and to see what we might be able to do militarily. Fawzi told me that we would be ready to open fire along the entire front within half an hour of the order being given. Before issuing orders to Lieutenant-General Fawzi I consulted Mahmoud Riyad who advised that a military step of this nature would have far-reaching effects on the political front and that it would be better not to embark on it at this time. But if what is meant is the degree of our forces' readiness to cross to the east bank of the Canal, then they still need time to complete their preparation. They also need nearly 20,000 ordinary and half-track vehicles which are going to cost approximately 60 million pounds.

Bahjat al-Talhuni: What will the political position be?

Nasser: I've already told King Husain that we will divide the loaf of bread into two halves – one half for you and the other for us. We will continue to support you, regardless of what happens. I'm pleased to say that I find the picture today very different from what it was yesterday. Even my personal resolve and morale have improved greatly since you last visited me at the end of 1967.

In my opinion the Americans are playing a very despicable game and want all of us as Arabs to sell out. Even the Russians have despaired of the possibility of achieving a political solution. For our part, we believe that we have offered the maximum we can to achieve a political solution.

Husain: What will the situation be if Israel approves Jarring's plan?

Nasser: In this case, contact will take place between our delegates and Jarring, provided that we are represented by the Arab delegates to the United Nations. We have Dr al-Quni [*head of the Egyptian Delegation to the UN*] there. Moreover, there shouldn't be any document to sign. In other words, I refuse to meet the Israelis openly or otherwise. What we will agree to is only a meeting with our official delegates to the United Nations.

Gen Khammash [*Jordanian chief of staff*]: It is true that the *fedayeen* operations are very important and that they have a very positive impact on the enemy. However, these operations are currently confined to the Jordanian front, and this gives Israel a good excuse to launch military operations against Jordan, particularly because the Israelis are deploying seventy-five per cent of their forces on the Jordanian front, five brigades on the Egyptian front and only two brigades on the Syrian front. During the battle at al-Karamah, an armoured brigade which they withdrew from Bir Sabaa [*Beersheba*] was sent to join the other brigades in the attack against Jordan. It is well known that Israel has eight armoured brigades and . . .

Nasser: I'm sorry to interrupt you, but I want to make sure of the number of the armoured Israeli brigades.

Gen Khammash: My information confirms that the enemy has eight armoured brigades.

Nasser: The reason why I ask is because Soviet intelligence had previously informed Marshal Amer that Israel had eight armoured brigades, but the former general command rejected the Soviet information and insisted on its own private information that Israel had only five brigades. Unfortunately it was on this basis that the former general command drew up its plans. However, let's return to what you were saying.

Gen Khammash: As far as armaments are concerned, we in Jordan prefer to acquire Western weapons because our troops, who are trained primarily on these weapons, can use them immediately.

Nasser: After this military and political review, I would like to say again that as long as we do not sign a peace treaty with Israel, then Israel has not won the war. What is important is for us to be patient and not to despair. Since Ben Gurion's days, Israel's strategy has been designed to force a settlement on us, but as long as we have not concluded any treaty with it, then Israel has not achieved its goals. An eastern front and western front must be created and we must move on both fronts simultaneously. I think we need to hold an Arab summit at which we will declare unanimously that the Arab land is sacred and that we will not relinquish a single inch of it. This means that we will mobilize all the Arab armies and all the Arab money to liberate the Arab land. We say that we are one hundred million Arabs but in fact this is not true, the fundamental reason being that there is no Arab political plan and no Arab military plan. This matter requires that we meet at a summit conference, to discuss, agree and then draw up a plan and a programme. It is inexcusable that we should remain silent and noncommittal.

As for the *fedayeen*, I recommend that you get together and coordinate with them. I know the Palestinians belonging to Fatah. They are good people and it is possible to cooperate with them. At the same time, there are those who stir up the *fedayeen* and tell them that King Husain is going to arrest and destroy them. Therefore, you will have to reassure them and create confidence between yourselves and them. You need to choose some dependable officials to contact them, and the basis on which such officials should be selected has to be that the Palestinians trust them. The people who are trying to sabotage the contacts between you and them must be kept away. I hope that you will avoid creating trouble for them and that you will not pursue them. [*The information at Nasser's disposal at the time indicated that the liaison officers between King Husain and the Palestinians were suspected of being in contact with the American Central Intelligence Agency.*] The final thing that I would like to say in our meeting today is that we should not give in to despair. We must also avoid any weakening of the Arab position.

Chapter 8

CONSTANT ACTIVITY
Rebuilding and launching
the war of attrition

During 1968 and 1969, the Council of Ministers and the Arab Socialist Union's Supreme Executive Committee held a great many meetings, a reflection of the intense political activity that was going on during those two years both at home and abroad. But the general military situation was Abdel Nasser's main preoccupation at this time. At one of the sessions of the Council of Ministers held in February 1968, Nasser asked Lt Gen Muhammad Fawzi, the new Commander-in-Chief, to review the military situation in detail. General Fawzi first gave his assessment of the June War.

Gen Fawzi: We had been expecting this war but there were several reasons why the armed forces were not ready for it. First, the main energies of the armed forces were directed towards the Yemeni front. Secondly, in the period preceding the war with Israel the upper echelons of the armed forces had abandoned their military duties, namely warfare and defence, and had devoted themselves to other pursuits outside the military sphere, while thirdly, there were too many command structures within the armed forces with the result that they had begun to quarrel with one another, and this made it practically impossible to prepare the troops for combat. Even though the army was of considerable size, its actual combat capability did not exceed 30 per cent of its potential, and there was no system of reserves.

General Fawzi then spoke of the current combat capability of the Egyptian soldier, referring by way of illustration to the battle that had taken place at Ras al-Ush between a small Egyptian force and armoured Israeli forces. The action had lasted six full hours at the end of which the Egyptian force had achieved its goal and defeated the Israeli forces. He also reviewed the position with regard to the Soviet military aid, saying that the Egyptian army had now reached 70 per cent of the size it had been before the outbreak of the June War and that the Soviet weapons had been supplied to Egypt at no cost.

Gen Fawzi: The picture has now changed and responsibilities have been defined at all levels in the army commands. The new conscription law has provided the armed forces with better-educated troops, and it has also been decided that division commanders, operation commanders, unit commanders, the war staff unit and the chief of staff should not stay in their positions for any more than three years. Trained pilots are now being provided on the basis of 1.5 pilots per aircraft – in other words three pilots for every two aircraft. After the plan for military preparation has been completed, the war with Israel will not last only for hours or even days but is going to be a violent, savage and protracted war. The fact that the Israelis are unable to withstand long-drawn-out battles needs to be taken into account. They are not prepared for such battles, and this is another of the factors that will mean possible victory for us. As far as the navy is concerned, I am able to confirm that Egypt now has full control at sea. On the question of the troops that will be needed for going to war with Israel, the numbers have been established as a result of careful calculations, and these forces are now available. However, I must insist on the need for all military steps to be taken within the framework of a combined Arab operation, and under a unified military command. In this context the Syrian land-based forces cannot be relied on but we can depend on Syria's air force. As for the Iraqi forces, they can be trusted to defend and support the eastern front. Unfortunately we lost nearly 13,000 ordinary and half-track vehicles, and we now need that number of vehicles before we can go to war in Sinai.

Meeting of the Council of Ministers, 18 February 1968

On the evening of Sunday 18 February, President Gamal Abdel Nasser called a meeting of the Council of Ministers to undertake an urgent review of the Arab position. The Arabs at this time were divided and Nasser believed that such disharmony would put numerous obstacles in the path of his plan. He asked Mahmoud Riyad, the foreign minister, to speak at this meeting about his recent tour of Arab countries, and Riyad's realistic assessment of what he had observed confirmed Nasser's belief.

According to Riyad, Syria was the obstacle to any form of joint Arab action, and he confirmed that in Lebanon, Jordan and Iraq he had heard fierce criticism of Syria's attitude. He also said that he had been told by Bahjat al-Talhuni, the Jordanian prime minister, that Jordan had offered to cooperate fully with Syria but that this had been refused by the Syrians who considered Jordan a traitor to the Arab cause, adding that the Syrians on their part had complained about Iraq's failure to send military forces to the Syrian front. The Iraqis, however, had told Mahmoud Riyad that the Syrians had distributed leaflets to the Iraqi troops calling for the overthrow of the Iraqi regime. Riyad then praised the Kuwaitis for their eagerness to set up a national air force that would take part in any future war against Israel, and concluded his assessment by suggesting that at this time the most important goal was to re-establish the eastern front by encouraging cooperation between Jordan, Syria and Iraq. Riyad also told the meeting that Saudi Arabia had indicated its willingness to make available whatever was requested of it for the battle.

Mahmoud Riyad: Mr President, they want to improve relations with us. I explained Egypt's position on the Arab Gulf emirates to King Faisal in detail and assured him that Egypt's primary concern was to see the British driven out of these emirates and for their stability to be assured. King Faisal responded by proposing that an alliance should be set up between them and Saudi Arabia with the aim of creating a political entity whose leadership would be assumed by the emirate shaikhs alternately, as is the case in Malaysia. Faisal described this formula as a way of guaranteeing the Arabness of the Omani coast and to protect it from Iranian ambitions. Mr President, King Faisal declared his readiness to recognize Southern Yemen and to provide it with economic aid. At the same time, he has expressed his extreme concern over Syrian and Algerian aid to Northern Yemen.

Meeting of the Council of Ministers, 24 March 1968

At the session of the Council of Ministers on 24 March, Nasser had several comments to make on the Arab situation, based on what Mahmoud Riyad had told the Council earlier.

Nasser: There is a possibility that as a result of political pressure from America, certain Arab countries will stop paying their share towards the economic aid arrangement decided by the Khartoum conference. [*An amount of 95 million pounds was to be paid annually to Egypt to compensate it for losses incurred during the war of 1967.*] This is why I have asked Abbas Zaki [*minister of the economy*] to secure the largest possible amount of hard currency to enable us to face such an eventuality and so that we may continue our steadfastness. I have information indicating that America is applying strong pressure on Libya to stop it paying its part of the aid [*Libya then was a monarchy*].

Meeting of the Council of Ministers, 25 March 1968

On 25 March 1968 Abdel Nasser called a special session of the Council of Ministers in the light of developments in Jordan, and particularly the massive attack on the village of al-Karamah by the Israelis on 21 March.

Nasser: I learned from General Fawzi about Israel's plan to attack al-Karamah the day before the raid, and I passed on the information obtained by the Egyptian intelligence services to the Jordanians. We asked the Soviets how accurate this information was and they confirmed that it was genuine and told us that the aim of the operation at al-Karamah was to drive a wedge between Jordan and Syria. When the Israelis went into action the Jordanian troops did not engage the attackers although the *fedayeen* did. The Jordanian army only joined in later on. The Fatah commander had been in al-Karamah to organise and direct the resistance operations personally but had left the village shortly before the attack. [*Nasser did not mention the commander by name.*]

al-Nabawi al-Muhandis [*minister of health*]: Is it possible for Jordan to be armed by the Soviet Union?

Nasser: King Husain's position is very difficult. If he asks for Soviet weapons, America will punish him by setting Israel on him. Moreover, it takes five years to rearm the military with new weapons. On the other hand, there are numerous reasons why King Husain is not able to conclude a separate peace treaty with Israel, which is why, as I've already said, his position is so difficult.

At this Council meeting Nasser described frankly and at length the difficult circumstances that he had had to face both before and after the 1967 war.

Nasser: I can't forget what I went through during the first few days after the war in June. I felt intensely, indescribably bitter. There is no doubt that what happened in 1967 has affected all of us psychologically, morally and materially. I had to meet dozens of presidents, visitors and journalists, as well as the gloaters. We were going through very difficult circumstances and we had to deal with a lot of conspiracies against us. I was responsible for reviewing everything that was happening on the domestic front and for making all the foreign contacts. I wished in those days that I had actually stepped down from power and from the position of such responsibility.

I know that the coming days will be very difficult both at home and abroad because our enemy is strong and since he is well organised he is ready to act against us. He also has all the money he needs to destroy us. When I reassumed power on 11 June, I felt so vulnerable that I sent my family away from Cairo and kept my gun beside me to use at the final moment and to the last bullet. That day, when I asked how many tanks were left in Cairo I was told that there were only seven tanks in the whole city. In spite of this information, I set off, with the military commands, along the difficult path of completely rebuilding the armed forces. I used to speak to General Fawzi every night before I went to bed, and at six o'clock every morning to go over with him the state of the forces and of the commands and the names of the officers responsible for every position. If I had not resorted to this method of doing things, everything would have got out of control.

Another problem that I had to face was the fact that certain military command structures were opposed to strengthening our political organisation [*i.e. to widening political participation through the ASU and other institutions*]. Their objections were based on the prevailing view that the army was the sole support of the revolution and that it should continue to be so, and that strengthening the political organisation would place the regime in a contradictory position. This has all stopped now. What Husain al-Shafei mentioned in today's session is true – that there was an attempted coup against me in 1962 and that it was led by Marshal Amer. It is quite true. At the time I refused to confront the plotters because there was no way of predicting the outcome, and in any case nobody knew what was going to happen to the country. I have always avoided such situations so that matters won't get out of control. If you cast your minds back, you will recall who introduced the expression 'centres of power' and who called for 'revolutionary purity'. When I used these terms before 1967 I was referring to many things that you were not aware of. People imagined that I was capable of doing everything by myself but this was not so. This is why I said after the defeat that our country should have an open society. In fact there has been a real change in the armed forces which have now become a part of this nation. There has also been real change introduced in the General Intelligence Service and that too has become a part of our nation. This change has also affected numerous groups within the government organisations.

Before 1967 the army existed independently of the country. If we want to safeguard the future then there must be a single authority in this country, and this cannot be achieved unless the army becomes part of this country. How? So far I have not found a solution to the problem. I think that when the National Congress and the Central Committee are formed, the army will have to be represented in them, and here we face another problem, which is that it is impossible to hold elections in the army. In any event, the army should not be against the political organisation and the political organisation should not be against the army because both of them form the two wings of the same authority.

Meeting of the Council of Ministers, 7 April 1968

On 7 April 1968 the Council of Ministers held a session to discuss military affairs.

Nasser: I would like to inform you that during his visit to Cairo, Podgorny agreed to send us a number of Soviet pilots. But the Soviets later turned down the request and decided not to send pilots. Afterwards they changed their minds again and agreed that we could use the 56 pilots who are here in Egypt as advisers. We are still pressing them to send a larger number of pilots but they have not yet agreed to this request. I will not be giving away any secrets when I tell you that until recently we have been living with the threat of the Israelis being able to reach Cairo in a matter of four to six hours, which is why I have persisted in asking for the Russian pilots. I was also trying to do something else, which was to make the Americans feel that the Soviets had come into the region of their own accord. This is an extremely important psychological factor as far as the Americans are concerned, and one which they take very seriously.

Our forces are now in good condition, but we can't go on the offensive because of the superiority of Israel's air force and armoured troops. Moreover, we haven't got enough vehicles and half-tracks to be able to go very far into Sinai. We have begun to form two extra military divisions and the Soviets have agreed to arm them fully. I would also like to advise you that some materials and equipment for crossing the canal have already been delivered. As for supplying us with new aircraft, the Russians have promised to discuss our request and I believe that they will agree to it. I may go to Moscow after the meeting of the National Congress on 23 July to persuade the Soviet leadership to approve the new requests for armaments. I would like to stress one fact to you, and that is that there is no source other than the Soviet Union that can supply us with the weapons, equipment and munitions that we need, and there are two reasons for this – we do not have the cash to purchase all these weapons from Western markets, nor is there any other country apart from the USSR that would supply us with this quantity and with this quality of weaponry. By and large we are moving ahead with our military preparation, but there are critical days ahead of us and we must stand fast and must prepare ourselves to achieve victory. But to go and sit with Israel and sign [*a peace treaty*], is something that we will never accept and that will never happen as long as I live.

Meeting of the Council of Ministers, 5 May 1968

At the meeting of the Council of Ministers on 5 May 1968, Nasser announced that the Soviet Union had agreed to place 120 Russian pilots in Egypt under Egyptian command.

Nasser: This number of pilots will give us the opportunity to put our efforts into training the number of Egyptian pilots that we require. Meanwhile, I have intentionally declared Egypt's official support for the Palestinian *fedayeen* so as to strengthen them against the reactionary forces and because the Palestinians themselves asked me to do so. I would also like to inform you that time has turned against Israel and that the Israelis are now losing fifteen lives every week as a result of *fedayeen* action. Two days ago I had a secret meeting with one of the West Bank leaders who told me that he had met Eshkol, the Israeli prime minister, and Abba Eban, the foreign affairs minister, and that they had told him that provided they could meet with us for negotiations to solve the problem, they were ready to make concessions which the Arabs would not expect.

Meeting of the Supreme Executive Committee of the ASU, 28 October 1968

At the meeting of the Supreme Executive Committee of the ASU held on Monday 28 October 1968, Dr Mahmoud Fawzi, President Nasser's assistant for foreign affairs, asked what was being done about the status of Jerusalem and what was being said about giving the city an international status.

Nasser: King Husain cannot conclude a separate agreement with Israel though he wishes he could. Moreover the West Bank people do not approve of King Husain's proposals and they are quite capable of opposing his plans. Our brothers in the West Bank have sent me several messages asking us not to take any military action until we have completed our military preparations.

Dr Mahmoud Fawzi: Mr President, how do you view the Soviet Union's position towards the Palestinian resistance?

Nasser: I once secretly took Yasser Arafat with me to Moscow, and they promised at that time to help him and to arm the *fedayeen*. This, as far as I know, was the first contact between the Palestinian resistance and the Soviet Union.

Meeting of the Council of Ministers, 31 October 1968

At the session of the Council of Ministers held on 31 October 1968 General Fawzi informed his colleagues that four Israeli Mirage aircraft had been shot down that week and that around one hundred 240-millimetre missiles had been destroyed at their bases in Sinai. Fawzi also said that the officers and the troops had regained their confidence and that the enemy had begun to realise that he was now facing military forces that were capable of positive performance.

Meeting of the Supreme Executive Committee of the ASU, 4 November 1968

On Monday 4 November 1968 the ASU's Supreme Executive Committee held a meeting at which Abdel Nasser spoke about the importance of forming a popular army to protect major targets in Egypt.

Nasser: We must hurry up with establishing a popular army which will consist of one million men. The Russians have promised me that they'll arm it. Our regular army is now capable of crossing the canal and of taking positions in the territory immediately to the east, but our ability to advance deep into Sinai is still limited by the shortage of vehicles and half-tracks. What is important now is that we cross and stand fast and that it becomes clear to everyone that we are resolved never to capitulate. This is what I said in 1956 and what I am still saying now. There are those who believe that the solution is in the hands of the Americans. I have heard from one of the members of the Revolutionary Command Council who has left us [*Nasser did not mention his name*]. I myself once told King Husain to go and kiss the hand of the Americans to save the West Bank, but even though he did just that, nothing has been achieved; they have not given him the West Bank. I have received information today indicating that the Americans have asked King Husain to stop the activities of the Palestinian *fedayeen* and that they have prepared plans to wipe out the *fedayeen* movement. I believe that it is necessary to make the Americans feel that their Middle East interests are threatened and that their current policies will speed up the spread of Soviet influence in the region.

Abdel Muhsin Abu al-Nour [*member of the Supreme Executive Committee*]: I would like to ask why we cannot coexist peacefully with America and why we should close the door on coexistence at any future time?

Nasser [*with emotion*]: Never. There will be no coexistence. That former member of the Revolutionary Command Council says that as long as Abdel Nasser is in power, the Americans will not try to reach agreement with him. With others, it is possible. I would like to tell that member that the Americans are first and foremost sympathetic to Israel and that the two countries have common interests. We have a clear example in King Husain. He is not a socialist and does not subscribe to our system, yet the Americans have not come to any agreement with him nor have they returned a single inch of his territory. As far as we are concerned our policy is fundamentally one of patience and steadfastness. As for the relationship between King Husain and the Palestinian *fedayeen*, I consider this a very important issue because if King Husain strikes at them, there will be trouble between us. The Palestinians have promised me not to interfere in Jordan's domestic affairs and I have asked them not to involve themselves in the problems of the Arab countries and to concentrate their efforts instead on operations inside Israel. What is important to us now is to identify what the country's vital targets are and to prepare and train the people's army to protect them.

Abdel Muhsin Abu al-Nour: There are now 10,000 volunteers thoroughly trained to fight under the command of Abdul Magid Farid who coordinates fully with General Fawzi and Shaarawi Gomaa [*minister of the interior*].

Discussions in the Council of Ministers and the Supreme Executive Committee of the ASU in 1969

For Nasser, 1969 was a year weighed down with hardship and with enormous labours. Immediately after the 1967 defeat he had thought that within a year he would be able to strike the enemy and drive him back. But by 1969 he had realised that this estimation had been a fantasy, and the reasons why this was so were numerous and diverse. The process of rebuilding the armed forces was taking longer than had been reckoned, notwithstanding the determined efforts of the leadership, but the main reason was the fact that when the process of rebuilding the army got under way, General Fawzi had had to begin from scratch. Not only had the army lost all its equipment but it had also lost its morale. Even before that, it had lost its discipline. So from the outset the situation required a strategy of engaging the enemy in small skirmishes to show that his apparent superiority was simply a myth.

These scattered operations entailed crossing the canal and challenging the enemy in the Sinai desert and trying to capture his men, and even though they had little material impact on the enemy's army, their psychological yield for the Egyptian army was considerable. On one occasion a five-man Egyptian patrol captured an Israeli officer with the rank of colonel after killing the men who were with him. The Israeli colonel had been hit by a bullet in the left side of his chest but he survived the journey back to the west side of the canal, near Ismailia. On the way to the hospital he was shaking and kept repeating one sentence over and over again: "I have not committed any crimes against the Arabs, I have not committed any crimes against the Arabs." The prisoner finally died in the military hospital in spite of receiving intensive treatment (the Egyptian command was keen to keep him alive). Word immediately went round the Egyptian troops that the Israeli officer had died not from the bullet wound but from fright. Moreover, the fact that he was a high-ranking officer indicated that the Egyptians had penetrated deep into enemy territory, which by itself was considered no mean feat. This was a great morale-boosting episode, and many enthusiastic volunteers came forward for operations across the canal.

After the June war, Nasser had had to sleep with one eye open and the other only half closed. The Americans were concocting a number of strategies to topple him, and American agents were all over the place. This was why Nasser had assumed the premiership himself so that there would be no gap through which any of his adversaries could infiltrate.

In 1969 the war of attrition, which was reckoned to be the fourth war between the Arabs and the Israelis, got under way, while it was also the year of the Sisco plan. This purported to be a 'peace initiative', and proposed a bilateral settlement between Egypt and Israel, rather than an overall settlement that involved all the parties. The Sisco plan was the culmination of a series of signals and insinuations which included a number of bombing raids by the Israeli air force on the electrical installation at the Nag Hammadi barrages in Upper Egypt and on the radar station outside Suez, as well as a concentration of raids all along the canal front and the killing of hundreds of Egyptians who had been working desperately to complete the ground-to-air missile system for the defence of Egypt. The raids also hit at the very heart of the regime's prestige.

However, and contrary to many expectations, reaction to Israel's aggression was immediate and strong, and came, in many forms, from outside as well as from inside Egypt. Sudan reacted with the May revolution, Libya with the September revolution, and Egypt itself suddenly opened fire with 100,000 guns at the enemy across the canal. This signalled the start of the war of attrition, and it was at this point that Nasser, possibly due to severe stress, suffered a heart attack which kept him bedridden for seven weeks. But what was going on in Nasser's mind before he collapsed at the end of the year? Certainly there was much to contend with, as the records of his many meetings during this period reveal.

Meeting of the Council of Ministers, 26 January 1969

Nasser: We have a critical period ahead of us before we can solve the problem in our region through political and military action. We really have to make a great effort at home to solve people's problems because otherwise I'm afraid that they'll start to feel aimless and hopeless. We really do need assistance from the World Bank but we will not allow its experts or any other of its officials who visit Egypt to tamper with our economy or to exceed the limits of our security procedures with regard to the information that they are demanding. I have learned from Hegazi [*Dr Abdel Aziz Hegazi, minister of finance*] that the World Bank delegates are asking for very many detailed statements from the ministries and other departments. Most of these representatives work for the American Central Intelligence Agency and have to gather extremely accurate information for it. From today we must be very careful about supplying material. To sort out this matter I believe that the director of General Intelligence [*mukhabarat al-ama*] Amin Hewedi should regulate the supply of information to the World Bank officials according to the country's security needs. I also think that they should not be allowed to visit companies and organisations until they have been given official permits to do so. In any case, I don't believe that the World Bank will offer us aid at the present time except within narrow limits, and moreover, the Bank will not even keep its promise to deliver the water condensation plant to us.

Meeting of the Council of Ministers, 16 February 1969

Nasser: On the subject of the domestic front, the utmost efforts must be exerted to wipe out corruption and to bring every culpable official, regardless of his rank, to account. There are rumours going around the country about the conduct of certain officials in the trade and economy sectors [*these words were addressed to Hassan Abbas Zaki, the minister of the economy*], claiming that enormous commissions are being paid to some high-ranking officials in these two sectors. I believe that people in top positions in these sectors should not be left there for long periods and that they have to be changed from time to time. We must also constantly examine deals and transactions with great vigilance and we shouldn't leave loopholes that can lead people into corruption and deviation. Unguarded property encourages stealing. It is disgraceful that we, who are in the process of socialist transformation, should allow some people to amass enormous fortunes of 300,000 or 400,000 pounds, and then also let them get away without even paying taxes. We would be letting our society slide backwards and destroying what we have already accomplished.

I will now move on to foreign policy. We must understand that America and the Soviet Union are both afraid of military confrontation, and this is why neither of them wants to heat up the political and military situation in this region. We should see where our interests lie and work for them. At the present time the Israelis are reassured by the fact that we are unable to start a war with them because of the lack of fighter pilots, military vehicles and other equipment that is needed to enable us to cross the canal. However, this shortage will be made up over the coming months when the delivery of new Soviet equipment, weapons and military aircraft starts next month. It is my view that whether the Americans and the Soviets wish it or not, we should go ahead this year and escalate the situation with Israel and in particular step up the commando operations in Sinai because, as part of the war of attrition, such operations have a significant impact on the enemy's military deployment and morale. Operations of this sort will force the enemy to keep large numbers of troops under arms, which runs counter to his military policy and stretches his capabilities. Now that we can rely on a strong defence line west of the canal, let us intensify the commando operations until we are militarily capable of crossing the canal and launching major operations.

Meeting of the Council of Ministers, 15 April 1969

At the meeting on 15 April, Mahmoud Riyad, foreign affairs minister, informed the Council of Ministers that the first quadrilateral meeting between the four major powers – the United States, the Soviet Union, Britain and France – had been held in New York to discuss proposals for the solution of the Middle East conflict. The French delegation had suggested the publication of 'a declaration of principles and intentions' whereas the Americans had tried to avoid the text of the terms of the Security Council resolution in an attempt to force the Arabs to make greater concessions. At the same time the Israeli government was trying to focus on the so-called issue of the Egyptian borders of 1906 which ran from Arish to Ras Muhammad. President Nasser offered very little comment, instead steering the discussion towards military matters.

Nasser: All this is political talk. We must continue our military preparations. At the Armed Forces General Command a few days ago, we started preparing a complete plan for the elimination of all traces of aggression. During the coming weeks, I have agreed to adopt some urgent military steps at the front. General Fawzi will sum up these steps for you now.

Gen Fawzi: The president has approved an urgent plan for the front. The backbone of the plan can be summarized as follows: first, to provoke bloody clashes with the enemy with the aim of killing the biggest possible number of enemy personnel; that is to say, priority will be given to [*weakening*] Israeli manpower in preference to weapons and equipment because loss of lives causes greater concern to the Israeli military command. The second element of the plan is to step up land, sea and air reconnaissance over enemy territory. The third thing will be to create a genuine atmosphere of battle for all our field units and to expose the men to bloodshed so that in future operations all of them will actually have had the experience of facing and fighting the enemy. Fourthly, we will send patrols deep into Sinai to shake the enemy's confidence in the Bar-Lev fortifications and show them that there is no way of stopping Egyptian patrols from getting behind their lines. We will also be stepping up other aspects of psychological warfare. [*At times during this period, the Egyptians had more than 20 patrols operating behind enemy lines.*] Fifth, our fighter pilots will be sent up for dogfights against enemy aircraft whenever there's a suitable opportunity.

Dr Sayed Gaballah, the minister of planning, then presented the broad outlines for the next development plan.

Nasser: The plan should not look for economic contraction because of the war conditions, and nor should it promote uncontrolled expansion. Rather it should always take into account one fundamental consideration, which is that the Americans will continue to work against us and will not leave us alone unless we adopt a completely rightist philosophy. They will then find certain politicians and intellectuals in Egypt who will be prepared to dress up whatever policy they dictate with some sort of political and economic ideology.

Meeting of the Council of Ministers, 18 May 1969

Nasser: These days the Americans are trying to make us believe that they have reached a secret agreement with the Russians on the Middle East problem. But from my conversation with the Soviet ambassador today it has become obvious to me that this is untrue, and that what the Americans are claiming is a plot designed to damage our relations with the Soviet Union. The ambassador has repeated the promise made to me in 1967 that the Soviets will not agree to any solution of the conflict without our prior approval. I have received new information about increased activity inside Egypt by American intelligence and about a serious attempt that has been made to approach certain officers in the armed forces. We must continue to work day and night to prepare the country for war. You must not forget that the Israelis want us to lose all hope, so we must work ceaselessly to make them lose all hope of ever achieving their goal.

Meeting of the Council of Ministers, 8 June 1969

Nasser: It has become obvious to us that America's attitude towards the Arabs, whether at the United Nations or in the quadrilateral committee, is gradually going from bad to worse and that the US has finally reached total partiality for Israel and complete agreement with Israel's views, since it constantly repeats that it is essential for us to negotiate directly with Israel.

Gromyko will be arriving here the day after tomorrow. In my opinion we should continue our policy of encouraging ongoing face-to-face dialogue between the Americans and the Russians until the Russians eventually realise that it is impossible to reach a peaceful solution. They will thus be compelled to continue to supply us with military equipment and weapons and meet all our other requests.

Dr Hilmi Murad, the education minister, asked whether it was possible to make direct contact with the Americans in order to change their political attitude towards Egypt.

Nasser: Any such contact will achieve nothing because Israel is considered an American satellite [*here he used the English word 'satellite*] and the Americans will not abandon it. However, we have recently sent Dr Mahmoud Fawzi to the States to continue contact with them and I have also sent a cable of congratulations to Nixon. But for us to enter into dialogue with them and to engage in bargaining about making concessions, this is something that I will never do, especially as it is clear that the United States believes that the opportunity is now favourable for achieving Israel's ambitions in the Arab lands. The United States also believes that the time is ideal for getting rid of our political system and thereby achieving victory for itself and for Israel. A dialogue with the Americans now will be of no benefit to us and will indeed do us harm. They have already offered us a 13-provision plan but unfortunately it requires us to make numerous concessions in return for some foodstuffs and some wheat shipments, and this is unacceptable. I can see no hope with the Americans until they have become completely convinced that we are capable of both steadfastness and confrontation. Another thing is that any dialogue with them will only be productive when they are sure that they are unable to replace this regime. As for West Germany, it is stepping up its cooperation with Israel, and it is trying to distract us with a 50 million pound loan. This is why I am going to recognise the German Democratic Republic, and I will announce diplomatic representation with it after you have approved the plan appended to the papers for today's session. [*Approval was duly given in this session to the proposed resolution.*]

Meeting of the Council of Ministers, 26 July 1969

Nasser: Joseph Sisco [*the US assistant secretary of state*] presented a new plan for the Middle East problem this week, consisting of a number of provisions which basically include the following points. First, Israel will withdraw from the lands it occupied, not to the 5th June lines, but to positions to be agreed upon by Israel and Egypt. Reference is made to Israel possessing secure borders which will be drawn on maps. Secondly, all the areas from which Israeli forces withdraw will be demilitarized. Third, UN forces will be stationed in Sharm al-Shaikh, while Sinai will be demilitarized and the Straits of Tiran recognized as international waters. Fourth, the state of war between Egypt and Israel will be terminated as soon as the agreement documents are deposited with the UN Secretariat, and next the parties concerned will agree on a timetable for the clearance of the canal and on the withdrawal of forces. Then the Gaza area will also be demilitarized and it will be placed under temporary UN administration. Seventh, all ships will be guaranteed the right of free passage along the Suez Canal and the Straits of Tiran, provided that no reference is made to the Constantinople Agreement [*Article 10 of which gives Egypt the right to close the canal when in a state of war*].

The eighth point is that the Palestinian refugees from 1948 will have the right to return to Palestine or to be resettled where they are now living, within the framework of an agreement which will set the number of refugees permitted to return annually, and provided that the first batch arrives not earlier than three months after the agreement has been concluded. Ninth, Egypt will undertake to establish peace with Israel and to eliminate all forms of hostility towards it as soon as it has signed this new agreement. Tenth, the agreement will be an Egyptian–Israeli agreement. There will be other agreements concluded simultaneously with the other Arab countries concerned, which means that there will be a Jordanian–Israeli agreement and a Syrian–Israeli agreement.

Meeting of the Supreme Executive Committee of the ASU, 28 July 1969

The Sisco plan was submitted to the Supreme Executive Committee on 28 July at a session chaired by Anwar al-Sadat who was deputizing for Gamal Abdel Nasser. Following extensive discussion, the members of the Committee agreed unanimously – in the absence of the president – to reject the plan.

Dr Mahmoud Fawzi: This plan needs neither comment nor analysis because everything it contains is bad. I believe that the best answer to the plan is to step up our military preparations and to continue along the path of struggle. I will not forget the words of the US Secretary of State when I met him during my recent visit to Washington and asked him to submit reasonable proposals to the Arabs. He said: "Don't forget that you lost the war and that you have to pay the price." The formula of the Sisco plan has been prepared with the utmost cunning. The plan stipulates more than one subsidiary issue that has to be settled finally through direct negotiations between Egypt and Israel, such as the issue of secure borders and of the number of Palestinian refugees to be permitted to return annually.

Anwar al-Sadat: I agree with every word and every aspect of the analysis made by Dr Fawzi regarding this bad plan.

Meeting of the Council of Ministers, 10 August 1969

At this meeting Abdel Nasser expressed his opinion of the Sisco plan and his own view of what Egypt should do.

Nasser: The Sisco plan is not much different from the American plans that preceded it, all of which seek our surrender to the Americans and to Israel. This is why I consider that there is no other way open to us except to concentrate all our efforts in the following three fields. First, the military field, and here we should continue with our plan to rebuild our armed forces and to raise their combat capability, while at this stage avoiding any escalation of military activity against the enemy unless the outcome and the potential gains of every action have been carefully evaluated and also after taking into account the fact that American Phantom aircraft will reach Israel next month – September. But at the same time don't forget that in the same month we will receive the new missiles for the air defence network from the Soviet Union, especially missiles to deal with aircraft flying at low altitudes which used to inflict such heavy losses on our forces and positions.

Second is the home front, and I consider this to be particularly important because high morale among the public will bolster the nation's determination. This will mainly require political action among the masses and a first-rate performance by government departments, and in this way we will be able to gain people's confidence. It means we will have to get rid of bourgeois behaviour and pretension in the country, to call to account unhesitatingly all those guilty of negligence and deviation, to submit everybody to customs inspection when entering or leaving ports or airports, and to ban gifts to high-ranking officials, even including the gifts of mangos and grapes handed out by the Ministry of Agrarian Reform.

Third, the Arab sphere. Here we should devote a great deal of effort to sustaining a comprehensive Arab movement in which every state, and particularly the frontline states and Iraq, will shoulder a specific responsibility in the battle. The challenge facing us is enormous and there is no place for a peaceful solution. Winning a military battle against Israel is going to require a great deal of effort and coordination, and as for America, even though we know that it is 99 per cent in Israel's embrace, we should keep Muawiya's hair intact with it [*keep some contact with the US*], if only for the remaining one per cent and in a manner similar to the weak contact that exists at present between Israel and the Soviet Union.

Meeting of the Council of Ministers, 31 August 1969

Nasser: You will remember what I said in the previous session about the need to act in all spheres. This is why we are going to take part in the Islamic Conference which will be held in Rabat next month. I imagine that since it will discuss the Israeli aggression and the burning of al-Aqsa Mosque, the United States will take a stand against it. As for us, we have supported the Islamic movement since the beginning of the revolution, as is evident in my book *The Philosophy of the Revolution.* We were opposed to the Islamic alliance which the United States was attempting to build as part of its policy of creating coalitions that would act within its orbit.

As for the Arab movement, the Arab foreign affairs ministers failed to reach agreement at their last meeting, and Saudi Arabia has not agreed to the holding of an Arab summit conference. But we will not remain idle. A small summit will be held here in Egypt tomorrow, in which Syria, Jordan and Iraq will take part. There is also talk about the Sudanese participating, now that the Sudanese revolution which took place three months ago has been consolidated.

> *In spite of the many worries that Nasser had to cope with, he did enjoy a number of pleasant occasions. His first meeting with the leaders of the Sudanese revolution leaders was like a real holiday since the changes in Sudan represented a personal victory over those trying to harass and ultimately to destroy him. At this first meeting Nasser told Babiker Awadallah, the Sudanese revolution representative: "You must keep your eyes wide open and remember that while Sudan's annual budget is 100 million pounds, American intelligence has a budget of 2 billion pounds every year. Plots against revolutions and revolutionary governments will continue, and it is important that we maintain our self-restraint."*
>
> *Nasser was also delighted by the successful four-state conference in Cairo, at which he announced that the Egyptian army would soon number one million men. He also warned against the stand adopted by the Egyptian isolationists, who were calling for the liberation of Sinai alone. In Nasser's view, liberation had to be total.*

Chapter 9

RENEWED RELATIONS
Rebuilding the eastern front, 1969

The quadrilateral conference on the eastern front which was held on 1 September 1969 was one of the cornerstones of the Arab movement in that year. Nasser had already had a number of meetings with King Husain, with Salih Mahdi Ammash of Iraq, and with Dr Nur-al-Din al-Atasi, but the conference was to be an important step towards establishing an eastern front.

Nasser's Meeting with the President of Syria, 15 August 1969

The meeting between Nasser and President al-Atasi of Syria was one of the preparatory sessions organized by Nasser in advance of the quadrilateral conference convened in Cairo. At this preliminary meeting Egypt and Syria signed a political agreement which incorporated the 'battle's political command', and it was decided that this agreement would be kept secret. Its most important provisions were that first, the command was to be set up straight away, and would consist of the presidents of Egypt and Syria, the two ministers of defence and the two ministers of foreign affairs. Secondly, the command would appoint a senior military officer who would be responsible for planning for the conflict. In planning and in preparation, priority was to be given to the air forces and to air defence. Thirdly, this agreement would not conflict with any other agreements that might be reached either at the eastern front or at the Arab level.

Having agreed its provisions and signed this agreement the two presidents spoke together briefly.

Nasser: Some people may criticize this agreement. However, the political situation is far more important, especially as Israel is not going to withdraw from the occupied territories in months or even in a year. This is why joint planning is required. To us, the issue is an issue of life or death.

Another matter is the importance of mobilizing all the political trends inside Syria. This issue is going to require speedy action on your side, and I hope that you won't think that this is an interference by us in your domestic affairs.

al-Atasi: There is absolutely no sensitivity about this matter because we believe that bringing the whole issue to a conclusion will constitute a guarantee for us all. We will apply as much pressure as we can on all the domestic groupings to achieve what is required.

Nasser: The latest UN discussions and the attack against Lebanon clearly show us how hostile America's position is towards all the Arabs. Golda Meir will be going to them [*the Americans*] on 23 September. Moreover, there are US Senate elections next year, and President Nixon needs the Jewish vote. If we can implement today's agreement, Israel will face a big dilemma in a year or two because it will be forced to fight on two fronts simultaneously. We must also press the Russians to give us more aid so that we can get more of their experts to participate in the air defence. Lastly, it is very important not to let this agreement of ours displease Iraq and not to let it become a source of aggravation for the Iraqis, particularly since they will be taking part in the quadrilateral conference about the eastern front and we have to encourage and reassure them by all possible means.

Nasser's Meeting with King Husain of Jordan, 31 August 1969

Nasser met King Husain at al-Qubbah Palace on 31 August in the last of the subsidiary meetings before the major quadrilateral conference that took place the following day, 1 September. Nasser was enthusiastic about the quadrilateral meeting, since he believed that Israel would be defeated if it was forced to fight on several fronts simultaneously and also felt that the time was right for creating a strong eastern front that would include Iraq, Syria and Jordan, matters that were to be raised at the quadrilateral conference. The two leaders held a brief conversation before having to interrupt their discussions to enable Nasser to meet President al-Atasi of Syria at Cairo Airport.

Nasser: We do not want war for the sake of war. We want a peaceful solution, but with conditions, namely the return of the Palestinians to their lands and the return of our occupied territories to us. But when there is no way to achieve our goals by peaceful means, then war becomes the only way. We in Egypt join hands with King Husain unreservedly and without conditions until we have liberated Jerusalem and the occupied lands.

King Husain: As far as the political solution is concerned, I am with you on the one essential condition, which is the restoration of the land occupied by the enemy and the return of the Palestinians to their territories. This is why we should thoroughly coordinate our positions. It's important that we maintain as much self-control as possible and that we do not allow the Israelis to drag us into a battle whose timing and location they have planned. The next battle should be our battle, and it is we who should choose its time and its place.

Nasser: Our military position is very different now from what it was after the June war. You remember that at that time our people were determined to stand fast and to continue the struggle. But the state of our forces was very bad. There were not even rifles available for many of the troops. Now, however, we have rebuilt and rearmed our forces. We now have half a million fighting men and we are attempting to increase this number to one million men. Two essential elements are needed for achieving a peaceful solution. First we need Arab unity and Arab solidarity. The United States places considerable importance on Arab solidarity and is afraid of the ultimate outcomes of any such solidarity. Secondly, our military strength. Israel will reconsider its calculations if it becomes convinced that we can check and resist its plans.

But if we are not able to achieve our aims through a peaceful solution, then inevitably we must apply the military solution to stamping out the traces of Israel's aggression, and it must be clear to everyone this means the liberation of all the occupied territories. There are some isolationist voices in Egypt that are calling only for the liberation of Sinai. We must go into the next confrontation with a unified command and we must force Israel to fight on all fronts. I would like to reassure you that our anti-aircraft defence is now thirty times what it was before the June war. As for the conference, I do not think that it will be helpful at present to raise the issue of Iran, given that I have already told Iraq that I am willing to send some naval units to the Basrah area as well as some bombers to strengthen their air capability.

King Husain: On the problem of Iran, we have been trying very hard to calm the situation along the Shatt al-Arab. I will ask Abdel Monem al-

Rifai, our minister of foreign affairs, to give a complete picture of the situation to Mahmoud Riyad, your minister of foreign affairs.

Nasser: There is one more thing. We have agreed with Syria to unify our air and naval forces. I would also like to make a quick comment to you about the Islamic conference which is being held in Rabat in a few days' time. This group of countries is supposed to be helping us either through the actual participation of their troops or by offering us financial aid. But for these countries to join the battle just with words alone is unacceptable.

Here the meeting between Nasser and King Husain ended and the quadripartite conference between Egypt, Syria, Iraq and Jordan began its attempt to set up the eastern front, an ambition that was never to be successfully realised.

The Quadrilateral Conference, 1 September 1969

In addition to the leaders, the accompanying delegations included a number of senior officials. The Jordanian group included Abdel Monem al-Rifai, the minister of foreign affairs, and Major-General Ali al-Hiyari, the minister of defence. Dr Ibrahim Makhus, the minister of foreign affairs, and Major-General Hafiz al-Asad, the minister of defence, were included in Syria's delegation, while Lt Gen Salih Mahdi Ammash attended on behalf of President Ahmad Hassan al-Bakr of Iraq who was ill, accompanied by Lt Gen Hardan al-Tikriti. Egypt's delegation included Anwar al-Sadat, Husain al-Shafei, Dr Mahmoud Fawzi, Mahmoud Riyad, the minister of foreign affairs, Lt Gen Muhammad Fawzi, the minister of war, and Dr Hassan Sabri al-Khuli. The conference was held in the main conference chamber at al-Qubbah Palace and after welcoming the delegates, Nasser opened the proceedings.

Nasser: In the light of my initial contacts with the chairmen of the delegations I propose the following agenda for this conference. First, we must define the strategic goal of our forthcoming plan. Secondly, we need an analytical study of the current political situation, followed by the formation of a political command for the military forces that are participating on the various fronts. If there is no objection to these topics [*there was none*], perhaps you will permit me to start the discussion.

It is evident to all of us that the political solution has not achieved our goals for us. So now we need to complete our military preparations – which will require us to unify the military command of all the fronts in order to guarantee full coordination – and to force Israel to fight on all fronts. We have contacted the Arab countries to ask them to participate in the unified military command but some of them, such as Libya, Morocco, Saudi Arabia and Kuwait, for a variety of reasons have not agreed. Unfortunately the recent conference of foreign ministers is not going to reach any positive resolutions, so we must move quickly, as the political command structure of the countries taking part in the battle, to draw up a very clear strategic plan and to review all the positive and negative aspects in full. I now propose that we move to a discussion of the military situation [*and the proposal having been approved, Lt Gen Fawzi read the military report to the conference*].

Salih Mahdi Ammash: It is obvious from the report that the most important negative feature is the inadequate preparation of the air forces that are needed for the eastern front.

Nasser: I would like first to salute the Iraqi revolution and the eagerness of its leadership to participate in the eastern front, even though Iraq has no borders with Israel and even though the enemy occupies no Iraqi territory. Indeed Iraq could stand idly by with, as the proverb says, 'an ear of clay and an ear of dough'. But they have come to the conference to participate constructively in the planning and preparation for the fight. I believe that the next battle will be a battle of life or death for Israel because Israel realises that we are preparing seriously for this confrontation. On a practical note, we can mobilise two million troops. Egypt now has half a million troops under arms. As far as tanks are concerned, there are two and a half thousand tanks on the eastern front and fifteen hundred tanks in Egypt, thus bringing the total up to four thousand. This figure surpasses the number of the enemy's tanks.

Another point that I would like to touch on is that there is no need at present for one-upmanship or for attempts to try to find other people's mistakes because we are now passing through a decisive stage in the future of the entire nation.

There are also questions that require definite answers. Can the air operations be stepped up at present? What is the reason behind the Americans supplying Israel with long-range bombers? Why is there no air defence for Baghdad and for other vital targets? We have stood fast for two and a quarter years since the defeat and we can stand fast for two more years, but only if our goal is entirely clear and if we plan to move from a position of defence to one of offence on all fronts. We also have to settle on something with regard to the deterrence policy because that is a political and not a military process and we need to decide this thing now.

Salih Mahdi Ammash: I repeat President Ahmad Hassan al-Bakr's apologies for not attending this important conference because of his illness. We in Iraq understand the seriousness and the importance of this phase and we agree with you on the need for a clear vision and for defining the entire plan because the battle with Israel is going to be a long struggle with formidable dimensions. I propose that the plan be divided into two phases – the phase of steadfastness and then the phase of liberation and of ridding ourselves of the source of the permanent aggression against us. We must rid ourselves of regional sensibilities when discussing the issue of the unified command. For example, if the eastern front is infiltrated and if, God forbid, the enemy should reach Damascus or Amman, then this should be no reason for Syria or Jordan to withdraw from the war. The battle should continue to the end.

Nasser [*teasingly*]: I think it's a bit too late now to discuss the issue of the enemy entering Damascus and Amman. Therefore, I suggest that the session be adjourned until six o'clock tomorrow evening, provided that allows enough time for the ministers of foreign affairs to meet beforehand and draw up a comprehensive appraisal of the political situation to present to us at tomorrow's session.

The Second Session, 2 September 1969

The second session started on the evening of 2 September, and Mahmoud Riyad presented the political report that had been prepared by the foreign ministers in which they proposed that an appeal from the conference should be sent to all the Arab leaders urging them to take a positive part in the next battle.

Nasser: Concerning what the report has to say on the element of time and the solutions that are available to the enemy, I do not believe that the enemy will move straightaway to occupy Damascus or Amman because he is currently in a more advantageous position and because he finds it is easier to maintain the status quo through a specific cease-fire agreement and with severe deterrence operations when necessary.

Hardan al-Tikriti: I believe that Israel's current policy is to destroy the Arab armed forces wherever they may happen to be. This is why Israel will not allow our armed forces to expand. This obliges us to decide at what point we will put an end to the military race between us and them. Nor should we forget Israel's superior ability to arm itself, which certainly exceeds that of the Arabs.

Nasser: [*provoked by Hardan's misgivings*]: So then, what is to be done? As long as we remain doubtful about our Arab capabilities, what is the proposal?

al-Atasi: I don't think that the arms race between us and Israel is the only decisive factor, because there's another more important factor, which is the human element.

Salih Mahdi Ammash [*in an attempt to reduce the effect of al-Tikriti's words*]: I do not think that Hardan is unaware of the impact of the human element. What he meant by his remarks was that America will always stand by Israel and will prevent the Arabs from becoming superior.

Nasser: Another factor is time. Is it in our favour or in Israel's favour? In my view, the time factor favours us because we will reach equality in armament with the enemy at some point in time, and at this point we can launch our offensive. Moreover, all the combat forces should be placed under one capable command that will be in control. Quite simply, the issue is that we have certain forces and that we should use them in the best manner possible.

> *Here Lt Gen Muhammad Fawzi read the important three-point summary of the military report that had been prepared by the ministers of defence. First, there would be the phase of steadfastness and of ensuring the security of the domestic fronts. This would be followed by exhausting the enemy forces and carrying out deterrence operations. Thirdly, there would be an offensive on all fronts to liberate the land.*

Salih Mahdi Ammash: The report is very good theoretically, but what is important is how it is to be implemented practically. It is also important to guarantee that there will be a follow-up of the implementation, and this is why I recommend that a follow-up committee is formed which will be attached to the office of the general command.

Nasser: The report of the defence ministers maintains that the effective factor in the battle will be the air force and the air defence system. Even though the total number of aircraft in the four Arab countries exceeds the number of Israeli aircraft, there are difficulties that prevent the necessary air challenge being mounted. I suggest that the air forces are immediately unified in preparation for unifying the ground combat troops.

King Husain: I welcome such a step and I propose that the command structure should be the prerogative of the state with the largest air force.

The proposal was approved by King Husain, President al-Atasi and Lt General Salih Mahdi Ammash. However, Lt Gen Muhammad Fawzi expressed some reservations, declaring that the proposal would remain theoretical and would be impossible to implement before April 1970, the date that had been set for completing the construction of the air bases on the eastern front. The meeting was then adjourned till the following day.

The Final Session, 3 September 1969

The final session was held at six o'clock on the evening of 3 September, by which time numerous subsidiary meetings had been held. This session, which did not go on for long, was joined by a Sudanese delegation led by Major-General Jaafar Numairi, chairman of the Sudan Revolutionary Command Council. Lt Gen Fawzi summed up the conclusions that had been reached by the defence ministers and stated that the only point on which agreement had not been reached concerned the need to strengthen the local reserves on the Jordanian front.

Lt Gen Hafiz al-Asad: We are ready to offer the Syrian Sixth Armoured brigade which is currently in the area of al-Mafraq for this purpose.

Salih Mahdi Ammash: I disagree with the suggestion of moving the Syrian Sixth Armoured brigade from al-Mafraq because this key area is vital and its loss would separate the Syrian front from the Jordanian front.

King Husain: I suggest that we leave the task of deploying the reserves on all the fronts to the general commander.

Nasser [*addressing himself to Ammash*]: I myself, you and indeed all of us who are present here are considered politicians, regardless of the fact that some of us have a military background, and we must therefore let the military commanders decide on military matters. In conclusion, I would like to submit the resolutions that this conference will approve, on the understanding that the drafting committee will formulate them later on. First, the conference approves the appraisal of the political situation submitted by the foreign affairs ministers, and secondly, it approves the appraisal of the strategic position presented by the ministers of defence.

Thirdly, the conference ratifies the strategic goal on which it has agreed, which is to carry out interception operations with the aim of destroying the enemy forces and reaching the lines of 5 June 1967. Fourthly, the conference approves "the present task" of the joint forces, namely to secure the current defence lines on the eastern and western fronts and to intercept and destroy any enemy force that tries to attack them.

Fifth, the conference approves the size of the armed forces of those Arab countries taking part in the conference, as stated in the appraisal carried out by the defence ministers. Sixth, Lieutenant General Muhammad Fawzi shall be appointed general commander and shall be given full powers to achieve the goals stated in these resolutions. Seventh, the drawing up of the plan of interception will begin immediately in order to achieve the strategic goal, and a timetable for implementation shall also be drawn up.

Eighth, the member countries pledge to speed up the process of implementation by preparing and training their armed forces as required to carry out the plan, with special recommendations for fulfilling the requirements of the air defence and of the air forces. Ninth, efforts shall be exerted to complete the air bases on the eastern front on schedule. Tenth, a meeting of the participating leaders shall be held once every four months and of the ministers of defence or the chiefs of staff once every two months.

These resolutions having been approved, they were then passed to the drafting committee to be written in their final form.

Salih Mahdi Ammash: Is it not possible for Sudan to participate by providing extra reinforcements to the troops that have been allocated for this plan?

Numairi: We do actually feel that it is important for us to participate in this plan. But after our successful revolution four months ago, we found serious flaws in the preparation and armament of our armed forces, and this is why we immediately started reorganizing and rearming them, with the assistance of the Soviet Union and the United Arab Republic. We hope that in two years' time our forces will have reached the size and the standard that will enable us to send substantial numbers actually to take part in the fighting.

Nasser: To conclude our activities, I believe that our meetings have been positive and that they have resulted in the mobilizing of all our resources for the confrontation. In your name I also salute the steps taken by the

Sudanese revolution to attend this conference, even though Sudan is far from the battlefield. We hope that in the near future all the other Arab countries will reaffirm their positions for this national battle. We also hope that the number of countries participating with us will increase by the next meeting.

I thank all of you for honouring your countries and on behalf of the people of the United Arab Republic I wish you all success and victory, God willing.

Both King Husain and President Numairi made appropriate replies, wishing Gamal Abdel Nasser and the people of Egypt victory and prosperity, and the quadrilateral conference came to an end.

Nasser Suffers a Heart Attack

After seeing off the leaders, Nasser felt extremely exhausted. The man had been living on his nerves for months. After all, he had been moving from problem to problem ever since the defeat in 1967 and right up to the day when he managed to get the army standing on its feet again and launch the war of attrition which was to inflict substantial losses on the enemy. This process had culminated in the quadrilateral conference the aim of which was to draw everything together, to mobilize all the energies and to coordinate all the strands. Sitting at his desk he suddenly felt sharp pains in his chest, and the hastily summoned doctors all confirmed that he was suffering from a severe heart attack and that it was essential for him to stop work completely and rest for at least the next seven weeks.

As a result of this enforced rest his physical condition may have improved somewhat, but his emotional state worsened. He wanted to know every little detail to do with the armed forces. He did not want to die before he had scored a victory against his enemies. He felt that all the plans were coming to fruition and insisted that the coming battle should not be delayed even by a day. Although the majority of the population believed the story that Nasser was suffering from influenza, those around him and everybody in authority knew the truth of course. Tense, long-drawn-out weeks went by during which Nasser left the overseeing of domestic matters to a committee of his aides. But he did not stop for one moment communicating with the military commanders and familiarizing himself with the latest reports coming in from the front.

Another odd thing was the relationship of Nasser's illness to crucial events

*in the Arab world, possibly because he was not the kind of leader who would
remain at one remove from the events taking place around him; nor would
he adopt the attitude towards events of an official refereeing a game between
two teams. Rather he became part of those events, influencing them and
being influenced by them, until the pressures wore him out.*

*The doctors allowed Nasser to resume work at the beginning of November,
his first political engagement following his recovery being the Council of
Ministers meeting on 12 November. He had been forbidden to smoke
although he had previously consumed sixty cigarettes a day, and before going
into the meeting that day the ministers had agreed, out of concern for the
President's health, not to smoke themselves. However, on discovering this
'agreement', Nasser insisted that the ministers should smoke as usual.*

*At this meeting, and in spite of his two-month absence, Nasser summed
up the political situation for his ministers, based on the latest information he
had received. The Americans, he said, had not changed their position of
favouring Israel. They had presented another proposal to Ashraf Ghorbal (the
temporary representative of the foreign affairs ministry in Washington) that
very day which contained nothing they had not already put forward apart
from confirmation that they would recognize Egypt's international borders.*

Nasser : It is clear from all sources that the United States still insists on
putting our area under its influence and control. This is why it plans to
change the current Egyptian regime, and also the regime in Syria, in the
hope that it will reach an understanding more easily with the new regimes.
As for the Soviets, they have finally reached the conclusion that there will
be no help from the Americans in reaching a peaceful solution, and this is
why they will start to prepare and to arm our troops so that they can
become an aggressive force. Furthermore, the Soviet experts that are now in
Egypt are making great efforts to train the armed forces and especially the
pilots whose numbers have increased and whose combat capability has been
enhanced.

As far as the war of attrition is concerned, our continuation of this war
has greatly affected the morale of the Israeli troops. They have been forced
to change their defence operations policy and have entrusted such
operations to the air force instead of to the ground forces. We have gained
another advantage from the war of attrition which is that our soldiers,
having become accustomed to the enemy, are now facing up to and
crossing swords with the enemy soldiers, and are living a normal daily life
in the thick of the battle and the sounds of grenades and attacking aircraft.
We are now capable of moving a fully armed and equipped infantry

division across the Suez Canal and to fight the enemy under the tough conditions of war.

The Soviet armament contracts are proceeding satisfactorily, and the ones that have been finalised during 1969 are equal to those that were concluded between 1955 and 1968. Today, our forces have risen to thirty thousand officers and half a million soldiers.

Addressing the session, Sayed Marei [minister of agriculture] congratulated the president on his recovery and informed the Council that agricultural production had increased during the year, in spite of the war conditions. Cotton production had gone up by one and a half million qintars and corn production by forty thousand ardabs.

At the conclusion of the session, Nasser spoke of his plan to benefit from all the military resources of the Arabs. He told the meeting that he maintained contacts with Libya and Sudan and that both wished to unite with Egypt. Syria had asked to join this unionist movement, but as Libya had expressed disquiet about the Syrian Baath Party, it had been agreed that Syria's participation in the talks would be postponed until the Libyan regime's fears had been calmed.

Nasser also informed the Council that contacts had been kept up with King Faisal and that relations between Egypt and Saudi Arabia were showing signs of improvement. Indeed, King Faisal had immediately accepted the invitation conveyed to him by Minister Hassan Abbas Zaki to visit Egypt, and the dates had been fixed for 18 and 19 December. Political talks would begin as soon as the king had arrived in Cairo.

The Restoration of Relations with King Faisal, December 1969

This visit was particularly significant, coming as it did after a period of lukewarm relations that had been preceded by a period of open hostility culminating in the Yemen war in which the Saudis had supported the royalists against the new republic. Moreover, the visit would take place immediately before the Arab summit at Rabat – potentially an explosive occasion because of the vast number of political difficulties, especially between Riyadh and Cairo. Despite all this, Nasser continued to believe in the need for unity among the Arab ranks to confront the common enemy. He was keen for King Faisal's visit to succeed so that the way would be blocked against all the conspiracies that were trying to spread dissent and disunity.

I was given very specific instructions on the need to give King Faisal a warm popular welcome, and indeed we were able to do so after much heated debate with our political cadres. The picture of King Faisal standing in the open car next to Abdel Nasser and saluting the population of Cairo who had turned out en masse to greet Egypt's important guest caught the attention of many people. The king was pleased by his warm reception which eased the way for candid and open talks between the two sides.

Discussions continued over two days, 18 and 19 December, and the joint communiqué issued at the end of the talks certainly marked a turning-point in Arab relations.

The First Session, 18 December 1969

The first few minutes of the first session were indeed critical. The two delegations sat facing each other, and there was a brief period of silence which felt like years. There had been no serious dialogue between the two sides for seven years, there had been a vicious and wasteful war in Yemen, and each side had plotted and conspired against the other. Perhaps the silence was due to the fact that neither side knew where to start or how to bridge the chasm before them. It seemed to me from my customary vantage point behind Nasser that the silence would continue forever. It was Nasser who suddenly spoke.

Nasser: Once again I welcome his majesty the king and his delegation, and I extend to you our sincere hopes for the success of this meeting and for the arriving at a common understanding on issues that are of concern to us and to you. For our part, we have been trying since 1967 to improve our relations with you. Our people have welcomed this, as they made clear to you today when they gave you such a lively reception: they feel that our interaction with you has not been normal, and that Arab interests require that relations return to normal, particularly as Egyptian–Saudi connections have stood firm over the centuries.

There is no doubt that this meeting and your visit will close the door in the face of all those who have benefited from the disagreement. We also believe that this visit will have far-reaching effects, not only in our two countries but throughout the Arab world. Even though the Yemen war harmed our relationship, it has ended now and there is no longer any reason why relations between us should not improve and grow.

I welcome once more our brother King Faisal and the companions who are accompanying him and I pray that our meeting will be beneficial to both our countries and will be one of the causes of the success of the forthcoming summit at Rabat.

King Faisal: I thank you for your welcome. I also thank your noble people. I would like to affirm that everything you have said about the relations between us is correct, and that the disagreement between us is an anomaly. From the days of King Abdel Aziz, our relations were normal and strong, and what happened afterwards was not normal. I always say that whenever there is disagreement between two sides, a third party must be behind this disagreement.

It is our hope that relations will return to their previous state. We consider this as something essential and inevitable that we must each try to achieve, because the national and Islamic interest of both countries requires us to be one hand and one body. Officials in both countries should try to create the proper conditions for achieving this goal, and not simply leave it to individuals. We pray that God will help us in our endeavour, for God accepts only honest labour.

Nasser: The truth is that the conditions we experienced in recent years, and particularly the Yemen war in 1962, had a significant effect on our relations and directed them along a path which neither we nor you had planned. For our part, we consider the Khartoum meeting of 1967 to have been a turning-point in the relationship between us. Since that time my instructions to all our agencies have been straightforward and clear – there is to be no intervention in the domestic affairs of any Arab country, and efforts must be concentrated on fighting Israel on all fronts. I sent Minister Hassan Abbas Zaki to you to explain all aspects of our new policy to you, but he informed me after his return that you still entertained many doubts and fears concerning the activity of some of our organisations. I told Hassan Abbas Zaki to tell you that in this connection any person who departs from my instructions will be investigated by me in your presence. There is one important fact which I hope will not be overlooked, and that is that there will always be individuals who will go on trying to tarnish the relations between us.

King Faisal: Actually, we still have some of these dregs, and, moreover, there are some people who are trying to widen the discord between us. But these attempts must be stopped in the interest of both countries. For example, some people were arrested in the kingdom recently. When they were interrogated they claimed that they were in contact with Egyptian individuals and agencies, and they admitted this in writing. I and my colleagues in the kingdom were at a loss as to what to do with them. Should we try them? They will admit to their contacts in the courts and this may harm affairs between us. Should we sentence them secretly without trial? Should we pardon them and let them go free? Indeed we remained at a loss as to what to do. Finally, we chose not to make a decision in their case and kept them in detention. There is also a small group of communists who also say that they have contacts with Egypt and other countries. I have postponed making a decision in their case too. I wish I could avoid bringing up these issues but perhaps bringing them up will be of benefit to both sides.

Nasser: I would like to mention a fact that we do not try to hide, and that is that we have no party branches outside Egypt, and that we have not established any regional leaderships [*for the Arab Socialist Union*] outside Egypt, unlike other Arab parties such as the Baath Party.

King Faisal [*interrupting with some passion*]: The Baath Party . . . may God destroy the Baath Party.

Nasser: Even where the *fedayeen* organizations are concerned, we have refused to let any of them follow us, as is the case of al-Saaiqah organization which follows Syria and receives its instructions from Damascus.

King Faisal: As long as we are talking frankly, we have documents that implicate a person who works for you of having suspect contacts with individuals in the kingdom. This person's name is Sami Sharaf, and it is said that he acts upon your personal orders. [*Sami Sharaf was the President's secretary for information.*]

Nasser: I am ready to conduct an investigation on this matter. However, I would like to assure you that at the present time we are not engaged in any hostile activity in your country or in any other Arab country. We have now to take a step forward in our bilateral relations, otherwise fears and suspicions will continue to control us.

Nasser dealt with this issue after Faisal's visit, at a meeting of the Supreme Executive Committee on 12 January 1970. He also spoke about the outcome of the Rabat summit and about the superficial participation by some Arab countries in the mobilization required for the battle. He said: "Concerning Saudi Arabia, I believe that King Faisal's visit to our country last month was for the purpose of throwing dust in our eyes, because they are still plotting against us. We have recently got hold of some documents that prove that the Saudi royalist regime continues to conspire against us. As for what King Faisal said during the talks about our plotting against him and his alluding to the fact that some persons had been arrested in Saudi Arabia and had admitted that they were in secret contact with an individual working in my office, namely Sami Sharaf, this is true. However, it happened in 1963 and 1964 when we were fighting in Yemen and when our respective countries were engaged in hostile activities. Such contacts were routine. In fact the contacts to which the king referred actually took place in Copenhagen between Sami Sharaf and some Saudi officers who were not happy with the royalist regime in Saudi Arabia. In 1965, I terminated my office's connection with this issue and instructed that anything that involved Saudi Arabia was to be dealt with by the General Intelligence Directorate as part of its normal activity.

King Faisal: There is another subject that I would like to discuss frankly with you, concerning what some of your information media publish, especially *Al-Ahram* and Heikal, its editor-in-chief. Heikal is said to be your official spokesman. This is not my personal theory but it is what the world's press and radio say and what some heads of state and prime ministers maintain.

Nasser: *Al-Ahram* is one of the Egyptian newspapers. It does not reflect my personal opinion. The Arab affairs page often publishes the opinions of Zakariya Neel, who is in charge of this section, which are very different from my personal opinions.

Indeed, Muhammad Hassanein Heikal did enjoy a special relationship with the President. When asked by his colleagues in the Revolutionary Command Council and in the Central Committee of the ASU why Heikal received preferential treatment, Nasser explained that although he had previously dealt with other journalists, he had found Heikal to be the one best able to express his thoughts and opinions. He also pointed out that he himself also benefited from the relationship, since Heikal used to telephone every morning to give the President an accurate and useful account of the latest news and current affairs, including political developments in the Arab world, as well as his own personal views on them. This relationship between the two men evolved over time to transcend what would be considered normal between a president of a republic and a journalist, becoming a relationship of friendship and trust.

Prince Nawwaf ibn Abdel Aziz: Will His Excellency the president permit me to repeat what His Majesty the king has said about *Al-Ahram* having a special status with you. For example, it is the one paper in the world to have beaten all the information media with the news of our visit to you.

Nasser: In fact the newspaper representing our government is *Al-Jumhuriyya*. *Al-Ahram* is an independent paper and Heikal, its chief editor, is the most active journalist in Egypt. He spends twelve hours in his office every day. As for the news of your visit, our foreign affairs ministry is the party responsible for the mistake because it was its responsibility to issue a press statement and to distribute it to the world information media. Furthermore, not all that is published in the press reflects firm facts. For example, at present the press is talking about a rapprochement between ourselves and South Yemen when in fact there are currently a number of differences between us.

King Faisal: I believe that our relations will improve from now on and that we will live up to the warm feelings of the masses that received us when we drove together from the airport to al-Qubbah Palace.

Nasser: Your Majesty, we are both responsible for doing away with any lukewarm relations that may crop up between us. I am confident that the exchange of visits will help a great deal in improving our relationship. Now, if His Majesty has no objection, we will adjourn the meeting until tomorrow.

The session was adjourned until six o'clock the following evening. Before the second session convened, King Faisal summoned me to his suite on the upper floor of al-Qubbah Palace. When I arrived at his private apartments, there were a number of fellow Saudis with him, among whom I remember Shaikh Ahmad Abdel Wahhab, head of royal protocol, as well as Minister Hassan Abbas Zaki who was accompanying the Saudi delegation. After a short period, King Faisal indicated, with the utmost courtesy, his wish to speak to me privately. When those present had departed, King Faisal told me that there were two extremely important issues that he wanted me to present confidentially to President Abdel Nasser, now that the hearts had been cleansed of ill feeling and that good intentions had prevailed. "I would like to warn the president against the Alawite rule in Syria, because Islamic history affirms that the Alawites are treacherous by nature and that they work only for their personal interest. Religiously, they are not considered true Moslems." When I indicated to the king that I would be interested in discussing some of his statements further, he said: "When you come to us in the kingdom, I will let you read some of the numerous Islamic volumes I have in my library." He then added: "The second issue is Abdel Nasser's relationship with the Russians. These people are atheists and Abdel Nasser's continued relationship with them will harm him gravely. The Russians do not wish him or Egypt either prosperity or success." He then reminded me of the story of the Soviet ambassador when he insisted on meeting Nasser on the eve of the aggression and assured Nasser that Israel did not intend to carry out any military action. After listening to his majesty, I said that the United States had also participated in deceiving Abdel Nasser until the last moment. My conversation with the king ended at this point because it was time for the second session to begin.

The Second Session, 19 December 1969

The second session started at ten o'clock in the morning. Tempers roused after the previous session had subsided, and the morning's discussions ignored the question of relations and went straight to the political and military issues and to the issues that were expected to be raised at the Rabat conference.

Nasser: We spoke very clearly and frankly yesterday about bilateral relations and I believe we attained a degree of complete understanding. Today, therefore, we shall move on to the fundamental issue which I asked Mahmoud Riyad to discuss initially with our brother Omar al-Saqqaf [*Saudi minister of state for foreign affairs*].

Omar al-Saqqaf: It is obvious from a review of the issues that are intended for presentation at the Rabat conference that you exclude the peaceful solution and that military action and the means of preparing this action are the proposed issue.

Nasser: When we approved the Security Council resolution in 1967, we were extremely short of time which was needed to rebuild our armed forces. For the sake of the truth and of history, Jordan and Egypt were the only two countries to approve the peaceful solution and the Security Council resolution. Today, we are the only country engaged in daily fighting in a bloody and unprecedented war of attrition.

America offered us a solution that split the issue apart and, as far as we were concerned, confined to Sinai alone. But we rejected it because if the issue had been a purely Egyptian one, it would have been easy to liberate Sinai. But as long as the issue is essentially at the pan-Arab level, we must accept comprehensive Arab action with all its commitments. We here in Egypt have paid dearly because of the war. Many of our installations and targets have been destroyed. We have more than four hundred thousand evacuees and thousands and thousands of our sons have been martyred.

Again for the sake of the truth and of history, I tell his majesty the king that if Egypt falters on this issue then the entire matter will come to an end.

We know that we are the people who have to pay the heaviest price and to sacrifice the most. Unfortunately there is no such thing as a peaceful solution. When we go to the Rabat conference and announce the mobilization of all the Arab forces for the battle, this does not mean that we will go to war tomorrow or the day after. This is simply because there are military matters that require some time to organize, such as the preparation of fighter pilots. We now have four hundred aircraft in Egypt but we do not have four hundred fighter pilots. Meanwhile, Israel faces no such problem.

Agreement must also be reached on the strategic plan that is to be achieved. We want the minimum degree of Arab solidarity from the Rabat summit. We are not going to this conference to create trouble for the others or to enter into fights against anybody. However, Syria has declared that it rejects any peaceful solution and talks about the armed struggle even though its guns are covered with rust and relative calm prevails on its front and even though it has so far not fired a single bullet against the enemy.

We, as Arabs, were successful at the Khartoum conference because we faced facts and acted accordingly. Had it not been for the aid agreed by that conference, we would not have been able to endure until the present moment, given that the losses we suffer greatly exceed the aid that was decided for us. In addition to losing the Canal revenues, we have also lost 170 million pounds from the industrial sector, not to mention the expense of providing the evacuees with the bare essentials. But we have not asked for the amount of that aid to be increased and we will not ask this of you or of any of the others. War is not an easy thing and the date of the battle cannot be fixed now because establishing this date depends on the growth of our air force. Moreover, the Arab military mobilisation which is to be decided upon by the Rabat conference is what will determine our ability to launch the war and what will set the date of the battle.

King Faisal: I do not believe that the issue of the peaceful solution or of setting the date of the battle will be brought up at the conference. All that can be discussed there is how to achieve Arab military mobilisation and the responsibility of each state in any such mobilisation.

Nasser: I have learned that there is a Libyan plan and a Sudanese plan concerning Arab mobilisation. As for us, we have no specific plan. We only have ideas. I have also learned that there is a Tunisian plan that confines military mobilisation to the Palestinians only.

King Faisal: This would have been reasonable in 1948, but not now – even though King Saud was one of the advocates of this opinion in the past.

At this point, much discussion took place on the issue of the unified Arab command and on the powers of the general commander to move and to use the forces of the various states. At the end, King Faisal and Abdel Nasser stressed the need for constant contacts and for the exchange of visits at all levels. Omar al-Saqqaf then read the joint statement drawn up by the foreign affairs ministers of the two countries. The statement having been approved, it was agreed that it should be broadcast simultaneously by Cairo Radio and Riyadh Radio.

Thus, the page was turned on the disagreement between Egypt and Saudi Arabia – a disagreement that at times had reached the point of bloodshed. It seemed to everyone that Nasser was moving closer to realising his grand dream of mobilization and liberation of the land. But fate had other plans, and less than a year later Nasser was gone. Even so, with the Arabs close to the abyss, he was still in control of the situation, directing matters towards the well-being of the nation.

Chapter 10

COMPLEX NEGOTIATIONS
Tactical considerations and the Rogers plan, 1970

We have seen how Nasser and the Egyptians and indeed populations throughout the Arab world resolved to continue the struggle and to rebuild, especially militarily, following the crushing defeat of 1967. Announcing the fourth war against Israel in 1968 Nasser's slogan was 'the battle continues', and indeed the protracted and bitter war of attrition that followed inflicted more losses on the Israelis than the three previous wars had done.

The year 1970 turned out to be unexpectedly eventful. The first surprise was that the widely anticipated union with Egypt, much desired by the pro-Nasserite revolutions in Sudan and Libya, failed to materialize. At the meeting in February 1970 between Abdel Nasser, Muammar Qadhafi and Jaafar al-Numairi it became clear that although impressive it would be a very difficult goal to achieve. As Nasser remarked, to establish unification without wide preparation and broad popular conviction would result in a feeble union that, once created, would then be resisted. It was also obvious that unification could not be promoted until the essential step of establishing a united Arab political movement had been taken. Even so, the lack of any progress in this respect did not prevent Nasser and Qadhafi from deciding on coordination at all levels between their two countries.

This was also the year of the Rogers plan, over which Egyptian and Arab popular opinion in general was divided. Without losing sight of the overall objective, Nasser approved the plan, seeing it partly as a tactical step and a key towards achieving his strategic goal of crossing the canal and ridding the land of the occupying forces. Others viewed the plan differently, regarding this 'tactical step' instead as a strategy for establishing security and peace. Thus, the strategic goal was forgotten in the breathless scramble for tactical moves.

Nasser's Meeting with Muammar Qadhafi and Jaafar Numairi, 12 February 1970

The meeting between Nasser, Muammar Qadhafi and Jaafar Numairi began at noon on 12 February 1970 in the conference chamber of al-Qubbah Palace, with each of the three leaders accompanied by a delegation of ministers and experts on the topics for discussion that included the 23 July revolution 1952, the 1 September 1969 revolution (Libya) and the 25 May 1969 revolution (Sudan).

Nasser was obviously delighted as he embraced his fellow revolutionary leaders. As he remarked later in a private meeting attended only by Egyptians, he saw in Qadhafi a true leader, unclouded by suspicion, genuine, unaffected, as yet untainted by the machinations of domestic or foreign policy, and although still lacking in experience, ambitious in his Arabist aspirations and willing to sacrifice for them. Nasser also felt that his advice to Qadhafi would not be particularly useful simply because only practical experience could polish the Libyan leader and turn him into a truly Arab leader, in spite of which he never failed to give detailed answers to any of Qadhafi's questions. At the same time, Qadhafi regarded Nasser like a student views his teacher or as a bedouin views the leader of his tribe, and was immediately ready to carry out whatever Abdel Nasser advised. He never hesitated in responding to Nasser, except once when Nasser pointed out to him the importance of improving his relationship with the Soviet Union and of meeting the Soviet leadership, given that the Soviet Union was the major power supporting the Arabs and supplying them with weapons and aircraft. Disagreeing with Nasser for the first time, Qadhafi said: "Mr President, ask me for anything but this, because in their ideology I see teachings that are in conflict with Islam and with God's book. Mr President, these people are atheists."

In Numairi Nasser saw at that time a leadership capable of dealing with the various Sudanese sects, although he also felt that the events and crises that had previously occurred between Egypt and Sudan had to some extent scarred Numairi's personality, and that these residual complexes had to be left to resolve themselves honestly and without compulsion, after which it would be easier to arrive at a genuine understanding with Numairi and the rest of the Sudanese leaders.

On this occasion, the discussions were started by Mahmoud Riyad, the Egyptian foreign affairs minister, who had already held talks with his Sudanese and Libyan counterparts in advance of the meeting. They now proposed the formation of joint committees of politicians and experts from the three countries concerned, in such fields as agriculture, education and industry. President Numairi was against the proposal, on the grounds that the committee method was slow and also inappropriate in certain instances such as in the military sphere. Instead he suggested that all issues relating to the battle should be put to a higher military committee consisting of the ministers of defence and the chiefs of staff.

Qadhafi: I endorse this proposal, provided that the decisions taken by this higher military committee take effect within two weeks of being issued unless any of the states have raised an objection before the end of this period.

Numairi: Another matter that I would like to deal with is the question of the solidarity of the popular councils and organizations and the need for them to be mobilised so that they can join the struggle alongside the military forces. There is also the subject of joint coordination in the field of information.

Nasser and Qadhafi both accepted Numairi's proposal, Qadhafi adding that concerning information a practical step would be to fix certain hours for simultaneous broadcasts by Cairo, Tripoli and Khartoum radio stations.

Qadhafi: Concerning the question of popular mobilization, I believe that it has become necessary to establish a single political organization in Egypt, Libya and Sudan that can confront the various ideological currents that are stirring here and there. We will thereby actually begin on the path of unity. I submit that a socialist union would be an appropriate single political organisation.

Numairi: I personally agree in principle to the creation of the single political organization. However, we may wish to differ in naming it in each country.

Nasser: I think that before we decide on any sort of single organization, we must define our objectives for establishing it, because if our aim is unity, our approach toward it will take a specific form. On the other hand if our goal is to establish some kind of alliance, some sort of cooperation or some form of commonwealth, then the approach will be different, and based on the type of relationship required. In my opinion the crisis of Arab unity will always be a crisis of disagreement about and struggle for power. I am also of the opinion that no form of Arab unity should be established until the political organizations have been unified, that is until the single Arab movement has been installed. There are numerous precedents for following this course. We can see, for example, that the Soviet Union is made up of several republics and governments but that it has a single political movement, namely the Communist Party.

There is another question too concerning the formation of a political organisation: should its development begin from the top or from the bottom? Almost all political organisations are formed from the top. The Communist Party started with a few thousand at the top and then gradually moved down to a broad base containing substantial numbers. While building this political organisation, we should distinguish between intelligent and stupid types of organisation. An intelligent organisation is one that does not permit opportunists to join its ranks, whereas a stupid organisation allows anybody to become a member, in spite of which circumstances may at certain times compel us to adopt the stupid organisation method. In Egypt, for example, we were forced at one point to follow this route and even to accept members of other groups into our own organisation.

Numairi: I think that at present we are still progressing within the stage of confidence-building among the Arab people in Egypt, Libya and Sudan and convincing them of the importance of their common interest. We have not yet passed this phase.

Qadhafi: I agree with President Abdel Nasser that we must decide now what our goal is to be. Do we require union, federation, a bloc, or something else? If our goal is in fact union, then it is our duty to take the immediate step of forming the single political organization in our three countries. At this point I would like to ask President Numairi whether at this stage Sudan agrees with the establishment of the single party?

Numairi: The political organization appropriate for Sudan at present is the 'single front' which will consist of all the nationalities, including southern Sudan, and will as a result be a strong and united front.

Major Awad Hamza [*from the Libyan delegation*]: I do not agree with President Numairi that creating the organization in the form of a 'front' will make it a strong political organization.

Nasser: I do not think either that the front will unify the various nationalities. Moreover, any nationality within the front that feels at any point that the front represents a danger to it will immediately break away and turn against it.

Minister Faruq Abu Isa [*member of the Sudanese delegation*]: I think it would be more appropriate if the proposed organisation was established in phases, especially as there are fundamental differences between us in a number of areas, such as the economic and the cultural fields, as well as others. What is important for now is that each revolution in each of the three countries strengthen itself by forming a political organisation that best suits its local conditions, as long as these organizations are gradually transformed into a single political organization.

Nasser: I would like to stress to my colleagues a fundamental principle concerning unity, namely that unless Arab unity is established on the basis of broad popular conviction, it will be a weak union created simply to be fought against. For example, between Sudan and ourselves there are numerous problems and complications dating back to the time of Muhammad Ali and of King Faruq that still have to be dealt with and settled before we can talk about the unity of Egypt and Sudan. This is why I believe that we shouldn't try to fabricate an artificial relationship before paving the way for unity, otherwise we will be helping to complicate matters even further. Therefore I propose that at this point we move on the basis of what the ministers of foreign affairs have decided about formation of the necessary preparatory committees. For my part, I will assign Hassan Sabri al-Khuli as political secretary to follow up the decisions of these committees.

Both Qadhafi and Numairi agreed to this, on condition that further moves could be reviewed in four months' time at the next tripartite meeting. This was set for 25 May, the anniversary of Sudan's revolution, and would be held in Khartoum.

Nasser's Meeting with Muammar Qadhafi, 14 February 1970

It was evident to the participants in the tripartite meeting that President Numairi was not ready to accept any form of unity or of union between the three countries, which is why Muammar Qadhafi asked to meet Nasser as soon as Numairi had left so that they could talk about the early formation of a supreme political leadership of the United Arab Republic and Libya which Numairi could join whenever he was disposed to do so.

The bilateral meeting was held on Saturday, 14 February, at al-Qubbah Palace, and Nasser took the opportunity to present a candid review to Qadhafi and his colleagues of the 18 years that had passed since the 23 July 1952 revolution and of the revolution's domestic and foreign achievements. He also offered them his personal views on the revolutionary actions that could be implemented within the framework of the prevailing situation within Libya.

Colonel Qadhafi began by reassuring Nasser that following the revolution the country was stable and that the population at large was fully committed to the Revolutionary Command Council. The Arab nationalists who had been active in Libya before the revolution were different from their counterparts in other Arab countries because, he maintained, they were unionists rather than individuals who had Marxist inclinations or who belonged to other factions hostile to Nasser at that time. As for the Baathists, they were Syrian Baathists who so far posed no threat.

Qadhafi: In view of the current Egyptian–Syrian rapprochement, the Baathists give no cause for alarm. The only dangerous elements may be the radical elements of the Moslem Brotherhood. Broadly, we have declared national unity in Libya and have also declared that there will be no partisanship from this time on. Even though there are worthy elements in the two parties, there is no place for their activities in our country at present.

I would also like to assure you that we are not middle-of-the-road people, as brother Numairi said in his conversation with you two days ago. We also believe that the adoption of unionist steps at this time is the most appropriate undertaking and that now is the most opportune time.

Nasser: I will start with the issue of protecting the revolution and its stability. When thinking about practical ways of protecting the revolution, you have first to define its friends and its enemies, while bearing in mind a fundamental consideration which is that the enemies cannot turn into friends and that some of the friends may take the side of the enemies. You must pay attention to reforming the economy and you must avoid creating any economic recession in the markets. You should also bear in mind the importance of permanent financial liquidity. As for your foreign relations, the major powers, especially those who have political or economic interests in you, will exert considerable efforts to get close to you. The United States will attempt to contain you in order to protect its strategic and economic interests, while the Soviet Union will work to support and back you, as it has done with us. Of course, the Soviet Union's attitude towards us is not inspired by love for our dark eyes but is based on our endeavours to eliminate Western colonialism in the region.

People will ask you about the meaning of the socialism that you have declared and they have the right to do so. It is my personal opinion that, on the basis of your economic and social situation, socialism in Libya means nationalizing only the banks and the insurance companies, as long as you begin to create a new public sector that will increase in size year by year, since your conditions are different from ours and in addition you haven't a structure of the size and form that we had.

They will also ask about the unity that you have proclaimed. I also think that you should explain to them that unity will be established fundamentally for the benefit of the Libyan people and of the Egyptian people.

Qadhafi: What is your opinion on foreign trade, on import and export policy?

Nasser: I think you need to plan carefully and to proceed gradually and without haste on the matter of foreign trade.

Qadhafi: And what about relations with the Soviet Union?

Nasser: I don't know why you are afraid of the Soviets. In our experience with them, there have been no attempts to recruit Egyptians into the Communist Party even though there were large numbers of them both in the armed forces and also around the area of the High Dam in Aswan for some years. During my latest visit to Moscow, Brezhnev asked me why you show such antipathy in your relations with them at the present time. Personally, I was unable to explain your position. However, I believe that time and actual experience will show you who are the friends and who are the enemies, and it will also become obvious who are the ones who support the Arabs and who are the ones that can be relied on.

Qadhafi: All right then, and what do you think about the relationship with China?

Nasser: We have a good relationship with China. They sent us a cable of support after the war, although these were only words and did not turn into tangible aid or explicit support either economically or politically. On the other hand, China insists that we refrain from favouring the Soviet Union. Is this sensible? But I don't mean to imply that your relationship with the Chinese should be bad. Rather, you should generally try to maintain a good relationship with them. Another point you should bear in mind while we are on the subject of foreign relations, is that less advanced countries do not always deliver all our requirements, which is why business has to be done with the major powers from time to time. For example, we have to import modern military equipment either from the United States or from the Soviet Union or at the very least with the approval of one of them.

Qadhafi: The fact is that I am uneasy about doing business with the major powers, given that there is always an ulterior interest behind their dealings with us.

Nasser: This is normal. You have to have relations with the major powers. However, try to work with more than one side and with more than one state so that you will guarantee an international balance and so that all of them will be competing to establish good relations with you.

Qadhafi: A final question about the war – are you going to leave the date undecided, and if so, for how long? What will be the effect of the date on the Mirage deal that Libya has concluded with France?

Nasser: The date of the war will depend entirely on our achieving parity in the air, otherwise it will be suicide for us. As for the Mirage deal, you must try to alter the contract so that the aircraft can be delivered during 1971 instead of in 1973, because we can't postpone the battle until that year. We have to begin the hostilities and cross the canal in 1970 or 1971 at the very latest.

Qadhafi: As soon as I return home, I will have urgent talks with the French to amend the Mirage contract so that the aircraft can be delivered at the necessary times.

Nasser and Qadhafi agreed to meet again at the end of March, either in Cairo or in al-Adm in Libya, to discuss two economic matters: the proposal to issue a unified currency in addition to the local currencies of Egypt and Libya, and the question of tariffs between the two countries. Dr Labib Shuqair, a member of the Supreme Executive Committee, was assigned to prepare a detailed study on these two issues.

Qadhafi: There is another thing, Mr President. Can you, without affecting the front line, lend us one of the Egyptian T-34 tank battalions and crews that have been designed to operate with the infantry?

Nasser: I think that it will be possible to send you a battalion without the front line being changed. I will take this up with Lieutenant General Fawzi. I have two final points before this meeting ends. First, I would like to assure all of you that we in Egypt are willing to offer you any help, including military support. You have Fathi al-Deeb [*minister of state at the presidential office whom Nasser had appointed to liaise between Egypt and Libya*]. He has my clear and explicit instructions to meet all your requests, whatever they are. But there's one thing I have to mention on this matter: we have developed a [*psychological*] complex from our earlier experiences of offering Egyptian aid to friendly countries, and we will not send any aid or Egyptian personnel unless it is at your personal request. The second point is that the sooner you explain your policy, whether in the political or economic field, to the people, the fewer enemies the revolution will make. Then you will attract an even larger number of the people whom the enemies of the revolution are trying to mislead and exploit.

The two presidents then parted on affectionate terms. Subsequently there were a number of meetings in Egypt and in Libya between Nasser and Qadhafi and his Revolutionary Council, and scores of joint ministerial meetings were held in both countries on a range of subjects as Egypt's ministers and military experts sought to pass on all the experience they had gained during the previous 18 years.

Another Meeting between Nasser and Qadhafi, 10 June 1970

In the early part of June 1970 Qadhafi visited a number of Arab countries to advocate the 'pan-Arabism of the battle' and to determine the contribution required for the war, and it was agreed during this tour that an Arab summit would be held in Tripoli on 20 June, attended by the heads of state of Jordan, Syria, Iraq, Sudan and Algeria in addition to the Egyptian and Libyan presidents. This conference took place from 20 to 23 June, and was attended by King Husain of Jordan, President Nur al-Din al-Atasi of Syria, President Ahmad Hassan al-Bakr of Iraq, President Gamal Abdel Nasser, Qayed Ahmad, chairman of the Algerian Revolutionary Council, on behalf of President Boumedienne, and Major Mamun Awad Abu-Zaid, chairman of the Sudanese Revolutionary Command Council, representing President Numairi. Qadhafi arrived in Cairo some days in advance of the summit, accompanied by Bashir Hawwadi and Omar al-Muhaishi, members of the Revolutionary Command Council, and Salih Buwaisir, his foreign affairs

*minister, to discuss the agenda for the conference with Abdel Nasser and to
present their view of the Arab situation following the tour. Their meeting on
10 June was, as usual, held in al-Qubbah Palace.*

Nasser: I am happy to welcome you here and to meet you after your
important tour through the Arab homeland. We applaud the efforts being
exerted by Colonel Muammar to achieve unified Arab action.

Qadhafi: I thank you for your greetings and I will try to give you some of
my observations on my recent visit.

First, I feel from the meetings that took place during the trip that there is
generally a crisis of confidence among us. If we can overcome this, we will
reach firm ground from which we will be able to solve the problems that
face us, and on which to stand with you in your forthcoming battle.

Another point concerns the Palestinian resistance. I have noticed
dissatisfaction with the Palestinian *fedayeen* action in all the Arab countries,
although at the same time nobody denies the success of certain *fedayeen*
operations, and particularly those whose impact on Israel can be judged by
Israeli reactions and the retaliatory operations that follow them. But it is
unsatisfactory that most of the *fedayeen* action is confined to mortar and
rocket shelling from the Jordanian or the Lebanese borders because such
shelling can just as easily be done by the guns and rockets of the regular
armies stationed on the borders. Even so, in spite of these comments, we
feel more optimistic than we did before our tour.

Nasser: The important issue for us and for the war is the creation of the
eastern front. Do you think, as a result of your tour, that there really is an
eastern front? As a military man, Lieutenant General Fawzi anticipated that
the creation of the eastern front would be possible as long as a proper plan
was drawn up and the various phases and dates were set, but I told him that
rather than being simply a military matter it was fundamentally a political
issue. This is why we have had a number of arguments that have delayed
the setting up of this front. For example, is this to be a defensive or an
offensive war? Is it a pan-Arab or a regional battle? Personally, I cannot
understand the debate over an offensive or a defensive battle when we have
not yet regained the territories occupied by the enemy.

As to whether the battle is pan-Arab or regional, then let us all ask
ourselves at the forthcoming summit what we have done to prepare for the
war since the 1967 operations. As far as we are concerned, we had an army
consisting of 170,000 men and now we have an army of 540,000 highly
trained fighters.

In the meantime, do you think that anybody has helped us to prepare this large number of armed forces? The answer is no. This is why we have been forced to raise taxes in our budget by 400 million pounds. The financial aid we receive according to the Khartoum summit resolutions, whether it comes from you, from Saudi Arabia or Kuwait, is channelled primarily towards making up for Egypt's economic losses resulting from the closure of the Suez Canal and the occupation of the Sinai oil fields by the Israelis. Israel's basic aim is to attempt to fragment the eastern front politically and thereby prevent it from turning into a military reality that will have a clear impact on the forthcoming battle. Therefore one of the most important subjects which the Tripoli conference will have to deal with is the issue of how the Israeli aim of breaking up the eastern front is to be thwarted.

These days we are also hearing comments about the so-called 'defeated leaderships of 1967'. What do these words mean? What is the significance of reiterating them all over the place? Lieutenant General Fawzi submitted his resignation to me, but I've turned it down and have asked him to offer it to the Arab kings and presidents at the forthcoming Tripoli conference. I imagine that these words are not meant for Lieutenant General Fawzi but that they are actually aimed at me. I don't think that any one of us has forgotten a lesson from the Second World War. Even though the attacking German forces were within a few kilometres of Moscow, Stalin and Zhukov stayed put in the capital. Numerous other commanders withdrew during the engagements at the beginning of the war and it was those same commanders that led the final victorious battles. Lieutenant General Fawzi is an excellent military commander. I know him well. He served with me in Palestine in 1948, and I also taught him at the Staff College when I was an instructor there. Even though he was one of the military commanders in 1967, he was not allowed to take any real command in that year. When I appointed him as general commander after the marshal [*Abdel Hakim Amer*], I told him from the outset that he would have the responsibility of building and preparing the armed forces for combat. But command of the military operations during the war will be assigned to another military commander.

Nasser's plan immediately after the 1967 defeat was to entrust the process of rebuilding and preparing the armed forces and of restoring morale and discipline to Lt Gen Muhammad Fawzi, because of his reputation for military strictness, for abiding fully by military rules and traditions, and for his superior abilities in implementation and follow-up. Command of actual military operations would then be given to Lt Gen Abdel Monem Riyad who was known for his intelligence and for his ability in planning and managing military operations. This is why Nasser had appointed Muhammad Fawzi as general commander and Abdel Monem Riyad as chief of staff, and the reasons were no secret to either man. The issue of the general commander of the Arab armies was brought up at the Arab summit in Tripoli on 20 June and the text of the fourth resolution of the conference read: "The conference has agreed to appoint General Muhammad Fawzi to the post of general commander. He shall be assisted by a joint chief of staff from the states signing this agreement."

Qadhafi: Mr President, I have great faith in the Arab countries and we must overcome the matter of the current crisis of confidence in whatever way possible, even if we have to apply some pressure here and there. I am also very hopeful about the possibility of mobilization for the war, and for victory. There are other provisos and comments on this issue but I would prefer to mention them to you in a more restricted session rather than in a meeting like this that will be on the record. Another thing I want to mention is that I visited the Iraqi front along the Iranian borders and saw the large Iraqi forces that have had to be stationed there because of Iran's deployment of three armies that extend all the way from Khanaqin to Basrah. I think that attempts should be made and pressures should be applied to persuade Iran to reduce its troop concentrations on the Iraqi borders so that Iraq will be able to take a larger part in the battle.

Mahmoud Riyad: Concerning this question, the Soviet Union has, at our request and after appeals to our Iraqi brothers, attempted to bring some influence to bear in this regard. Podgorny brought up the subject during his recent visit to Iran, and the Iranians expressed willingness to withdraw from the borders provided that Iraq started immediate negotiations with them. However, the Iraqis have at the same time stipulated the condition that Iran must refrain from abrogating the Gulf joint borders treaty. I also know that Jordan is trying to mediate between Iran and Iraq, but that the Iraqis have refused the mediation on the grounds that their position is much better than Iran's, both politically and militarily.

Nasser: There was actually a discussion between the Iranian foreign affairs minister and Foreign Minister Buwaisir at the Islamic summit conference in an attempt to restore relations between us. We had no objections but I stipulated approval by the Iraqis as a condition. The Iraqis objected and so I objected too and did not agree to relations between us and Iran being restored. In my opinion you can play an important role between Iran and

Iraq in freeing the largest possible number of Iraqi forces to participate in the eastern front or at least to become the strategic reserve for this front. Brother Muammar, I hope that you will not view the conflicts happening in the Arab world as "treason" since they are old conflicts that have been building up, along with all their clutter, for years. We in the United Arab Republic hope that Muammar Qadhafi will succeed in his efforts to resolve these conflicts so that, God willing, we may succeed in the major battle.

The meeting ended and Nasser rose, took Muammar Qadhafi by the hand and the two leaders walked from the conference chamber.

The Rogers Plan, June 1970

The Rogers initiative, delivered to the foreign affairs minister Mahmoud Riyad on 20 June 1970, was a strange sort of political measure that Nasser had never come across before. Since 1967 political proposals of this type had been submitted to the bilateral meetings between American and Soviet representatives at the United Nations, and then presented to Nasser through the Soviet Union. This meant that until this occasion none of Egypt's moves towards a political solution had ever taken place behind Soviet backs. As a result there had been no opportunity for any driving of wedges or sowing of discord between Nasser and the Russians or for arousing Soviet doubts about Nasser's actions; this explains why the Soviets had never had any excuse not to respond or even to delay meeting Nasser's economic or military requests. However, in June 1970 the situation suddenly changed and, with the ball thrown directly into his court, Nasser had to calculate and to tread very carefully before returning it, especially with regard to the ally that had stood by Egypt for so many years.

Domestically, Nasser proceeded first by distributing the text of the initiative to his colleagues on the Supreme Executive Council and then to the ministers, in preparation for a major meeting on the plan. He also tried to gauge the opinions of various popular political leaderships and of certain people in the mass media, at which point the important question arose of how the Soviets would react to news of the American initiative, especially if it was channelled to them by Nasser himself. On 29 June, having decided to convey the information personally to his friends, he left for Moscow, to exchange views with his ally and thereby to reassure himself on an issue that had been preoccupying him considerably: the degree to which the Soviets would be willing to continue their support and their supplies of weapons in the event of his agreeing to the initiative. At the same time, he was convinced that the United States was a crucial ally of Israel and that every previous step taken by the United States towards the Arabs and particularly towards Egypt had been suspect and not well-intentioned.

Nasser spent 18 days in the Soviet Union, from 29 June to 17 July, deliberating on all aspects of the issue. As soon as he returned to Cairo he called two meetings, one on 18 July with the Supreme Executive Committee of the ASU and the other with the Council of Ministers on 19 July, in preparation for the crucial meeting with the country's highest authority scheduled for 23 July.

During this period the main concern dominating Nasser's thinking was the military factor and his desire to organize all the appropriate resources and conditions required by the armed forces. He had been struggling for three years to rebuild the armed forces to the point where they would be capable of crossing the Canal and recovering Sinai for Egypt. The Rogers plan seemed to offer an accessible tactical opportunity to push the surface-to-air missile barrier forward to the west bank of the Canal in preparation for carrying out the crossing into Sinai. The escalating attacks in the continuing war of attrition had brought home to him that the Israeli air raids, equal in severity to those during the Vietnam war, would make it impossible to complete the SAM missile bases, since the Egyptians had suffered heavy damage as a result of the intense shelling and had lost more than 4,000 men during the construction of the bases. In addition, the missile crews would require nearly three months to complete their training at the special training centres in Egypt and the Soviet Union.

The American initiative provoked heated debates both within and outside Egypt and arguments sprang up all over the place on the topic of peace and war. In the opinion of Nasser, and of the political leaderships supporting him, there was no harm in moving politically to establish peace in the area, provided that certain fundamental supports were available to the peace-building process. These supports included first the international balance between the East and the West, and secondly the political status of the Arabs, and in particular Egypt's ability to maintain its political influence in the Arab world and to preserve the recognition of its pioneer status in the area. Third came military capability so that the enemy would realize that if attempts to establish a just peace failed, he would be exposed to grave losses in a savage military attack, especially personnel losses which the Israelis would find hard to accept. Then there was the option of holding back until the last possible moment from recognizing Israel as a state in the region in return for a just peace.

Even though all these alternatives were actually available to Nasser he was not particularly optimistic about this new American move given his previous experiences with American plans. For this reason he agreed to the initiative as a simple tactical step rather than as a strategic one, with the aim of utilizing the cease-fire period to redeploy the Egyptian–Soviet missiles to the west bank of the Canal.

At the same time, Israel was facing a certain amount of pressure which prompted the Israeli prime minister Golda Meir to announce on 26 July: "We are ready to observe the cease-fire and we call on the United Arab Republic and the other Arab countries to cease their shelling." This pressure was aggravated by heavy Israeli losses in the Canal Zone caused by Egyptian missiles shooting down unprecedented numbers of Israeli Phantom aircraft, to such a degree, indeed, that the world press called that particular week "the week of the falling Phantoms". The Israeli air force also lost a number of highly trained pilots, some of whom were taken prisoner by the Egyptian forces.

The operation to build the protective missile wall, to strengthen its combat capability and to move it up to the banks of the canal completely dominated Nasser's thinking and his actions. He exerted the utmost effort to supply the wall with the latest Soviet missiles, and utilized all his political skills to persuade the Soviets to deliver the required missiles and to send Soviet crews for the first time in Soviet history to fight on Arab territory. It was his stubborn determination that later, in 1973, enabled the Egyptian forces to cross the canal and to destroy the Bar-Lev line.

Before discussing how Nasser came to approve the American initiative it is useful to review five of the statements made over a six-month period by the President to the Council of Ministers up to the time of the 23 July meeting.

The first statement was made on 25 January 1970 .

Nasser: I have recently learned of a conversation between Abba Eban, the Israeli minister of foreign affairs, and a moderate Western journalist who is close to him, and this conversation to a great extent explains the position and intentions of Israel and of the United States towards us. The journalist asked why the United States and Israel are focusing on me, Abdel Nasser, personally, and Abba Eban told him, 'We are making a concerted effort to overthrow Abdel Nasser because we are convinced that the situation in Egypt will die down and that it will turn in our favour after he has fallen, in the same way that everything subsided in Indonesia after Sukarno's collapse and as things also subsided in Ghana after Nkrumah's fall. Some American circles [*by which I believe he probably meant the Central Intelligence Agency*] condemn us for our negative position at this time and for our failure to carry out positive action in Egypt. They have asked us to focus our efforts in the coming period on whatever may lead to overthrowing Abdel Nasser.'

Nasser's second statement was made on 8 March.

Nasser: We want to broaden our dealings with the Soviets so that their bond with us can become like America's bond with Israel. This means that we should take steps on this issue. It is evident that America is trying to push Russia out of the Mediterranean at any price, and this is why the Soviet Union is now compelled to stand with us and to support us. Russia's bond with us will enable us to draw up a new strategy.

The third statement was made at the Council of Ministers on 11 April.

Nasser: We have finally agreed to meet Sisco [*US assistant secretary of state*] and to talk to him so that we may prove to everyone that we speak to both the East and the West. Sisco asked me to hold discussions with the United States directly and not through the Soviet Union, as is the case currently. I told him that the reason why we had chosen this method was that: 'We don't trust you because of your bias towards Israel. You are also asking us for concessions whereas we made enough concessions when we approved Security Council Resolution 242.'

The fourth statement made by Nasser was made to the Council of Ministers on 19 July, that is after he had returned from his Moscow trip and his agreement with the Soviet leadership on approving the Rogers plan.

Nasser: I have already told the Americans: 'We do not want direct discussions with you because you are a major power and we can't outdo you, but the power that can surpass you is the Soviet Union. Moreover, you will use the statements made in any direct discussion with you to drive a wedge between us and the Soviets, the ones who are supporting us politically and economically and the ones who supply us with all the weapons and aircraft we ask them for.'

Our strategy relies fundamentally on the Soviet Union. Therefore, we must continue to have an understanding with them and the continuation of our relations with the Soviets is essential. But to say that we must rely on ourselves and on our own resources in the face of US science and technology would be no more than idle talk that the books of the Ministry of Education might find useful. Our latest movement and our approval of the Rogers plan has its advantages and its drawbacks. There are Egyptians who will oppose the plan and others who will reluctantly support it. We said long ago that the Americans are the ones who can solve the issue.

The Text of the Rogers Plan

It may also be useful at this point to give the text of the plan that was submitted by William Rogers, the American secretary of state, in June 1970. The text of the Rogers plan was delivered to Mahmoud Riyad and was conveyed in the form of a verbal message by Donald Burgess, US chargé d'affaires in Cairo, to Salah Gohar, under-secretary at the ministry of foreign affairs, on the morning of 20 June.

"Verbal message to His Excellency Mahmoud Riyad, the minister of foreign affairs, 19 June 1970:

"I have read carefully the statement by President Abdel Nasser on 1 May and the observations you made afterwards to Mr Burgess. Mr Sisco has also submitted to me a detailed report on the talks that he held with President Abdel Nasser and with you and we have given serious thought to what could be done in regard to the Middle East.

"I acknowledge that the situation has reached a serious point and I believe that it is in our common interest that the United States maintain and develop relations of friendship with all the area's peoples and states. We hope that it will be realized that this can be accomplished and we are ready to perform our part. We look to the other parties concerned, especially to your government which has an extremely important role to perform, to move with us to exploit this opportunity which, if lost, we will all suffer and will truly regret. With this spirit, I appeal to your government to study very carefully the ideas that I will present in the following:

"We are extremely concerned with lasting peace and we wish to assist the parties concerned to achieve this peace.

"We have submitted serious and practical proposals for this purpose. We have also advised all the parties of the need to accept a compromise and to create the atmosphere in which peace becomes possible. We mean by this last point reducing the intense tension on the one hand and clarifying the positions on the other hand so that the Arabs and the Israelis may have some confidence that what will be attained will preserve their fundamental interests.

"It is our opinion that the most effective means to achieve a settlement would be for the parties concerned to begin working under the supervision of Ambassador Jarring to reach the detailed steps necessary for the implementation of Security Council Resolution 242.

"Abba Eban, the Israeli minister of foreign affairs, has stated recently that Israel is willing to make concessions when the talks begin. At the same time, Egyptian participation in these talks will lead to a large degree to overcoming the Israeli doubts that your government is really seeking to reach peace with Israel.

"I am aware of the problems facing you in regard to direct negotiations. We have explained at the outset that we do not propose that such arrangements be put into implementation from the beginning even though we believe – and this depends on the progress made in the discussions – that the parties will find it necessary to meet at a certain point if peace is to prevail among them.

"With these ideas in mind, the United States presents these proposals so that the UAR may study them:

A   That both Israel and the UAR agree to resume a cease-fire, even if only for a limited time.

B.   That Israel and the UAR (and Israel and Jordan also) agree to the following declaration to be issued by Ambassador Jarring in the form of a report to Secretary General U Thant:
'The UAR (and Jordan) and Israel have informed me that they agree to:
a. Having agreed to and expressed their desire to carry out Resolution 242 with all its provisions they will appoint their representatives to the discussions to be held under my supervision in accordance with the procedures and in the place and at the time I may recommend, while taking into consideration, whenever convenient, the procedural methods preferred by the parties on the basis of the previous experiences they have had with each other.
b. The goal of the above-mentioned discussions is to reach an agreement on the establishment of just and lasting peace among them, based on:
1. Mutual recognition by the UAR (and Jordan) and Israel of the sovereignty, territorial integrity and the political independence of the other party.
2. Israeli withdrawal from territories occupied during the 1967 conflict in accordance with Resolution 242.

   c. To facilitate my mission to achieve the agreement stipulated by Resolution 242, the parties concerned will observe closely as of 1 July and until the beginning of October at least the Security Council resolutions concerning the cease-fire.'

"We hope that this proposal will meet with the approval of the UAR. We also hope to get Israel's approval. Until then, I am confident that you share with me the opinion on the need to exert utmost efforts to keep these proposals confidential so that the chances of their acceptance may not be affected.

"I am addressing a similar message to Minister al-Rifai. I hope to receive your reply at the earliest possible time.

"With my best wishes, Yours sincerely, William Rogers."

Explanations Concerning the Provisions of the Plan

In his meeting with Salah Gohar, Donald Burgess added some important explanations related to the plan's provisions:

"First, the cease-fire will cover both the ground and the air so that the UAR and the Soviet Union may refrain from changing the military situation existing in the western canal zone, meaning that no surface-to-air missiles or any new military installations should be set up [*by this he meant that the Egyptian missiles would not be permitted to move up to the west bank of the Suez Canal*], provided that Israel undertakes a similar commitment in a similar area east of the canal.

"Second, the UAR should take into consideration that according to this plan, the United States is asking Israel for important political concessions, especially in regard to agreeing to the principle of withdrawal before negotiations because the United States is aware that there can be no peace without withdrawal and no withdrawal without peace.

"Third, in regard to Israel's request for more US aircraft, the United States has decided not to exceed the limit to which it committed itself in the contracts concluded originally with Israel, during the period in which the American peace initiative is being discussed (i.e., the United States will not exceed the 50 Phantom aircraft agreed upon in 1968 and the 100 Skyhawk planes agreed upon in 1969). [*But while dealing with this point Burgess added a warning from his government that in case Egypt refused the initiative or failed to observe the cease-fire, his government had already prepared precautionary arrangements that would permit compensating Israel in the future for the aircraft it loses in case the situation required such action. He also added that he hoped that this point would remain undisclosed because at that time the United States did not want publicly to discuss the issue of its military aid for Israel.]*

"Fourth, that the US government presents this initiative directly to the UAR out of its desire to avoid any misunderstanding that could result from transmitting the initiative through a third party" [*by which he meant the Soviet Union, considering that the discussions and the proposals had earlier been transmitted by the Soviets*].

As for American opinions on the question of the Palestinians within the framework of the initiative, Mr Burgess explained these views in further discussions with the under-secretary at the ministry of foreign affairs on 25 June. The gist of his statements was that the USA recognized that the Palestinians were an interested party whose concerns had to be taken into account in any settlement. Resolution 242 provided for a just solution for the problem of Palestine refugees, and their legitimate interests were protected by the language in the American proposals, according to which the parties would undertake to carry out Resolution 242 'in all its parts'.

Nasser himself, in speaking of the Rogers initiative at a meeting of the Supreme Executive Committee on 18 July, made the following comments:

Nasser: I am confident that the Egyptians are astute; in my opinion, if the initiative is presented to them accurately on 23 July, they will rapidly understand that our acceptance of the initiative would pressure the Americans and put them in a corner [*here Nasser used the word 'corner' in English*]. This is in addition to the fact that in three months we will get from the Russians twice the number of SAM-3 surface-to-air missiles along with Egyptian crews that have been trained in the Soviet Union and that are in addition to the Soviet crews that we already have and that will be deployed at the heart of our country to bolster our air defences. Thus within three months our missiles will have reached the canal bank and our military position will have improved enormously.

The US initiative was announced by Nasser to the National Congress of the Arab Socialist Union, on 23 July 1970, and the President's statement was followed by a heated discussion between him and the members of the Congress who had lived for the past three years in the shadow of the conflict. Politically, it was not easy to gain the approval of the members for this step.

At dawn on 4 August, as the cease-fire came into effect, the guns went silent and the aircraft disappeared. However, only a few days were to pass before the implementation of the plan began to falter, Israel having discovered that, by approving the initiative, it had committed a serious error. There were two reasons for this conclusion. First, the initiative meant that delivery of new American Phantom and Skyhawk aircraft was withheld from Israel, thereby seriously exposing its strategy and undermining its military superiority over its Arab neighbours even as Nasser continued to strengthen his military forces, and particularly the air force and the air defence units. Secondly, Nasser exploited the cease-fire that had been stipulated in the initiative in favour of his military front, right from the first week, by secretly moving the Egyptian SAM missiles forward to the canal west bank. American protests and Israeli objections did not stop him from implementing the stages of his plan which, as the Israeli military soon began to realise, gave the Egyptians local air control over both the eastern and western canal zones.

Israel thereupon launched a savage propaganda campaign at the international level that persisted for two months and that, until the day of his death, continued to portray Nasser as a man who had not agreed to the initiative as a man of peace but as a man of war and revenge, intent only on launching his next battle.

Perhaps Nasser's remarks to the Council of Ministers on 7 September, a month after implementation of the Rogers plan had begun, best reflect the political attitude towards Israel at the time.

Nasser: Israel has been directing a vicious propaganda campaign against us which started a few days after it had approved the initiative. The Israelis are declaring everywhere that we have failed to keep to the agreement about avoiding making changes in the military situation during the cease-fire period. Through their rabid propaganda campaign they accuse us of having moved our missiles forward and of having built many new missile bases. We have replied to them and to the Americans that we reorganized our armed forces in the canal area within the limits of the preparatory period that was permitted by the initiative. As for the construction of bases, we told them that these come under the same interpretation – 'maintenance and repair of positions' – that America has allowed to the Israeli forces stationed east of the canal. I have entrusted the minister of information [*Muhammad Hassanein Heikal*] who is in charge of domestic and external information with preparing a complete refutation of their present campaign against us and with constantly following up this campaign.

I suspect that the real goal of the Israeli propaganda campaign, which is supported by the United States, is to prepare international opinion for responding to a new Israeli request for international observers to conduct inspections at the front and ensure implementation of the terms of the initiative. Naturally, we will not agree to such a proposal under any circumstances. I also think it is possible that Israel is trying to organise condemnation of Egypt to a degree whereby it will feel itself internationally authorized to carry out a new military operation against us.

Generally speaking, we are in an excellent position militarily and Israel cannot now attack us and cross the canal. We are also prepared for any commando operations against the missile sites. On 7 August we received the new SAM-3 missiles on which Egyptian crews have been training in the Soviet Union. The electronic equipment to jam the Phantom aircraft radars also arrived with the missiles. At the same time, our intelligence information confirms that the Israelis are politically and militarily exhausted. In a statement he made recently inside Israel, Abba Eban said: 'The Israeli air force had begun to deteriorate and this is why we accepted the ceasefire.'

> *The Rogers plan acquired a reputation at the time that other and much better plans never achieved. This was largely because of Nasser's response which had not been expected at either the international or at the Arab level, and partly also because of the reaction of the Arabs who were opposed to the Egyptian leader's move. Most of the Arab countries were afraid that the initiative would obstruct the restoration of the occupied Arab territories and that it would be a direct cause of any failure to regain the rights of the Arab people in Palestine, especially as it was an American move and because Nasser was in a better position than others to know about America's ill intentions towards the Arabs.*
>
> *Nasser himself was not surprised by Arab reactions to the plan, having anticipated such a response since June. However, he always felt that as soon as the Arabs were convinced of his seriousness in preparing for the liberation battle their suspicions would evaporate, and this explains his remarks after the virulent Israeli propaganda campaign had got under way: "You may hate something that is good for you. It is true that the Israeli campaign is irritating us a great deal at the international level, but I consider it the biggest proof to our Arab brothers who have expressed their fears and doubts over my acceptance of the Rogers plan."*
>
> *In a conversation with Dr Labib Shuqair on 18 July concerning the anticipated Arab reaction to the initiative, Nasser made the following comment.*

Nasser: I have no objection to the Palestinian resistance's attack against the initiative, but I believe that when the resistance takes power in Jordan, or in some other place, it will adopt a different position, because at the moment it speaks without responsibility and without considering any other factors. I also know that the Americans, and possibly the Russians, believe that it is better for the Palestinians to shoulder responsibility in order to face reality and act accordingly.

At the same meeting, Nasser explained his evaluation of King Husain's probable action on the initiative.

Nasser: King Husain will not approve the initiative publicly but he will send his approval to the Americans. On the following day, the world press agencies will quote US sources on the king's acceptance of the initiative.

Regarding anticipated Arab reactions against the initiative, in my view matters should not be pushed towards any sort of Arab tension. Arab tension will weaken us and it is in our interest internationally not to enter into a confrontation with any of the Arabs because if this should happen, the world will leave Israel alone and will direct all its political and media activity towards the subject of Arab discord and the benefits it may reap from such disagreement in the future.

It may be of interest here to look briefly at the reactions of the Soviet Union to this important strategic issue. What, for example, was the Soviet response to Nasser when he informed them of the American initiative and what was the effect of the initiative on Egyptian–Soviet relations? We will also note a novel idea by Nasser to settle the problem outside the framework of the American initiative, as well as details of his meeting with the Hungarian leader at the end of August.

As mentioned earlier, there were serious political and strategic considerations behind Nasser's 18-day visit to the Soviet Union. His discussions with the Soviet leaders following presentation of the initiative and its accompanying explanations lasted over four lengthy sessions, and the Russians objected even to the principle of accepting an American plan, telling Nasser that it would have been better for him to have accepted the Soviet plan that they had proposed to him some considerable time before.

Two meetings will serve to illustrate the position of Nasser and the Soviets towards the Rogers plan. The first was the meeting held immediately after his return to Cairo from the Moscow trip.

Nasser's Meeting with the Higher Executive Committee, 20 July 1970

The meeting at which he reported the results of his visit took place in al-Qubbah Palace at seven o'clock on the evening of 18 July 1970. There was an air of expectation as Nasser arrived, smiling and relaxed, and after he had exchanged greetings with his colleagues, discussion began on the sensitive topic of Soviet reactions to the American peace proposal.

Nasser: The Soviets have approved 95 per cent of our requests for new aircraft and missiles, helicopters and trucks, provided that we pay the price of some of these items, such as trucks, with hard currency. The rest will be paid for on soft terms, as usual. [*The Russians customarily requested payment in hard currency for certain items and equipment produced by their plants for civilian consumption, such as vehicles. Military weapons and equipment, such as tanks and aircraft, were paid for according to the old and comfortable agreement.*] I have also been able to get their partial approval for Russian pilots to take part with our Egyptian pilots in air sorties. As for the surface-to-air missiles, they had agreed only one day before my arrival that some of them, along with our missile crews, could be moved to the eastern side of the canal, even though they were not very comfortable with this issue at the first session.

The Russians have also agreed to deliver modern electronic equipment for jamming the Israeli ground radars and the radars with which the Phantom aircraft are equipped. Within a few days, a number of Soviet scientists will arrive to look at the technical aspects that will result from the use of the new equipment on the spot. This means that they have approved nearly 95 per cent of our requests, most of which will be delivered during the current year, 1970.

This is the way the Russians do business. I know that they like to move slowly and to deliver what is requested piece by piece so that they can make the Americans swallow the matter gradually and unsuspectingly in order to avoid stirring up the situation. This is as far as the military aspect is concerned. As for the political aspect, I talked to them very frankly and told them that it would be better for us to approve the American initiative now because it does not in fact contain any new conditions. Moreover we, and the Soviets with us, are at present being exposed to tremendous international pressure on the grounds that we want only war and that it is the Israelis who want the peaceful solution. Therefore, when we approve the initiative, it will be just as if we are answering all aspects of this deliberate campaign. Moreover, the three-month cease-fire provision means the abolition of the 1967 cease-fire resolution which called for an indefinite cease-fire. Consequently, it would be entirely legitimate to resume the fighting in three months' time.

The cease-fire period will also help us to build the new missile sites that we have been trying to construct since December 1969 but without success because of the unrelenting pressure of air attacks. This has meant that our missiles in the frontline area are still in the open instead of being under proper fortified cover to protect them from air raids.

In fact, when I presented the matter to the Russians, they protested and said: "Why are you approving an American plan whereas we had already submitted a peace plan to you that you turned down?" They also said that this would mean that the whole world would say that America was the one working for peace and that, through our approval, we would be giving the United States a prominent international position.

After these statements, there was a long discussion which ended up with my telling them that at the present time, the fact was that we had either to approve or reject the plan and that there was no compromise. We had also to remember that if we rejected the initiative now, we would be giving America a convenient justification for supplying Israel with more modern weapons and aircraft. I thought that from a practical point of view the issue of approval or disapproval would ultimately come to the same thing. However, our approval of the initiative in full view of the world would hedge in the Americans as well as Israel. After hours of discussion, the Russians agreed. But they asked me not to announce my acceptance of an American plan but rather my acceptance of a plan for a peaceful solution. I did not agree with this notion and explained to them why I didn't, bearing in mind that I would be standing in front of the members of the National Congress and in front of the whole Egyptian population on 23 July to inform them of the reasons why we had approved the American initiative. I would of course be obliged to explain the issue at length and in detail in order to persuade all these people. I also talked to the Russians about the American campaign against us, that is intensifying day by day – Nixon followed by Rogers, by Kissinger, by Sisco, by Fulbright and by Mansfield as well as the daily statements by the Israelis about how they're in real danger as a result of the Russian armament in Egypt, and so on. It means that we have to launch a rapid political action to counter them. [*Here Nasser spoke about the position of Syria in relation to the Rogers peace initiative, pointing out that the Americans had not excluded Syria from their plans.*]

Burgess, the US chargé d'affaires in Cairo, asked to see me on the evening of 28 June, which is the night I departed for Moscow, but I did not meet him. So he saw Mahmoud Riyad instead, and informed him that the time was now very favourable for seeking a peaceful solution, that the United States was the only country that could apply pressure on Israel and that he hoped that we would allow the United States the freedom of choosing the most appropriate method. He said that if the opportunity was lost on this occasion, there would be complications in their relations with the entire region and with the Soviet Union as well, and he also added that their plans did not exclude Syria and that it would be sufficient for Syria to declare its acceptance of the Security Council resolution to be included in the settlement issue. As for the matter that we were always raising with regard to the rights of the Palestinians, it would not be difficult to include the Palestinians in the solution processes in one form or another, while on the question of withdrawal from the occupied territories, American opinion concerning this issue was based fundamentally on the principle of non-acquisition of territories by war, as stipulated by the Security Council resolution. This was why they, with Israel, were searching for a suitable formula to achieve this principle in one form or another, with the likelihood of including Israel in the settlement of the situation in Gaza and in Jerusalem. With regard to Jerusalem, they had already proposed that it should remain undivided, provided that both Israel and Jordan would take part in its administration, while on the subject of the West Bank, they believed that slight changes should be made on its borders.

In view of all this information, I believe that I should face the people on 23 July and explain the political situation to them fully, pointing out to them that the Americans are now demanding implementation of the Security Council resolution which we approved in 1967. The Americans are also declaring their disapproval of the annexation of territories by war and aggression. The initiative contains no new provisions or anything that is different from the Security Council resolution that calls for establishing a just and lasting peace. I will then point out that our Charter calls for establishing just and lasting peace in the Middle East, and that this is why I propose that the initiative be approved, without ignoring the issue of the rights of the Palestinian people, provided that implementation of the initiative includes the following points. First there must be withdrawal of the Israeli forces from the territories they occupied in the latest conflagration. Secondly there must be the termination of all calls for and conditions of war, and recognition of the sovereignty, territorial integrity and independence of each of the area's states.

Mahmoud Fawzi: I think that the plan is being presented like propaganda and not in an objective manner. As for the cease-fire, why should we be worried about it as long as we are going to exploit it for our own interest?

Nasser: The cease-fire requires observers and this means that observers will be present. We will have no objection, but only after we have moved our missiles forward.

Mahmoud Fawzi: In which case, our air defence will have reached the canal bank. As a result, the day we have enough missiles and a sufficient number of personnel trained on them, it will become possible to cross the canal.

Nasser: During the period of the initiative, and specifically during the coming month of August, we will be receiving the new SAM-3 missiles with their full equipment and with the crews that have been trained in the Soviet Union.

Mahmoud Fawzi: Then from the military angle, we will benefit and we will be reinforcing our capabilities. Another point I'd like to draw attention to is that our announcement agreeing to the initiative should not convey the impression that we are saying yes and no at the same time. A declaration of this kind will be exploited by the people who want us to reject the initiative, particularly as there is some suspicion internationally, and notably in the United States, that Abdel Nasser is against the American initiative.

Nasser: In fact, I believe that the plan was originally presented in the region mainly for propaganda advantage. But we will surprise them by approving it. I will explain to the people, and to the Arabs in particular, why we are approving it, especially as there are Arab countries that will describe the plan as a 'liquidationist and capitulationist solution'. In my opinion such words will lead to a dead end. What will force them [*the Americans and Israelis*] to reach a positive solution is something else, and that is the degree of Russian participation with our military forces in Egypt. This means that the likelihood of reaching a just and peaceful solution will always correspond to our ability to involve the Russians in the Egyptian front 'to the limit of their commitments' [*these last words being said in English*].

The Russians are now here with us, their missiles are next to ours and their pilots are with ours. Naturally the Russians are not going to accept a military defeat, which is why I believe that our success in making the

Soviet troops participate with us can be considered of much greater value than any military deterrence operation. The Americans are very frightened by this form of Russian presence in the region, and it is for this reason alone that they will be compelled to think seriously about reaching a peaceful solution without giving major concessions or gains to Israel.

Abdel Muhsin Abu al-Nour: There are actually several advantages internationally to approving the initiative, but I believe that we will have to face numerous difficulties at the Arab and domestic levels.

Nasser: We mustn't forget that the three-month period during which the fighting will stop will help us considerably in achieving military control over the canal area, thanks to the large numbers of new missile battalions and to the continued presence of the Russian air defence units in the interior of the country. Even though the Russian units were expected to return home as soon as the Egyptian crews trained in the Soviet Union had arrived here, I asked the Soviets to keep their units in their current positions so that the Egyptian crews can acquire additional missiles and move them secretly to the bank of the canal. They agreed to my request, so we will have twice the number of missile battalions that we possess at present. The Russian units are going to stay with us for a further six months, and since it is not expected that a solution will be reached during the current year, we will be able to replace the engines on the MiG aircraft with new ones.

At the same time, we will be able to show the world that we want peace and that Israel wants expansion. We will offer practical proof of our position by accepting the peace initiative, as we previously accepted the Security Council resolution.

Saad Zayid [*he was not a member of the Supreme Executive Committee but Nasser had asked the Committee to agree to the presence of ministers Shaarawi Gomaa and Saad Zayid because of their status within the ASU*]: Mr President, what will be the position if Israel rejects the American initiative?

Nasser: In this case, it would be easy to pressure America politically, and I believe that it would then be possible to stir up the Arab oil-producing countries to apply such pressure. I clearly remember a recent statement by Moshe Dayan in which he said: "I am ready to carry out any military action against the Arab states, except in two instances; first, in the event of Russian units being present in Egypt and, second, in the case of the United States applying real pressure on us."

Ali Sabri: Mr President, I am afraid that after the initiative has been approved, people in Egypt will begin to feel that we are reluctant to embark on the battle. This is where the role of information comes to the fore. The way things are published domestically will have to be carefully reviewed, and particularly things that are published on the subject of the initiative.

Nasser: First of all I will explain to the people that there is no new solution and that there is no peace initiative, and that what is being presented to us is a procedural plan. I will also explain to them that if we reject this plan, we will be faced with enormous military aid being given to Israel. By and large, our approval of the initiative will be a major information coup. A detailed analysis of our political movement will appear in *Al-Ahram* and will point out that the submitted plan contains nothing new.

With regard to press reports, I also feel that it would not be proper to publish details of what we have acquired from the Soviet Union and that it will be enough to note in general terms that we have received everything we requested, bearing in mind that eleven Soviet ships are going to arrive next month loaded with Egyptian troops trained on the new missiles and accompanied by all their missiles and equipment. The Russians have asked for them to be unloaded at night but I think that it would be better for us to unload them during the day so that people can see them.

Labib Shuqair: What will the situation be as far as the Palestinians are concerned?

Nasser: Our acceptance of this plan does not in any way mean concessions where the occupied territories are concerned or any undermining of the rights of the Palestinians. There will not be any backing down from our previous positions and principles. There's nothing more to it other than that as long as there is a peace attempt, then we are peaceful.

Nasser's Meeting with the President of Hungary, 29 August 1970

The second meeting that illustrates the position of Nasser and the reaction of the Soviets to the Rogers plan took place between the Egyptian leader and one of the Warsaw Pact leaders. There is no doubt that Nasser's approval of the American initiative cast a certain cloud over Egyptian–Soviet relations and caused some apprehension in dealings between the two countries in spite of the public statements made by both sides and despite Nasser's prolonged stay in Moscow prior to the announcement of his approval of the initiative. Political observers raised doubts and spread rumours about the deterioration of relations between Nasser and the Soviets, and indeed between Nasser and the entire Eastern bloc, which was why the visit of Comrade Losonczi, President of Hungary and an influential Eastern bloc leader, was rather a slap in the face for the rumour-mongers. The timing of the visit was significant, coming as it did shortly after implementation of the peace plan had got under way, and furthermore the guest was accompanied by a large delegation of members of the Hungarian Communist Party and government officials.

The meeting was held at al-Qubbah Palace on 29 August 1970 and the dialogue between the two leaders was relaxed and friendly.

Nasser: I welcome you and hope you will regard our country as your own. In the name of the Egyptian people, I express our deep appreciation for the support given to us by the people and the government of Hungary since 1967, and our sincere gratitude to the Hungarian Communist Party which declared its solidarity and support for our struggle and for our rights.

Losonczi: Our friendship towards you is based on resolute common principles, and has stood firm since 1956 when the imperialist forces attacked both our countries. I and my colleagues will not forget the popular reception accorded us by the people of Cairo and we will try to convey its warmth to our people and our political leaderships in Hungary [*on arrival the Hungarians had been given a lively popular welcome, in addition to an official reception organized according to the now well-established formula for receiving heads of state and delegations from Arab, socialist and other friendly countries*].

Nasser: I believe that we should begin our review of the political issues by looking at the current Middle East situation, on the grounds that this directly affects most of the other political questions. We will then look at the situation in Africa and discuss bilateral relations between our two countries at all levels, although I believe that they are proceeding normally and that there are no problems or troubles between us. [*The guest president approved this agenda, asking Nasser to begin with the Middle East issue.*]

Nasser: On the problem of the Middle East situation or, to put it more precisely, the problem of Israeli aggression against the Arabs, we cannot exclude the United States from this aggression because it supplied Israel with weapons, aircraft and bombs, and gave it the latest equipment before the invasion took place. The United States has also supplied the Israeli forces with the latest sophisticated electronic equipment, such as equipment for electronic reconnaissance and for electronic jamming. The United States has continued supplying Israel with the latest equipment since the aggression, including a new consignment of electronic equipment that was delivered to Israel in recent months.

Israel has always sought expansion and has not concealed its ambitions to acquire more Arab territories. When the Security Council resolution was issued after the 1967 invasion, Israel refused to implement it and to withdraw from the territories it had captured. Mr Jarring, the UN secretary-general's representative in the region, went on roving around the region quite pointlessly for a year and a half.

For the sake of history, we have with the help of the Soviet Union been able to rebuild our armed forces, to stand fast and not to capitulate. Israel now wants direct negotiations with us while it is occupying our lands. This kind of negotiation, with the enemy forces still on our land, is considered some kind of surrender. At the same time, America every now and then makes statements reflecting the Israeli viewpoint. The United States is constantly declaring that it will guarantee Israel's military superiority over its Arab neighbours so that Israel will always be able to occupy Arab lands. Even over the last few months America has been focusing once again on the need for maintaining Israeli superiority in the region, which is why it has supplied Israel since 1967 with 50 Phantom aircraft and 100 Skyhawk aircraft, not to mention large numbers of tanks and modern weapons.

Israel constantly demands the implementation of the cease-fire called for by the Security Council resolution of 1967, whereas it ignores the withdrawal which the resolution called for at the same time. We felt that the situation was getting more complicated because suspending Jarring's mission and effecting a cease-fire were tantamount to nothing more than an entrenchment of the position that Israel wants and that best serves imperialist interests. The arms race between ourselves and Israel has been going on since 1967. The border attacks and the air battles, in which Israel applied lessons learnt from the American experience in Vietnam and used electronic techniques to jam our radar equipment and confuse our missiles, have also continued. The air war between us at that time was unequal because, unlike the Israeli pilots, our pilots were effectively going into the fights blindfolded as a result of the jamming operations. But now that we are able to carry out jamming operations with Soviet electronic equipment, the situation has changed. In the first attack in which we used this equipment, the Israeli aircraft fled as soon as our aircraft appeared.

The Western press has recently said that had it not been for the cease-fire in compliance with the Rogers plan, the region would have been seeing an electronic battle unparalleled in any other war before. We have also captured one of the latest American electronic systems that was installed in one of the Phantoms that we shot down four days before the cease-fire.

Brother and friend, I have told you all these details to make clear to you America's position and its alignment with Israel. Despite this, I sent an appeal to President Nixon on May Day this year and he answered it with the recent Rogers plan.

Israel has always rejected the word 'withdrawal' and has instead repeated the phrase of "secure and recognized borders" to every political figure that has visited it. Such personages find such phrases proper and reasonable but if they examined a little more deeply what these phrases meant and if they followed up the statements and ambitions of Israeli officialdom, they would find that by these phrases Israel means expansion in the Arab land.

When the Rogers plan was submitted to us as a new attempt to implement the Security Council resolution and its provision on withdrawal from the Arab territories, we accepted the plan on this basis. The information available to us indicated that Israel did not agree to the plan and that America itself had put it forward for the purpose of local consumption and for propaganda, thinking that we would not endorse it. So our approval has been a major surprise.

Our acceptance of this plan underlines our eagerness for a just peace in the region. However, Israel is still obstructing progress on implementing the various phases of this peace. Generally speaking, we will wait out the ninety-day period called for by the plan [*the plan stipulated that the three-month cease-fire would last from 4 August to 3 November 1970*] without violating the conditions and provisions of the plan, even though I am confident that Israel will ultimately demand that its borders are expanded to include Gaza, Jerusalem, Hebron, Bethlehem and other West Bank towns. This is why we are not optimistic and why we will work during the ceasefire period more seriously than ever to prepare for the future and for events during the coming period.

Where Arab reactions to this plan are concerned, most of the Arab countries have rejected it, as they previously rejected the Security Council resolution. The Palestinian resistance has also opposed it because implementing the plan means dismantling the resistance and raises big questions with regard to its fate and future. This is where the People's Republic of China entered as a new element in the picture when it contacted the resistance and supplied it with a limited quantity of weapons and ammunition. The PRC is also trying to persuade the resistance on the political front by telling it that a secret agreement has been concluded by the United States and the Soviet Union to divide the world, including the Arab region, between them. Regrettably, such words are meeting with a response from some Palestinian leaderships. With this meagre outlay, China can realise its goals in the region through these elements in the Palestinian resistance.

In the Arab East, there is a big dispute between King Husain and the Palestinian resistance, and this clash has reached the borderline of a struggle for power. This is why the problems and crises between them are continuing and escalating. Unfortunately, a degree of dissent has recently cropped up between the UAR and the resistance but we are on the way to clearing up and ending this disagreement altogether.

This, briefly, is the political and military situation of the Middle East question.

Losonczi: I thank you for this political explanation. I would also like to tell you our view on the subject of the Middle East. We in Hungary considered Israel's aggression against you was an aggression against all the progressive countries. There is no doubt that Israel cannot achieve superiority over its Arab neighbours by itself. But things changed as a result of American support which is based on the interests of Washington. This is why we adopted a definite position towards the aggression, why we severed our relations with Israel as an aggressor state and why we fully denounced the aggression and completely supported the Arab peoples' struggle, declaring this support both at home and abroad.

We understand that America had hoped for the downfall of the progressive Arab regimes in the wake of the battle. But the days following the battle proved that these regimes did not and will not fall. We in Hungary were certain of this, especially with regard to the UAR with its stature and its history of struggle.

We believe that the problem now, after three years of steadfastness, has reached a point which makes it necessary to change the method of operation, but on one fundamental condition which is guaranteeing withdrawal from the Arab territories without the use of the phrases of 'secure borders' and 'recognized borders' because such phrases have twisted meanings. In addition there must be the condition of repatriating the Palestinian refugees and finding a just solution for the Palestinian people.

Regrettably, America understands the balance of powers in the Middle

East on the basis of the concept of balance in favour of Israel whereas there should be a real balance in the region. American intelligence has become aware that the UAR is stronger than it used to be in 1967 which is why, and as a result of your position of steadfastness and struggle, America has been compelled to present the Rogers plan. We also believe that acceptance of the Rogers plan by all the parties concerned means acceptance of the UAR's view, in other words working to implement the Security Council resolution in full.

As for the general Arab situation, we are aware that Jordan, Sudan and Libya are the only countries supporting you on the issue of the plan. However, we are confident that the number of your supporters will increase day by day. As for the Palestinian resistance, we know that there are foreign forces that are in contact with some of its leaderships, and we also suspect that the US Central Intelligence Agency, in addition to the PRC, is playing an important role inside the resistance organisations. This Arab position does not help unity of the Arab ranks in the face of your enemy. Moreover, it is a position that greatly satisfies the United States.

Nasser: What do you suggest should be issued about our meeting in terms of information?

Losonczi: I propose that we issue a joint communiqué pointing out our mutual political positions, including the support for the Arab peoples and the people of Indochina.

I will now turn to explaining our political position on other issues. In Africa, we support the struggle of the African peoples to achieve their rights. We also try as much as we can to support them materially. We have nearly 500 experts in the African countries, and we also set aside large numbers of places in our universities for African students.

From your private conversation with me during dinner last night about your policy in Africa, I find no big differences in our points of view on most African issues. I hope that we will continue to exchange views on these issues. We are also confident that all the African countries will soon triumph in their struggle and will live as progressive independent states.

Nasser [*smilingly*]: I'm afraid we have taken up all your time with our problems in the Middle East and Africa and that we have not heard anything about conditions in Hungary.

Losonczi: We are living in entirely stable conditions. The Hungarians are making serious efforts to implement the five-year plan which will end this year. We have been able to increase the national income by 40 per cent.

Industry and agriculture have also realized most of their objectives. At present we are preparing the ground for beginning the new five-year plan which will increase the national income by 43 per cent. This plan also seeks to absorb all the unemployed. It also offers numerous facilities to the peasants and will increase individual incomes by 28 per cent.

We are now busy organizing the general congress of the Hungarian Workers Party which will be held in two months' time, in November. Our policy in the various spheres will be submitted to this congress.

Mr President, you have not visited Hungary so far, even though you have visited numerous other countries. This is why I hope that you will accept an invitation in my name and in the name of the party and of the government to visit Hungary at the earliest possible opportunity.

Nasser: I am delighted to accept this invitation but I hope you will allow me to postpone the date until the Israelis have left our territory. We are currently compelled to exert enormous efforts centrally because of our desire not to allow any negligence to occur at the domestic or foreign levels during this decisive period of our history.

Losonczi: There remains only one thing for us to discuss, which is the bilateral relationship between our two countries. In this sphere, we are prepared to proceed to develop and enhance the relations to the utmost because we consider the UAR a long-standing friend of the Hungarian People's Republic. This is why we are determined to support your struggle and the struggle of your people with all the resources we possess. I have forgotten to inform you during my review of the general political situation that we in Hungary will support fully the forthcoming conference of the non-aligned countries. In conclusion, I repeat my thanks and the thanks of my colleagues to you and to the people of the UAR for the official and popular welcome we have received in your country.

Chapter 11

CLOSING SESSIONS
End of an era

*Having faced his Russian allies during his visit to Moscow in July 1970,
Nasser had next to confront his own people and to present them with the new
political course that the decision to accept the Rogers plan would necessitate.
Although Nasser had consented to the American initiative as a tactical step,
it was not going to be easy for the ordinary Egyptian to distinguish between
tactical and strategic moves. Furthermore, the country had followed a steady
course for three years and would now have to deal with a complete change
of direction. Nasser prepared anxiously and punctiliously to face 1,600
members and other young people of the Arab Socialist Union leadership at
the approaching meeting on 23 July, asking many questions about the sort of
reactions to the announcement of the initiative that could be anticipated,
and on the day he was to make the major address, I could see him reviewing
his speech and selecting words and phrases with a degree of care that I had
never seen with his previous popular speeches.*

*Psychologically, these were difficult and unsettled days for Nasser and those
who were close to him were also anxious, and very concerned about the
precarious state of his health. We were all glad to learn that he had finally
agreed to take the advice of both the Egyptian and the Soviet physicians who
had been treating him and, after the speech scheduled for 26 July in
Alexandria, to give himself a two-month holiday in order to regain his
health. The following year was to be the year of the crossing of the canal, and
he would need all his strength. But he could not shake off his responsibilities.
Arab opposition to the approval of the Rogers initiative was growing, and
King Husain, with serious problems and dilemmas of his own, interrupted
Nasser's holiday to seek the Egyptian leader's assistance. The events which
flared up in Jordan on 16 September and the strain of trying to bring about*

a peace agreement were to contribute two weeks later, on 28 September 1970, to his untimely death.

That last meeting between King Husain and Abdel Nasser was of considerable importance, and political observers agree that it cannot be separated from the ugly events of 'Black September' that followed it in Jordan. However, there are conflicting opinions on the words spoken and the issues raised at the meeting: some people view them as a declaration and a warning from King Husain to Abdel Nasser, and others consider them as a warning to and an exposure of King Husain. Certainly many of the Arabs felt that Nasser had not protested sufficiently to prevent King Husain from carrying out his plans.

Nasser's Meeting with King Husain, 21 August 1970

The meeting was held in the main conference room in Ras el-Teen Palace in Alexandria on 21 August 1970, and lasted for three and a half hours. Nasser started the discussion by welcoming the guest on behalf of the Egyptian people, and expressing appreciation for the king's constant efforts to come to Egypt for consultation and for exchange of opinions.

Nasser: We in the United Arab Republic will not forget Jordan's stand in June 1967 when you came into the war with us, even though at the time I did not want to involve the Jordanian army in the conflict. Had circumstances permitted I would have refused the participation of your forces in the operation as I did in 1956. Certainly we will not forget this move on your part and we are fully aware of it in Egypt. Jordan took part in the war for our sake, as we took part in it for Syria's sake. Essentially, therefore, Jordan entered the battle for the sake of Syria, but it seems to me that our brothers in Syria have now forgotten about this. However, we declare that our people in Egypt will not forget what the Jordanian people suffered for their sake.

King Husain: We entered the 1967 war simply to fulfil our duty and to fulfil what our responsibility as Arabs dictates to us. We in Jordan appreciate your leadership and your patriotic stance which genuinely reflect the feelings of every true Arab. It is important now to do our utmost to develop our mutual trust. I will put our political and military problems to you so that we can reach the correct solution together.

Abdel Monem al-Rifai [*Jordanian minister of foreign affairs. It was evident* *from King Husain's signal to Abdel Monem al-Rifai to join in the discussion and to ask his prepared questions that there had obviously been a prior agreement between them to open the dialogue in this manner*]: We in Jordan lack a clear vision as to the present situation. Even though we have advanced some way, we still have some questions on which we need a certain amount of clarification. Has a political agreement been reached recently by the USSR and the United States? Does the Soviet Union have any idea about how to solve the problem? In light of the answers to these two questions I believe that we, as Arabs, can determine our future political moves since it is obvious to us from the policy and the positions of the United States, the Soviet Union and indeed all the major powers that they are not serious about reaching a political solution even though it is a month since we announced our approval of the Rogers plan. This is why we in Jordan recently closed down our information line about the initiative. It is also obvious that the problem is not influenced by our wishes only and that it is subject to so many other forces that we have become unable to define our Arab policy.

Nasser: The issue is of course very complex and is not easy to solve. However, the root of the problem is the fact that there is Israeli military superiority and at the same time there is Arab division. For example, if we calculate the size and the strength of the Arab armies, we find that we are superior to Israel. But we are several armies and several commands whereas they are a single army and a single command, in addition to the fact that there are those among us who do not want to contribute to or participate positively in the battle on the pretext that Palestine is the responsibility of the Palestinians alone. Generally, our strategic plan in Egypt at present is to exert efforts to remove the enemy from our lands and to liberate the occupied Arab territories and not to give up a single inch of this territory, including Jerusalem. Our plan is also to work for implementation of the Security Council resolutions concerning Palestine. Where military preparation is concerned, we are working to build up our forces so that they will reach one million fighting men. In fact our forces will number three-quarters of a million servicemen by December. Crossing the canal and liberating Sinai is not only our goal but also our duty.

As for political action, some have attacked my latest political move, asking how they can accept the existence of Israel? We should bear in mind the fact that we Arabs accepted the existence of Israel in the 1949 treaty. I told you [*addressing King Husain*] earlier to go to America and to appeal to Johnson to return the West Bank to you, but America ignored you because it was busy with something more important, specifically the wish of its ally Israel to annex more Arab lands.

It is my opinion that the peaceful solution is still very far from succeeding. The Americans are liars. However, we accepted the latest political initiative for one major reason, which was to complete our military preparations and to finalise the arrangements necessary for our military plan because ultimately we will fight. The Supreme Executive Committee of the Arab Socialist Union, then the Central Committee and then the National Congress all approved this initiative after lengthy debate and with complete confidence. Naturally, my faith in the United States is weak but it is likely, even if only by half a per cent, that there is an international game that may influence the solving of the problem in our favour. As for brother Abdel Monem al-Rifai's question regarding the likelihood of the existence of an agreement between the Soviet Union and the United States on our problem, the answer is no. There is no such agreement. We also record with the greatest appreciation the aid that the Russians have given us, as well as their positive military participation with us. We have decided in Egypt that once we have surmounted this crisis, we will erect a monument to the Soviet people to commemorate their help and their open backing for us.

Regarding brother al-Rifai's second question as to whether the Soviets envisage any way of solving the problem, the answer is that they are now proceeding on the basis of their dialogue with us and after we have endorsed every move. What is more, the Russians reject what we reject and approve what we approve.

As for the final question, namely: Is there a solution on which we have agreed with the Soviets? The answer is also no. We may agree with them on the importance of the peaceful solution but each of us views this solution from his own angle. We believe that the peaceful solution is very remote, that we have to stand fast more and more firmly and that the Americans must feel that they do not have a completely free hand as far as the Arab position is concerned. As for the liberation of Palestine, I do not believe that it will be done in six days or even in six years! Who will do the liberating from the river to the sea and how many years will it take? These are things that must be explained to our people with complete honesty. I believe that we now have a duty to remove the aggressor from our land and to regain the Arab territory occupied by the Israelis. We can then engage in a clandestine struggle to liberate the land of Palestine, to liberate Haifa and Jaffa.

Nasser then spoke about the Palestinian resistance movement and about the difficulties and the dissenting voices with which it had to contend.

On the subject of the position of the Palestinian resistance, I have met the resistance leaders and have informed them that they are free to reject the Rogers plan and to reject the peaceful solution even if these are approved by all the Arab countries, since as Palestinians it is their right to do so. As for the Voice of Palestine radio station, it was not my intention originally to shut it down in spite of their daily radio attacks against us, particularly from Cairo radio. What happened is that we intercepted a cable sent from their headquarters to their branch in Cairo asking the branch to escalate their condemnation of us from Cairo radio and to intensify their insults and vituperation against us, assuming that we would be afraid to confront them. Of course this was a faulty view of our attitude and a miscalculation on their part. I will again say that it is their right to reject the initiative and to reject any peaceful move, and this is why I appeal to King Husain not to attack them or to do anything against them. I also hope that he will prevent certain Jordanian officials from acting too vigorously against the Palestinian organizations, because the only one to benefit from such a situation will be the enemy, Israel.

Your Majesty, I hope that you will be patient with them, even if they go astray, for the sake of your people and the sake of the Palestinian people. Do not forget that the Prophet Job lived by the River Jordan. This is why I believe that you will be able to settle matters with them wisely and sensibly, in spite of the presence of various radical Palestinians, because at the same time, there are many well-balanced people among them. Generally speaking, I hope you will always consult on this matter because I consider it an Arab issue at the present time. You must also select Jordanian leaders who enjoy the confidence of the Palestinians, such as Dr Nabulsi. We must continue the dialogue on this question and refrain from becoming emotional and from taking the wrong steps. I will always be ready to receive any envoy you send to consult with him on resistance issues. Brother Faruq Abu-Isa, from the Sudanese revolution [*the Sudanese Revolutionary Command Council*], told me that he met the Central Committee of Hawatmah's faction and that their discussion with him was reasonable and constructive. My final recommendation on this issue is that you approach it through political action and not through police action. This does not mean that you desist from taking a negative stance towards the bad or opportunistic Palestinian elements, but it does mean that you will have to embark on a vast political movement. I am sorry that I have talked to you about your domestic affairs. But I have done so because any upsets in your country will cause numerous reactions on our front.

King Husain: Speaking of the patience of Job, this has been the hallmark of our policy for a long time. But patience definitely has its limits. The presence of all the Palestinian resistance organizations on our territory has shifted all the conflicts in the Arab world to our country. Moreover, peddling the slogan of "from the river to the sea" is a contentious act, the aim of which is to demolish whatever Arab resources remain to us for the liberation of our lands. The action against us by members of the [*Palestinian*] resistance is escalating daily and these elements are trying to sow doubt and confusion in our ranks and even inside the armed forces. But thank God, the military units remain unaffected so far. The provocations committed by the resistance members against the Jordanian government are endless. If your time permits, I can tell you many anecdotes about the insults to which our local authorities in the cities and villages are exposed every day. Just one example – the vehicles of the resistance drive in the cities without carrying any identification marks so that it is impossible for the local authorities to carry out proper procedures when there is an accident or when some innocent civilian is killed or injured. Another incident recently involved some resistance members who fired their sub-machine-guns in a bakery in Amman because the owner refused to give them priority when distributing bread.

Nasser: I have already spoken a great deal to the resistance leaderships about having to refrain from engaging in provocative acts against the Jordanian authorities. In fact, they are aware of the effects and consequences of such provocation. Unfortunately, however, there are some of them who actually want the provocation, and there may also be certain hostile forces among them that plan intentionally to sabotage the political situation in Jordan. Generally, these matters can be discussed again without our having to become too agitated, provided that the interests of all the parties are taken into consideration. Before the session ends, I beg to repeat what I have asked for in my discussion with you today, namely that you will use patience and wisdom. I am confident that after our patience and our determined and strenuous efforts for three successive years, God will ultimately give us victory in our battle against Israel. I also believe that the Arab situation is improving daily. We are ready for greater military coordination with you, and I have given Lieutenant General Fawzi all the necessary instructions to carry out this coordination straight away and to the extent that you request.

The session ended at this point, but it was evident from Nasser's words and from his personal approach to King Husain both before and after the meeting that he was afraid that the Jordanian authorities would engage in retaliatory acts against the Palestinian organizations based in Jordan. Using both gentle and stern words, Nasser tried to prevent confrontation with the Palestinians, but events had gone too far.

Black September: Confrontation between the Jordanian Army and the Palestinians

Less than three weeks after this meeting events erupted in Jordan. The history of these events dates back to February 1970 when differences between the Palestinian resistance and the Jordanian authorities first began to surface. Nasser intervened, using his influence to prevent King Husain from retaliating against the Palestinians, but the situation flared up again in June 1970 when the two sides clashed. Hundreds of people were killed or wounded and the fighting only died down after a meeting between King Husain and Yasser Arafat. But tensions remained high.

Almost two weeks after King Husain had met Nasser in Alexandria on 21 August, the situation deteriorated again. The king felt that his conscience was clear since he had informed Nasser that he intended to act according to circumstances. The king and his advisers insisted on total control of their territory, arguing that offering hospitality to the resistance fighters did not give the latter the right to take part in government or to exercise powers beyond those of the Jordanian government, such as the right to carry weapons on the streets of Jordanian cities away from the border areas.

Following an emergency meeting to discuss the volatile situation in Jordan, the Arab League set up a special committee which went to Amman on 7 September, but in spite of the committee's efforts, the situation suddenly worsened, and on 16 September King Husain declared martial law, appointing Maj Gen Muhammad Dawud to head a military cabinet. The following day, 17 September, Bedouin forces launched a brutal attack against the Palestinian camps and training centres, destroying everything in their path and pursuing all those closely or even remotely affiliated with the Palestinian resistance, and as the conflict moved from Amman to northern Jordan, thousands were killed or wounded in what has been described as one of the worst massacres in Arab history.

Nasser was deeply grieved by the reports he was receiving from the Egyptian embassy in Amman and, to begin with, wanted to go personally to Jordan in the hope of stopping the killing but because of the tense situation with Israel, the chief of staff Lt Gen Muhammad Sadiq was sent on his behalf to Amman to ask King Husain to stop the onslaught and to explain the dangers of wiping out the Palestinian resistance, pointing out that this would serve the American–Israeli plan in the region. But Sadiq's efforts were in vain and the fighting continued. Eventually Nasser felt the only solution would be to invite the Arab kings and presidents to come straight away to Cairo for consultation.

The Last Week of September

The last week of September 1970 was one of events and emotions. These can best be presented in outline to give some idea of Nasser's final acts and of developments in the Arab sphere.

Sunday, 20 September:

– The Jordanian army continued its shooting.
– The situation became critical for the Palestinian resistance in Amman because of the concentrated shelling of areas where Palestinians were concentrated.
– Thousands of Palestinians were killed.
– Yasser Arafat appealed to the Palestinian resistance fighters to stop shooting.
– There were telephone contacts between Nasser and Muammar Qadhafi on the serious situation in Amman.
– Nasser sent a message with Husain al-Shafei to King Faisal, asking the king to come to Cairo quickly to discuss the situation.
– Two cables were sent by Nasser asking King Husain to stop the attacks on the Palestinians.

Monday, 21 September:

– After receiving Nasser's messages, King Husain ordered a cease-fire, giving his orders from his office in his palace in front of Lt Gen Sadiq and the Egyptian ambassador in Jordan (Othman Nuri).
– The situation in Amman, both in human and material terms, was extremely painful, especially as the spectre of US collusion with Israel gradually began to become clearer.
– There was extensive destruction in Amman, with black smoke rising from its damaged buildings.

– The battles began to spread into northern Jordan, and King Husain again accused Syria of allowing its forces to enter the northern part of his country.

– From six o'clock in the evening, the presidents began to arrive in Cairo in response to Nasser's appeal. The first to arrive was Muammar Qadhafi, followed by Nur-al-Din al-Atasi, and then al-Bahi al-Adgham (the Tunisian prime minister on behalf of President Bourguiba). President Jaafar Numairi arrived at midnight. As soon as these presidents had arrived, meetings began between them and Nasser, continuing until long after midnight.

Tuesday, 22 September:

– Yasser Arafat estimated the victims under the debris of Amman at some 20,000 people killed or wounded.

– On the sixth day of the fighting the picture in Amman was grim. The fighting in northern Jordan entered a critical stage.

– The meetings between Nasser and the Arab presidents at al-Qubbah Palace went on all day long. More leaders arrived in Cairo – Amir Sabah al-Salim al-Sabah, President Charles Hilu, President Salim Rubayyi [South Yemen] and Judge Abdel-Rahman al-Iryani [North Yemen] – and joined in the meetings.

– The meetings were interspersed by telephone calls to King Husain from Nasser and several of the conferring presidents.

– It was decided that a delegation representing the Cairo meeting would go to Amman, headed by President Numairi and including al-Bahi al-Adgham, Shaikh Saad al-Abdallah al-Salim and Lt Gen Muhammad Sadiq, and that the delegation would approach both King Husain and Yasser Arafat to put an end to the fighting.

– Nasser's meetings and contacts with the Arab leaders and his communications with Amman continued until early the following morning.

Wednesday, 23 September:

– There were furious tank battles around Irbid in which the air force also took part. President al-Atasi raised the possibility of the Syrian forces taking part in the action in northern Jordan.

– President Nixon discussed the development of events in Jordan with the US congressional leaders. The United States placed nearly 10,000 troops on alert to intervene in Jordan. (Nixon later wrote in his memoirs that the United States had come closer then than at any other time to military intervention in the Middle East.)

– The Soviet Union warned Washington not to interfere in events in Jordan.

– Numairi and his delegation returned to Cairo from Amman without having reached a decisive solution.

– King Faisal arrived in Cairo and joined the Arab meeting at the Hilton Hotel where Numairi reported the results of his mission to the assembled Arab kings and presidents. This meeting continued until two o'clock the next morning.

Thursday, 24 September:

– In spite of the assertions made by the Jordanian government on ending the fighting, shelling continued in Amman, and Irbid was threatened by another massacre.

– Maj Gen Muhammad Dawud, head of the Jordanian military government, who was in Cairo, resigned after his daughter had convinced him that it was not right for him to let himself be used to wipe out the Palestinians.

– King Husain met the US ambassador, and the American Sixth Fleet, based in the Mediterranean, declared a state of maximum alert.

– Sulaiman Franjieh, the new Lebanese president, arrived in Cairo to participate in the Arab meeting.

– The conference decided that the situation was grave and sent President Numairi to Amman a second time, accompanied by a large delegation that included Husain al-Shafei, Rashad Faraon [King Faisal's adviser] and Saad al-Abdallah al-Sabah representing their heads of state. Faruq Abu-Isa, al-Bahi al-Adgham and Lt Gen Muhammad Sadiq also went with them.

– Bilateral meetings between Nasser and the kings and presidents went on until two o'clock on Friday morning.

Friday, 25 September:

– The delegation returned from Amman having negotiated a cease-fire agreement which in the event lasted no more than a few hours.

– Yasser Arafat, disguised as a Kuwaiti citizen, arrived in Cairo with the members of Numairi's delegation.

– Numairi and Arafat presented an evaluation of the grave situation that was worsening by the minute to the kings and presidents, in a meeting that continued until four o'clock in the morning of Saturday.

– Nasser explained to the participants in the conference that he had become convinced that events in Jordan were the result of planning by the

CIA and Israeli intelligence, with the help of certain suspect local elements, and informed them that the American Sixth Fleet and Israeli forces were in fact ready to intervene at once.

– At half past four on Saturday morning Nasser sent an urgent message to King Husain informing him of the American–Israeli plan and declaring that the continuation of the Jordanian attack on the Palestinians would be regarded as actual participation in that plan and that he would be held responsible for the consequences.

Before the cable was sent Nasser discussed its content with the kings and presidents, some of whom – especially Qadhafi – thought it was wrong to even contact King Husain because of his attitude towards the Palestinian issue. But Nasser, who was visibly shaken every time I read him the cables describing the horrifying events that arrived regularly from our embassy in Amman, insisted that positive action was needed to stop the fighting instead of prolonging the discussions and debates in the comfort of the air-conditioned Hilton Hotel. When one of the Arab leaders suggested that Nasser should send Egyptian forces, along with other Arab forces, to occupy Jordan, he replied: "I sent our forces to Yemen, where we lost more than 10,000 men, and Israel is still occupying our lands. I am not prepared for a single Egyptian soldier to die on Jordanian soil. Anyone who wants to send his forces there is welcome to do so." After a long discussion between the Arab kings and presidents, Nasser asked me to send an urgent cable in their name to King Husain demanding that the shooting should stop immediately and that the Palestinians should be protected.

Saturday, 26 September:

– The fighting in Amman entered its tenth day.
– The fighting in northern Jordan continued although the Palestinian resistance fighters controlled most of the towns there.
– Nixon announced that Jordan would be compensated for its losses in the fighting against the Palestinian resistance, confirming that Jordan was to be given five million dollars in emergency aid.
– The Arab kings and presidents drew up a resolution holding King Husain responsible for the bloody events that were taking place in Jordan.
– At an international press conference in Cairo, President Numairi reported on the meetings and the consultations he had had in Jordan and announced the decision of the Arab kings and presidents to hold King Husain responsible and to inform the Arab masses of this fact.
– King Husain contacted Nasser at midday to inform him that he wished

to come to Cairo to explain his position to the Arab kings and presidents. Nasser delayed his reply until he had discussed the King's request with his fellow leaders.

– At six o'clock in the evening, King Husain contacted Nasser again for the same purpose.

– Heated discussions lasting more than four hours took place between the Arab kings and presidents on the question of calling King Husain to Cairo. Qadhafi led the faction which refused to invite the King, considering him personally responsible for the blood bath in Amman. Nasser, heading the other group, meanwhile pointed to his watch saying that while the minutes were passing and while the leaders were failing to reach a positive decision, the numbers of innocent victims continued to increase. Given that it was impossible to send Arab forces to invade Jordan and stop the fighting, the only solution was to call King Husain to Cairo and actually to compel him, in their presence, to bring the conflict to an end. Shortly after midnight, a resolution was issued by the Arab kings and presidents approving King Husain's request to come to Cairo and confirming that they would hold a major meeting on the following morning that would be attended by King Husain and Yasser Arafat.

Sunday, 27 September:

– King Husain arrived at Cairo airport at eleven o'clock in the morning and was met by Abdel Nasser, even though Qadhafi had objected to the president going to receive him at the airport. However, Nasser received him personally, according to the customary traditions of hospitality.

– Having requested at the outset that the meeting should be confined to kings and presidents only and that other representatives and crown princes should be excluded, the Arab kings and presidents met King Husain and Yasser Arafat at one o'clock in the afternoon. Nasser asked that I should be allowed to stay in order to follow up on the discussions and the resolutions that would be issued.

– Discussion was heated and King Husain had to listen to some embarrassing remarks, especially from Yasser Arafat. King Faisal attempted to calm things down, and asked that the guns that the two men carried should be given to me for safe keeping, so that the shooting would not be transferred from Jordan to the Hilton Hotel.

– After more than five hours of discussion it was agreed, first, that the fighting on all fronts was to be stopped immediately, and secondly that the Jordanian army and the resistance fighters were to be withdrawn from all the cities before sunset of the same day. Thirdly, a committee headed by al-Bahi al-Adgham, the Tunisian president's representative, would go to Jordan the following day (Monday, 28 September) to oversee implementation of the agreement.

– An open session, attended by all the leaders, was held at nine o'clock that evening, and representatives of the international and local press and broadcasting stations were also invited to be present at the signing of the agreement by all the kings and presidents, including King Husain and Yasser Arafat. When Nasser came out of the conference room he was obviously delighted and chatted cheerfully to some of his fellow leaders before going up to his suite on the 13th floor of the hotel. He spent almost an hour with members of the Egyptian delegation, exchanging notes with his colleagues Anwar al-Sadat, Husain al-Shafei and Ali Sabri. He and Muhammad Hassanein Heikal, the minister of information, also drew up a news report for the agreement, after which he sat next to the Zenith [Russian-made] radio that accompanied him all the time and tried to hear what the world broadcasting stations were saying about events in Jordan following the signing of the agreement.

Before leaving his suite, Nasser went out on to the balcony and looked at the Nile flowing silently below, the lights of Cairo and Giza reflected in the black water. Standing next to him, I could see that he was contented, and proud of the beautiful city. He looked at me and said: "This is the first time in my life that I have seen this marvellous view. Compared to this place, a person in Manshiyat al-Bakri [where he lived in a modest house] is not alive. Is it fair, Abdel Magid, that I should not have seen Cairo's beauty until tonight?" He spoke gently, and with a smile, but I knew that he must have been totally exhausted. By pushing the other Arab leaders into taking positive action, Nasser had succeeded in stopping the bloodshed in Jordan, and in doing so had prevented the Americans and the Israelis from intervening directly in the matter in the way that they managed to do in Lebanon some years later. He had also pushed himself to the limits of endurance and beyond.

He talked to me when I was the only Egyptian with him during the closed session with the kings and presidents. He talked to me during the recesses which he requested every couple of hours so that he could walk about for a few minutes and ease the severe pain in his legs caused by long hours of sitting still. From what he said, I felt that he was blaming himself for the way the state of affairs in Jordan had come about. He said: "If it hadn't been for the defeat in 1967, what has happened in Amman and

Jordan would not have happened and were it not for that defeat, thousands of innocent people and children would not have been killed." I tried to play down the events, to change the subject, to deny that he was in any way personally responsible, but he remained much troubled by his conscience.

Before he left the hotel that evening to see Qadhafi off at the airport he shook hands with the hotel management and staff, thanking them for the services that they had performed for Egypt's guests during the days of the conference.

Nasser went straight from the airport to his office in Manshiyat al-Bakri where he stayed until the call for dawn prayers in order to work on the financial and administrative arrangements for the new committee that would monitor the situation in Jordan. Shortly before midnight Khaled Abdel Nasser, his eldest son, stopped by the office. This was a little unusual, since although his children often passed Nasser's office at night they rarely stopped, preferring not to disturb their father. But Khaled had missed talking to him during his week-long absence. Nasser put aside the papers and the telephone calls to chat with Khaled about how things were going at the university and with his studies, to ask about the activities of his brothers Abdel Hamid and Abdel Hakim, and to talk about Hoda and Mona, his sisters. Neither the father nor the son could have been aware that this ordinary conversation was in the nature of a farewell.

The Final Day, 28 September 1970

All countries expressed interest in the Cairo agreement, except for Israel which tried to sow dissent by hinting that, practically speaking, it would be impossible to implement it. In Cairo, arrangements were put in hand for the work of the Higher Committee for Supervising Implementation of the Agreement which included a military, a political and an aid subcommittee within it. Al-Bahi al-Adgham, the committee chairman, went to Amman, set up radio communications with Cairo, and got straight down to work. The city gradually began to quieten down.

Nasser left his office at dawn and went upstairs to snatch a few hours' sleep before going to the airport later in the morning to see off, at half-hourly intervals, President Franjieh, then King Husain, then King Faisal and then Jaafar Numairi. He returned to the airport again halfway through the afternoon to see off the Amir of Kuwait. Though feeling very faint and dizzy during the farewell ceremony, he forced himself to stand tall, on behalf of his fellow Egyptians, until the Amir's plane had started to move.

Only then did he ask his accompanying secretary, Fuad Abdel Hayy, to bring the car to where he was standing and to drive him straight home to Manshiyat al-Bakri. A major heart attack was confirmed by the doctors, but their efforts to save him were unsuccessful. At a quarter past six that evening Gamal Abdel Nasser died.

The Significance of Septembers

By way of a footnote to this account, it is interesting to see that the actual month of September has a long story with Abdel Nasser. It tended throughout his career as leader to be a month of troubles and crises that often affected him very seriously.

– On 28 September 1961, the United Arab Republic was wrecked as a result of Syria's secession. This was a severe shock that could have aggravated his diabetic condition.

– On 14 September 1967, he lost a very close colleague and friend when Marshal Abdel Hakim Amer committed suicide. The death of his lifelong friend had a profound effect on him and on the measure of his confidence in those surrounding him. He could not imagine that Abdel Hakim Amer would ever have plotted against him personally. For days after Amer's death Nasser could not eat properly because of his constant mental image of his friend sitting and sharing food with him.

– On 9 September 1969, at a time when he had the greatest confidence in the ability of the newly-armed forces to confront the enemy, the Israeli forces carried out a highly successful commando operation in the vicinity of al-Zafarana on the Red Sea coast, inflicting heavy losses on the Egyptian armed forces, killing the Red Sea region's governor, and managing to carry off a modern radar system by helicopter to their own sector.

– On 10 September 1969, he suffered a heart attack that confined him to bed for several weeks. That attack constituted a major and a final warning on the exhausted state of his heart.

– On 16 September 1970, the events of Black September began with the massacre of the Palestinians in Jordan.

– On 28 September 1970, Nasser's heart finally failed.

INDEX